Price, Principle, and the Environment

This book argues that while economic theory can inform the design of institutions and processes for settling disputes, it cannot measure the value of environmental goods. Environmental economics fails as a science of valuation because preference-satisfaction, its normative basis, has no relation to any value not trivially defined in terms of it. It fails because preferences cannot be observed but must be inferred from arbitrary descriptions of behavior. It fails because market prices are settled largely on the supply side and thus do not correlate with consumer benefits. Maximum willingness to pay represents a conceptual will-o'-the-wisp about which people have no estimate even for ordinary purchases. It fails because economists have no better information than market players and thus cannot second-guess or "correct" market outcomes. The book contends that environmental policy turns not on preferences revealed to economists but on principles that are identified and applied through deliberative political processes.

Students and professionals in environmental studies, whether in law, philosophy, politics, or science, along with informed readers generally, will find that this book, written with clarity and humor, thoroughly debunks economic valuation and explains the normative foundations of environmental policy.

Mark Sagoff is Senior Research Scholar at the Institute for Philosophy and Public Policy, School of Public Affairs, University of Maryland, College Park. He is the author of *The Economy of the Earth.*

Price, Principle, and the Environment

MARK SAGOFF

University of Maryland

CAMBRIDGE
UNIVERSITY PRESS

PUBLISHED BY THE PRESS SYNDICATE OF THE UNIVERSITY OF CAMBRIDGE
The Pitt Building, Trumpington Street, Cambridge, United Kingdom

CAMBRIDGE UNIVERSITY PRESS
The Edinburgh Building, Cambridge CB2 2RU, UK
40 West 20th Street, New York, NY 10011-4211, USA
477 Williamstown Road, Port Melbourne, VIC 3207, Australia
Ruiz de Alarcón 13, 28014 Madrid, Spain
Dock House, The Waterfront, Cape Town 8001, South Africa

http://www.cambridge.org

First published 2004

Printed in the United States of America

Typeface ITC New Baskerville 10/13.5 pt.   *System* LATEX 2$_\varepsilon$ [TB]

A catalog record for this book is available from the British Library.

Library of Congress Cataloging in Publication data
Sagoff, Mark.
Price, principle, and the environment / by Mark Sagoff.
p.   cm.
Includes bibliographical references and index.
ISBN 0-521-83723-5 – ISBN 0-521-54596-X (pb.)
1. Environmental economics.   2. Environmental policy.   I. Title.
HC79.E5S222   2004
333.7–dc22   2004043560

ISBN 0 521 83723 5 hardback
ISBN 0 521 54596 X paperback

For Kendra

"Nothing matters in the end but the quality
of the affection that has carved its trace in the mind."

Contents

Acknowledgments

A fellowship year at the Woodrow Wilson Center of the Smithsonian Institution, to which I am grateful, gave me an opportunity to begin this book. I wrote most of it as a researcher at the Institute for Philosophy and Public Policy at the University of Maryland, College Park, which has given me an incomparable opportunity to pursue sustained philosophical analysis of the environmental sciences. I am indebted to the director, William Galston, the current editor, Verna Gehring, and our past editor, Arthur Evenchik. Colleagues at the School of Public Affairs, in which the Institute is located, have been constant sources of criticism, encouragement, and advice, especially Herman Daly, Robert Nelson, and Robert Sprinkle, whose help I deeply appreciate. Carroll Linkins, as always, cheerfully and patiently assisted me with the secretarial problems I created.

I am grateful, too, to friends outside the University of Maryland, including Philip Bobbitt and Peter Jutro, for helpful discussions, and to two economists, Alan Randall and Clifford Russell, whose intellectual clarity and open-mindedness helped me to frame some arguments and to avoid some errors. The National Science Foundation (NSF), in partnership with the Environmental Protection Agency, through its program on environmental valuation and decision making, provided two crucial grants (SES9975770 and SBR9613495). As always, I am grateful to Dr. Rachelle Hollander, who as a brilliant program officer at NSF has helped to create and to sustain the study of ethics and values in science and technology. I also want to thank the Pew Charitable

Trusts, particularly their former program officer Susan Sechler, for support given to the Institute for Philosophy and Public Policy over many years, some for work represented in this book.

I thank my wife, Kendra, to whom this book is dedicated, and my children, Jared and Amelia, for giving me time and energy to write it. They are for me the Heaven and earth that are more than what is dreamt of by philosophy.

In writing this book, I have built on, revised, or otherwise borrowed from several essays published previously. Parts of Chapter 1 appeared in the *Hastings Center Report* 21(5) (September–October 1991): 32–40. Chapter 2 appeared in the *Arizona Law Review* 42(2) (Summer 2000): 434–62. Chapter 3 combines material that first appeared in *Land Economics* 70(2) (May 1994): 127–44, and as "On the Relation between Preference and Choice" in the *Journal of Socio-Economics* 31(6) (2003): 587–98. Chapter 5 draws on material from "Four Dogmas of Environmental Economics," *Environmental Values* 3(4) (Winter 1994): 285–310. Chapter 6 combines elements from "On the Value of Natural Ecosystems: The Catskills Parable," *Politics and the Life Sciences* 21(1) (March 2002): 16–21, and "Can We Put a Price on Nature's Services?" *Report from the Institute for Philosophy and Public Policy* 17(3) (Summer 1997): 7–13. Chapter 7 borrows from material that first appeared in *BioScience* 45(9) (October 1995): 610–20. Chapter 8 appeared in *Environmental Values* 12 (2003). Chapter 9 revises a chapter appearing in Robert K. Fullinwider, ed., *Civil Society, Democracy and Civic Renewal* (Lanham, MD: Rowman and Littlefield, 1999), pp. 151–83. I wish to thank the editors of these publications for permission to revise and reprint copyrighted and previously published material.

1

Zuckerman's Dilemma

An Introduction

Many of us recall from childhood – or from reading to our own children – E. B. White's story of the spider Charlotte and her campaign to save Wilbur, a barnyard pig.[1] Charlotte wove webs above Wilbur's sty proclaiming the pig's virtues in words – "TERRIFIC," "RADIANT," and "HUMBLE" – she copied from newspaper advertisements salvaged by a rat named Templeton. Wilbur, Charlotte wrote in her web, was "some pig." He won a prize at the fair. Moved by these events, Zuckerman, the farmer who owned Wilbur, did not slaughter the pig for Christmas dinner. Charlotte saved Wilbur's life.

"Why did you do all this for me?" the pig asks at the end of *Charlotte's Web*. "I don't deserve it. I've never done anything for you."

"You have been my friend," Charlotte replied. "That in itself is a tremendous thing. I wove my webs for you because I liked you. After all, what's a life, anyway? We're born, we live a little while, we die. A spider's life can't help being something of a mess, what with all this trapping and eating flies. By helping you, perhaps I was trying to lift up my life a little. Heaven knows, anyone's life can stand a little of that."[2]

Three Kinds of Judgments

In the following chapters, I want to call attention to a distinction between three kinds of judgments. First, we make judgments as individuals about what is good for or benefits us. For example, Charlotte could tell which flies were the tastiest, and she trapped those she wanted the most. Wilbur wondered, in this context, why Charlotte chose to save his life, since he could do nothing to benefit her or make her better off.

Second, we form judgments about what is good in general, right as a matter of principle, or appropriate in view of a particular situation. Charlotte thought it morally better that Wilbur live out his life in peace than show up with an apple in his mouth at Christmas. She valued Wilbur's friendship as a good thing in itself, and she recognized the obligations and responsibilities friendship creates.

Third, we make aesthetic judgments about what is beautiful or is worth appreciating and protecting for its expressive, symbolic, and formal properties. In describing Wilbur as "some pig" and in other ways lauding his aesthetic qualities (his intelligence was not much to speak of), Charlotte convinced Zuckerman to spare Wilbur for his intrinsic qualities rather than to slaughter him to provide ham for Christmas dinner.

Judgments of the first kind – those we make in view of our own well-being – answer the question, "What is good for me?" Judgments of the second and third kinds – moral and aesthetic judgments – answer questions such as, "What is good or right in view of the situation?" and "What is wonderful or beautiful because of its intrinsic properties?" These kinds of questions turn not on judgments about what is good for the individual but on judgments about what is good in general, good from the perspective of the larger community, or good in itself.

Charlotte formed moral and aesthetic judgments about almost everything except flies. She apparently cared about flies solely on the basis of the good they did her. She dealt with most other creatures, such as Wilbur, with respect and appreciation. Her idea of what is valuable went far beyond what she thought enhanced her well-being.

In this book, I shall assume – and sometimes argue – that there is an important difference between saying that something is *good for me* and saying that something is *good in itself, good from the point of view of the world in general,* or *good because of its intrinsic qualities.* I shall take it as a premise that in our political lives we do not pursue merely private conceptions of *the good life* but also public conceptions of *the good society.* We are not concerned only about the way a social decision or outcome affects us. We are also concerned with whether the decision or outcome is right, fair, or good in view of values or reasons we believe carry weight with society as a whole.

We can assume that the individual is the best or the most legitimate authority, except in special cases, about what is good for her or him.[3] I do not challenge, then, the assumption of welfare economics "that individuals understand fully how various situations affect their well-being and that there is no basis for anyone to question their conception of what is good for them."[4] Judgments about what is good in itself or good from the perspective of a larger social community, in contrast, depend on deliberative political processes that reflect the force of the better argument. Some may believe that a society that maximizes utility – whatever that means – has found the right direction. Others may support opposing principles, for example, that society ought to pursue justice, end discrimination, promote education and the arts, and so on. In this context, society is concerned with resolving contradictions in public opinion, not conflicts of private interest.

Welfare Economics and the Public Interest

A democracy is constantly seized with disputes that reflect disagreements in moral or aesthetic attitudes – differences in conceptions of the public interest. Moral and aesthetic questions in the news include, for example, whether to permit abortion, pursue policies of affirmative action, allow physician-assisted suicide, fund religious groups to provide public services, enable single-sex marriage, assist those with disabilities, engage in preemptive military action, legalize marijuana, condone certain kinds of genetic and reproductive research and technology, support the sciences and arts, and so on. Debates over these questions reflect disagreements about the principles we should respect as a society – not differences about how to achieve an agreed-upon goal, such as welfare-maximization. To be sure, politicians ask if you are better off than before, but they also ask whether as a society we are going in the right direction.

For the welfare economist, society is going in the right direction only if its policies "depend solely on concerns for human welfare."[5] Human welfare "is presumed to be a function of individuals' well-being," which, in turn, is determined by "relying on individuals' existing preferences, as revealed by their behavior."[6] That social policy aims at the satisfaction of each and any preference, taken as it comes on a willingness-to-pay (WTP) basis, is the essential thesis of welfare economics and its subdisciplines, including environmental economics. Social policy, on this view, should act as a prophylactic on a free market, correcting it when it fails – as it often does – to allocate resources to those who value them most in the sense that they are willing to pay the most for them. The goal of social policy would be to emulate the outcome of a competitive market, in other words, the goal of economic efficiency.

In fact, society does support the satisfaction of certain kinds of preferences, for example, those that involve educational, religious, eleemosynary, and health-related activities. Society taxes and otherwise discourages other preferences, for example, those that involve smoking, gambling, prostitution, and the use of illicit drugs. A libertarian typically argues that the government should give people the widest freedom to satisfy their own preferences, whatever they may be, as long as they respect the rights and freedoms of others. This does not imply, however, that the satisfaction of preference is the business of the government. The libertarian sees nothing but trouble in the power of bureaucracies to second-guess market outcomes in the name of economic efficiency.

Consider, for example, Janis Joplin's famous prayer, "Lord, won't you buy me a Mercedes Benz?" Perhaps the good Lord feels a responsibility to satisfy this preference, but why should the government? Having a preference gives the individual a reason to try to satisfy it, and he or she should be free to do so under rules that are convenient, efficient, and fair. This does not explain, however, why social policy has the task of satisfying preferences ranked by WTP and taken as they come.

Economists should say why society should make preference-satisfaction a goal. To refer to "welfare" or "well-being" is not to answer but to dodge this question, if these terms refer to nothing and mean nothing at all other than "preference-satisfaction."

Microeconomists, as we shall see, propose that WTP – rather than argument, deliberation, or reflection – can adjudicate questions of environmental and other social policy. The use of WTP or utility "to measure preferences can be applied quite generally," three economists explain. "Utility or preference exists for any activity in which choice is involved, although the choices may themselves involve truth, justice, or beauty, just as easily as the consumption of goods and services."[7] Louis Kaplow and Steven Shavell, in a recent book, similarly state:

> The notion of well-being used in welfare economics is comprehensive in nature. It incorporates in a positive way everything that an individual might value – goods and services that the individual can consume, social and environmental amenities, personally held notions of fulfillment, sympathetic feelings for others, and so on.

According to the welfare-economic approach, I am able to state an objective thesis – rather than express a subjective want – when I say that environmental policies should be assessed exclusively in terms of their effects on the well-being of individuals. If I defend an opposing principle, for example, that we should protect species to honor God's creation, my statement is irrelevant to policy except insofar as it expresses a welfare-related preference. "The hallmark of welfare economics is that policies are assessed exclusively in terms of their effects on the well-being of individuals. Accordingly, whatever is relevant to individuals' well-being is relevant under welfare economics, and whatever is unrelated to individuals' well-being is excluded from consideration under welfare economics."[8]

When Kaplow and Shavell argue that social policy should be assessed solely on its effect on the well-being of individuals, they state a judgment or thesis they expect to be considered and accepted on its merits. They do not believe that this preference about the goal of social policy is to be assessed in terms of how much they are willing to pay for it. What would they say about the views, judgments, arguments, and positions of those moral philosophers, policy analysts, and others who disagree with them? There are two ways welfare economists may respond to these opposing opinions. First, they may regard them as subjective preferences for some "intangible," "soft," or "nonuse" value for which advocates may be willing to pay. Second, if these opinions do not reflect the welfare effects of a given policy, Kaplow and Shavell dismiss them as irrelevant. They state that under welfare economics, "philosophers' or policy analysts' views . . . are irrelevant."[9]

In this book, I shall emphasize the extent to which disagreements about environmental policy arise from differences in principle, that is, differences in the general rules people believe should govern social policy. The principles that underlie and justify environmental law rarely if ever embrace the efficiency norm. For example, pollution control law, as I shall argue, responds to the widely held principle that people should be free from unwarranted coercion. I shall propose, in any case, that society regulates pollution as a kind of trespass or tort – a sort of assault – not as a market externality or social cost. If some pollution has to be permitted to keep the economy running, it should be tolerated as a necessary evil, not welcomed as a welfare-enhancing utilization of resources.

Environmental law expresses a respect for nature as well as for persons. In one survey, 87 percent of the public agreed with the statement, "Our obligation to preserve nature isn't just a responsibility to other people but to the environment itself."[10] Biologist Michael Soule has stated that the "most fundamental postulate" that motivates scientists like himself is that "*biotic diversity has intrinsic value,*" irrespective of its instrumental or economic worth. Other biologists have argued that a "quasi-religious" view of the value of the environment impels them to revere and therefore to study the natural world.[11] In emphasizing the intrinsic value of biodiversity, these biologists do not implicitly accept but explicitly reject well-being – whatever that concept means – as the principal *desideratum* of endangered species policy. Views such as these have to be considered on their merits, not dismissed as irrelevant or treated as indicators of utility.

Demands people make to benefit themselves, such as consumer demands, conflict in the economic sense that there are not resources enough to satisfy all of them. Differences in what we believe we care about as a society present contradictions that would remain even if resources were infinite. For example, people would disagree about the morality of capital punishment even if there were plenty of rope to hang everybody. Sorting out by deliberation our moral intentions, aesthetic judgments, and spiritual commitments as a society is basic to making environmental policy. The satisfaction of preferences per se – "all this trapping and eating flies" – is hardly the principal purpose or policy goal of a civilized society.

Value in Use and in Exchange

Although I want to emphasize the importance of ethical and aesthetic judgments in justifying environmental policy, I do not mean to dismiss consumer preferences, that is, preferences that reflect what the individual believes is good for her or him. I will emphasize, however, that value of this kind – economic value – can be construed in two quite different senses. For example, Zuckerman understood that Wilbur could serve him either by providing the Christmas ham or by fetching a good price at the marketplace. In this book, I shall conceive of economic value in these two ways. A good can be valuable economically for the benefit it provides or because of the money it fetches in a market.

Adam Smith explained the concept of economic value in terms of these two different meanings – either "the utility of some particular object" or "the power of purchasing other goods which the possession of that object conveys." Smith called the first sort of value – the benefit or utility an object provides – "value in use." He called the buying power associated with owning an object – its price – "value in exchange."[12]

In this book, I shall argue that value in exchange (price) can be observed in a way that value in use (benefit) cannot. To find the price of a Christmas ham, one checks the advertisements. How can an economist measure the benefit a Christmas ham provides? I shall contend that economic "valuation" (as it is called) cannot venture much beyond price or value in exchange. Economists have no plausible way to measure – or to adjudicate conflicts that arise between attempts to measure – value in use or benefit.

Adam Smith thought that economic science does not and cannot measure benefit or value in use but focuses on the "principles which regulate the exchangeable value of commodities."[13] Economists may analyze the conditions that account for exchange or "marginal" value, in other words, the prices buyers of the next units of a good pay sellers who compete for their business. This amount – the price of a good – is set largely by competition on the supply side and thus may not tell us much about consumer benefit. I shall argue (as Smith does) that economic science may help us to understand the conditions that determine value in exchange, but it cannot measure the benefit, value in use, or the utility an object provides.

One of the principal goals of environmental economics today – an effort that receives large amounts of public research support – is to measure the benefits of environmental improvements. This book argues that research aimed at measuring value in use rather than value in exchange should not be attempted because it cannot succeed.

In subsequent chapters I shall argue, moreover, that terms fundamental to the theory of environmental economics, such as "benefit,"
"preference," and "willingness to pay," refer to conceptual constructs
that – unlike market prices – cannot be observed or measured. These
terms have no meaning or referent outside of the tautological and
circular formulas of the theory of welfare economics. To be sure, the
prices people actually pay for goods can be observed and measured.
If competition drives these prices down to producer costs, as is often
the case, these prices do not measure consumer benefits.

We observe that people in general pay and seek to pay the lowest prices they can conveniently find. These prices vary with market
conditions, especially production costs, and offer no reliable basis for
assessing the utility or benefit goods provide. People are said to be
"willing to pay" – whatever that means – an amount equal to the benefit or utility they expect a good to provide. The thesis that goods
should be allocated to those willing to pay the most for them because
this maximizes welfare – when WTP is the measure of welfare – is then
tautologically true. This principle draws as perfect a circle on earth as
can be found in Heaven.

I shall argue that the immense effort economists have invested over
decades in trying to measure the benefits of environmental resources
and services has resulted and can result only in confusion. This book
will argue that there is no need to measure environmental benefits
anyway. Insofar as the goals of environmental policy can be construed
in economic terms, cost-benefit analysis could arguably be helpful.
Cost-benefit analysis, however, relies on market (or "shadow" market)
prices, not maximum WTP. The kind of maximum WTP that is stipulated to be equal to utility is not required for or relevant to cost-benefit
analysis, which is defined on market prices.

The Varieties of Goodness

This book describes three ways people find value in the natural environment. First, we *use* nature: it serves our needs and wants. Second,
we *respect* nature: it commands our moral attention and loyalty. Third,
we *appreciate* nature: it is the object of aesthetic admiration and wonder.

Welfare economics presupposes an instrumental conception of
value – that nature is valuable only as a means to the end of

well-being, defined as the satisfaction of preferences. The goal of social policy on this view is to raise the level of welfare – or to maximize the social aggregate of utility – as much as resources allow. From this perspective, individuals (other than economists) are not thought to have views, beliefs, or ideas worth considering on the merits. Rather, individuals are seen as locations where preferences – or WTP to satisfy them – can be found.

In *Charlotte's Web*, Templeton embodies the welfarist point of view. He exemplifies the individual who is the best judge of how well off he or she is in a given situation. Ask him to do a favor, and he will ask what you will do for him in return. Near the end of the book, for example, Wilbur needs Templeton's help to save Charlotte's egg-sac. In exchange for climbing a wall to retrieve the sac, the rat exacts a promise from Wilbur to feed him the best morsels from his trough. Templeton supposes that the more he acquires of the things he wants, the happier he becomes; as a result of this assumption, he is always miserable. He does not think of himself as a citizen of a barnyard community, bound by its norms or responsibilities. E. B. White observes, "The rat had no morals, no conscience, no scruples, no decency, no milk of rodent kindness, no compunctions, no higher feeling, no friendliness, no anything."[14]

Eban Goodstein, in his textbook on environmental economics, explains that the "consumption of market and nonmarket goods" makes people happy. "The relation between consumption and happiness can be conveniently expressed in the form of a utility function."[15] Templeton, however, was miserable. The most confirmed hypothesis of social science research may be that money does not buy happiness and that the satisfaction of preference has no relation to perceived well-being, once basic needs are met.

The word "satisfaction" in the phrase "the satisfaction of preference" may mean either of two different things. It may mean that a preference is met or fulfilled; in this sense terms, conditions, equations, and predictions may be "satisfied." Second, it may mean that the person who has the preference is content or happy. Satisfaction in the first sense has no known relation to satisfaction in the second sense, once basic needs are met. On the contrary, one should beware of getting what one wishes for. When one has satisfied a preference, one may experience dissatisfaction and disappointment as much as the reverse; as Keats points out in his "Ode on a Grecian Urn," the fun is in the striving. I shall try to show that normative concepts that occur in welfare economics, such as "welfare," "benefit," "utility," and "willingness to pay," are little more than stand-ins for each other and have no relation to happiness or any other substantive concept of the right or the good.

We need not think of nature simply as a source of welfare. Rather, we respect nature: we treat it with loyalty, affection, even reverence. In an interview, Tom Finger, a Mennonite, expressed the position of many Americans. "We are exterminating God's creatures," he said. "All these nonhuman creatures . . . have a certain intrinsic worth because they are part of God's creation."[16] Mr. Finger believed that if God created a species, that is a reason not to destroy it. A society that respects nature, Mr. Finger may reason, is *better* than a society that does not – even if he and other people are not *better off* in an economic sense. As I shall argue in Chapter 3, people act on norms and principles – and this has to be distinguished from seeking to satisfy preferences. Moral duties and religious affections matter. Well-being, however defined, is hardly the only value or goal or principle that informs environmental policy.

The ethical good directs attention to the object itself, not to the use to which it is put; unlike the instrumental approach, it engenders loyalty, love, and respect. Many of us think of nature as a kind of mother – one at least as fierce as Charlotte was in her way – and therefore we may recognize an obligation to care for whatever is left of it. Affection and loyalty often embrace particular places, the historical characteristics of which people have come to cherish. The love of place is called "topophilia," and the love of nature "biophilia."[17] Wilbur thought his barn was the best place – "this warm delicious cellar, with the garrulous geese, the changing seasons, the heat of the sun, the passage of the swallows, the nearness of rats, the sameness of sheep, the love of spiders, the smell of manure, and the glory of everything."[18]

We also *appreciate* nature: we admire its aesthetic properties. We find value in nature as an object of knowledge and perception. This is the aesthetic good.[19] Aesthetic judgments cannot be reduced to what the individual happens to desire or prefer. Rather, even if people desire or admire an object or action, they should still ask whether it is desirable or admirable. Aesthetic judgments, like moral ones, are open to criticism and correction; in this regard, they have a public dimension. The aphorism "*de gustibus non disputandem*" reminds us that in many personal matters – for example, the clothes one wears – each person chooses for him- or herself. Yet each judges for all (and therefore must engage with others in a deliberative process to get at consensus) in matters that concern the aesthetic quality and character of the shared or public environment.

The basis of aesthetic value lies in the object itself – in qualities that demand an appreciative response from informed and discriminating observers. Aesthetic judgment requires perception, not preference; it appeals to reasons and insights with which others can agree or differ, not to conceptions of one's own benefit, about which each person may claim to be the final authority. Even if one cannot prove an aesthetic judgment true or false, one can surely inform and educate one's taste. There are better and worse aesthetic judgments, and so making decisions involves deliberation, discussion, and reflection. We often rely on expert judges, panels, and committees to help us decide which environments and objects to preserve because of their intrinsic historical and aesthetic qualities. The judges who awarded Wilbur a prize, for example, saw in him qualities that made him a pig to be appreciated rather than a pig to be consumed.

Noneconomic Value

Objects of ethical and aesthetic judgments do not as such have economic value but moral and aesthetic value; as the eighteenth-century philosopher Immanuel Kant wrote, they have a dignity, not a price.[20] These things are said to be good from the perspective of the world or from the perspective of a particular moral community. For example, we think of hallowed places, such as the battleground at Gettysburg, as being important because of what happened there – because of sacrifices that occurred in the past, not benefits that may accrue now or in the future. We may think of some places as being so beautiful or majestic that they are worth preserving for their expressive and symbolic properties and not just for the uses we may make of them or the prices people might pay, for example, to visit them.

We also make moral judgments about the way we treat each other. Charlotte thought that Wilbur deserved respect and concern even though he was a pig. It did not seem right to her that Wilbur should be used simply as a means to the end pigs usually serve or meet. It appears that we have made a similar judgment as a society that a person – or his or her kidneys, liver, etc. – should not be used as a dumping ground for the effluents and emissions of others. Pollution, in other words, crosses moral boundaries that we have decided to police. Laws that regulate pollution explicitly protect public safety and health; they do not maximize net utility or balance benefits and costs. In a later chapter, I shall examine principles that underlie pollution-control law and discuss some of the problems society faces in implementing those principles.

I shall argue that environmental law serves primarily two purposes: the protection of personal and property rights, especially with regard to pollution, and the preservation of places. Laws controlling pollution serve the first goal; they constrain the risks one person can impose on another. Statutes that pursue the second purpose seek to preserve national forests, landscapes, and landmarks; to protect historical districts; to maintain biodiversity; and to defend the integrity of ecological systems, such as rivers and wetlands.

In the United States, these two statutory goals – the protection of rights and the preservation of places – emerge from two foundational traditions in our political culture. The first draws on the values of property and autonomy; the second, on those of community and diversity. A tradition of libertarianism would protect people from involuntary risks and harms. Pollution-control law may be understood in this context. The second tradition, which we associate with Madisonian republicanism, permits Americans to use the representative and participatory processes of democracy to ask and answer moral questions about the goals of a good society. Americans, most of whom are immigrants or descended from immigrants, find in the natural environment a common history – a *res publica* – that unites them as a nation. Policies that protect the ecological and historical character of the shared environment do not necessarily maximize its economic product, but construct a common heritage.

Just as Charlotte found in Wilbur qualities worthy of admiration and respect, so may we appreciate the intrinsic qualities of the natural world. These qualities appeal to our perception of what is valuable in itself, and they lead to actions that make us better (by lifting up our lives a little) but not necessarily better off.[21] The decision to protect the natural environment is often a decision to act on the basis of principle, not in response to preference, and thus to forgo an economic gain. We act through political processes in response to common ethical, aesthetic, or cultural intentions and convictions, though we look for cost-effective ways to pursue them.

This book criticizes the penchant of economic analysis to conflate beliefs with benefits, that is, to assimilate the moral and aesthetic judgments people defend on the merits with the consumer preferences they may pay for at the margin. By misconstruing ethical beliefs as economic benefits – and then elaborating arcane methods to measure these so-called "intangible" values – economic theory tries to "price" moral attitudes and judgments that are inconsistent with its own assumptions. People bring ethical judgments and commitments into political and legal deliberation and negotiation. Rather than recognizing the realm of the political and the possibilities of democracy, economic theory too often describes as market failures it must correct cultural and aesthetic judgments it implicitly rejects. This misconstrues the value of nature by misunderstanding the nature of value.

The Market and Democracy

The market mechanism provides the best framework we know for maximizing the instrumental or economic value of nature. Competitive markets are marvelous institutions for allocating resources, and I have nothing to say against them. I think it is plain, however, that market allocation has to be balanced with political deliberation with respect to social policies that involve moral or aesthetic judgment. This is true, in part, because people who take positions about public policy often have the social good rather than their own good in mind. For example, some people support the death penalty because they believe certain murderers deserve to die. Others denounce capital punishment because it violates the sanctity of life. Whatever you believe, your reasons are likely to have nothing to do with your welfare. The choice society makes will reflect or contradict what you believe is right, but unless you are on death row, it may not affect your well-being.

A distinction between a political compromise and an economic tradeoff may help make this point.[22] A political compromise, at least in principle, responds to reasons; an economic tradeoff, in contrast, weighs preferences. Political compromises may be said to be legitimate insofar as they emerge from democratic processes structured to ensure that all sides get a fair hearing. Economic tradeoffs, in contrast, may take place between strangers who make exchanges in a market. The trick is to tell which environmental problems are to be resolved by a political process and which by a market – and then to design the appropriate process if it does not already exist. Both political and market institutions can be involved. For example, to set a "cap" or ceiling for a pollutant under a cap-and-trade approach, society would rely on political compromise in order to balance the principle of freedom from coercion with the necessity of economic activity. Society might then design a market in which to trade pollution allowances under the cap.

I do not cavil with "free market" environmentalists and others who find that market-based, entrepreneurial, and voluntary activities can help to protect the environment. Rather, I inveigh against welfare economists who reject both markets and political processes as ways to govern the environment. Market failure is so ubiquitous with respect to environmental public goods, they argue, that markets should be viewed more as the cause than as the cure of environmental problems.[23] At the same time, politicians are not to be trusted. "It is the politician's job to compromise or seek advantage," while economists "produce studies that are . . . as objective as possible."[24] One gets the impression that these economists believe society should rely upon them – or their science – rather than upon either markets or political processes to protect the environment.

The point of democratic or political deliberation is not to maximize satisfaction, whatever that means, but to match rules to recognized situations, which is to say, to figure out how to classify a problem and then on what principle society should respond to problems of that kind. The way the problem is defined or categorized often determines how a solution is formulated. One may ask, for example, whether pollution represents a trespass, which would call for one kind of rule, or an external cost of production, which calls for a different kind of regulation. Ethical and aesthetic judgment is as important as economic calculation in formulating and addressing environmental concerns.[25]

Decision theorist James March summarizes this point as follows. When society allocates resources to maximize the welfare of individuals, it chooses among policies "by evaluating their consequences in terms of prior preferences."[26] To do this, society should either leave matters to the market, create markets when they are "missing," or, if necessary, try to figure out how a market would allocate the resources in question. The last possibility, which introduces the prospect of cost-benefit analysis, presents a difficulty. We must recognize that when the stakes are high enough, all sides to a controversy will hire their own economists and present dueling or conflicting cost-benefit analyses. In Chapter 8, I shall describe an example of the way environmental and industry groups may commission opposing economic analyses – in other words, how interest groups can obtain the WTP they are willing to pay for. I know of no research that shows how differences of expert opinion in this context can be resolved, although it is reasonable to suppose that the side that hires the most Nobel laureates may eventually win in court.

When society seeks to respond to or act upon its members' opinions, arguments, and principled beliefs, it must turn from economic calculation to political deliberation. It must allow citizens to engage each other in the task of determining the nature of the problem they confront and the rules that they should apply to problems of that sort. A society through negotiation and collaboration identifies itself as a community committed to recognizing individuals as legislators, not simply as consumers. The reasoning process "is one of establishing identities and matching rules to recognized situations."[27] The search for shared intentions constitutes the basis of democracy.

The Wealth of Nature

Throughout history, humanity has prospered by controlling and conquering nature – by turning forests into farms, savannas into cities, seashores into commercial strips. Welfare was served when trees were felled, animals domesticated, and swamps drained. Property values increased when wild areas were developed and in that sense "improved." Developing countries wish to transform their landscapes to the same commercial uses that created great wealth in the developed world. Within the next few decades, we shall decide the fate of many estuaries, forests, species, and other wonderful aspects of the natural environment. Can we with honesty connect human well-being and economic growth with preserving rather than with exploiting these environments?

Consider whales. Two centuries ago, whale oil fetched a high price because people used it in lamps. Whales had instrumental value. Indeed, many of the great New England fortunes were built on whale oil. If you look at the universities of New England, you see institutions founded in large part on investments of the income gained from whaling, logging, and other activities that exploited nature. Was this exploitation of nature – whale stocks depleted and forests denuded – wrong? Why?

What if hunters in the early 1800s had protected whale stocks so that people today could have more oil or blubber? In other words, what if people back then put whales off-limits in order to preserve "natural capital" for future generations? We might have access to marginally more blubber and whale oil. We might not have the great universities, libraries, hospitals, mansions, and other assets that began with the fortunes earned by the whaling industry. Would we be better off as a result?

It made economic sense for New Englanders to harvest the whales and invest the money in the institutions that supported the prosperity of that region. It would have made no economic sense for our ancestors to do more than they did – virtually nothing – to preserve "natural capital" for future generations. In 1820, people could confidently expect that if human beings did not destroy their lives through war, they would no doubt improve their lives through technology. Advances in technology – for example, in food production, antibiotics, dental care – have made people today infinitely better off than their great-grandparents. The bourgeoisie today enjoys a far better standard of living than did the royalty of earlier centuries. We can confidently expect that technology will continue to advance exponentially – so that future generations, if they do not end the human adventure in the holocaust of war, will look back on our lives with pity, as we look back on the miseries of, say, the thirteenth century.

Today, we need whales no more than Charlotte needed pigs. Why, then, do so many people care about saving whales today? Are they concerned about maintaining a strategic reserve of blubber? Do they worry that the seas might fill up with krill? No; as whales have lost their instrumental value, their aesthetic and moral worth have become all the more evident. We respond to moral and to aesthetic judgments in seeking to preserve these great mammals. Their aesthetic value and moral value have increased as their instrumental value has diminished.

Much is written about nature's free services.[28] Yet we have come to depend increasingly on the productive capacity of technology and decreasingly on nature's free and spontaneous largess. Indeed, nature tends to specialize in disservices as much as services – flood, drought, storm, fire, pestilence, heat, cold, and whatever else it takes to kill every living thing, for universal death is nature's only way. The Pilgrims found out how well nature's services support human welfare. According to Governor Winthrop, half of his people died horribly of hunger, cold, and disease during the first winter, and all should have perished had not the native tribes fed them and taught them to raise corn. Today, few economies subsist on nature's free beneficence; lumber is likely to come from high-tech tree plantations, fish from aquaculture. Although technology makes us less dependent on wild nature, it does not lead us to value it less; rather, the value of nature changes from instrumental to aesthetic, ethical, and spiritual. We may therefore regard with dismay the extent to which we have transformed nature for economic or instrumental purposes and thus displaced ourselves from our own natural history.

Whale oil has substitutes in a way that whales do not. The industries that exploit whales have little economic importance. Nevertheless, we know that it would be shameful – not inefficient but blameworthy – to drive these creatures to extinction. Aesthetic and moral value attaches to the animals themselves, not to any benefit they confer on us. The intrinsic value of whales matters to us a lot more than their instrumental value. No one worries about the sustainability of whale oil, but we do care about the survival of whales. As Charlotte knew, the most valuable things are often useless.

Aesthetic Judgments Are Disinterested

Someone may say that aesthetic value counts as a kind of instrumental value because it produces pleasure. On the contrary, as Kant argued, aesthetic perception, even if it occasions a slight and subtle pleasure, is disinterested. That aesthetic perception is disinterested, in other words, is independent of any benefit one may seek, does not mean one is indifferent to it. It means, rather, that aesthetic appreciation cannot be traced in any way to self-interest, that is, to a concern with one's own well-being. We do not find the aesthetic object valuable because we enjoy it; rather, we enjoy the object – we take pleasure in it – because we perceive it to be valuable. The pleasure or satisfaction we feel functions not as the *end* or *purpose* of our experience; it is not *what* we value. Rather, pleasure or pain serves as the *means* by which we perceive aesthetic qualities of an object – qualities we may expect others to perceive with approval and therefore to enjoy as well.

In the context of instrumental value, a person finds an object to be good because it contributes to his or her well-being. But with the aesthetic good, just the reverse is true. An object contributes to well-being because it is perceived to be good. Its very qualities are valued, not its possession or use. Aesthetic judgments are intersubjective, moreover, in a way that simple enjoyment is not. That you enjoy chocolate, for example, in no way suggests that I should. But if you find some painting, song, novel, or the like admirable or awful, you may expect me to agree or, if not, show you how or why you are wrong. Music, the arts, and the beauty and complexity of nature train our emotions to discern moral qualities. The education of feeling constitutes the value of aesthetic experience.

If pleasure were itself the point of experience – what gives it value – it can be had far more easily, in far greater intensities and quantities, and at much less expense by means of sex or drugs than by discerning and appreciating aesthetic differences. Evolution prepared the pleasure centers for procreation, not poetry. Kant understood that welfare or happiness are good things, but he did not consider them to be good in any context and however they arose. Rather, he believed that it is less important that we be happy than that we strive for lives worthy of happiness.

Likewise, the nineteenth-century Utilitarian John Stuart Mill knew that what is valuable about pleasure is not that we get lots of it but that it is appropriate to its object.[29] For example, if you take pleasure in the suffering of others, this does not make that suffering better. Rather, it only makes you worse. Mill famously wrote, "It is better to be Socrates dissatisfied than a pig satisfied." (Would he have said this if he had known Wilbur?)

The quiet satisfaction you take in an accomplishment, to use a different example, is a way you perceive the value of what you have done, but this pleasure is not what gives it value. The contemplation of an achievement – unlike the intense pleasures caused, for example, by drugs – rests on judgment and understanding and is never merely a matter of stimulus and response. Pleasure can be had in the falsest circumstance, but then it has no worth. To maximize pleasure is hardly an important goal. Morally speaking, the goal is not to lead pleasurable or happy lives but lives worthy of happiness. If pleasure or satisfaction were itself the goal of experience, a good biochemist could provide more of it at less cost, and the Big Lie would be better than the hard truth.

Zuckerman's Dilemma

Zuckerman confronted a dilemma. He had to choose whether to butcher Wilbur (or sell him to be butchered) for economic reasons or preserve him for aesthetic and moral ones. I think this is the dilemma we confront today with respect to whatever is left of our evolutionary and ecological heritage, for example, old growth forests, wetlands, estuaries, and so on. Instrumental values pull in one direction, aesthetic and moral considerations in the other. We also face this dilemma in trying to accommodate economic activity while protecting people from the involuntary risks associated with pollution.

Solving environmental problems – or resolving environmental conflicts – often requires designing for Zuckerman's dilemma, that is, finding ways to honor shared aesthetic and ethical beliefs while accommodating legitimate economic interests. The literature of environmental economics, however, generally rejects the proposition that anything like Zuckerman's dilemma arises in environmental policy. Mainstream environmental economists – at least insofar as their textbooks and other literature suggest – believe that all tradeoffs, even those that involve ethical and aesthetic judgments, are susceptible to welfare calculation and cost-benefit analysis. Zuckerman's dilemma would pose at most a technical problem of attaching monetary equivalents to "non-use," "existence," or "commitment" values – the sorts of values that might be supposed to somehow connect Zuckerman's own welfare with his decision to spare Wilbur's life.

A large and growing group of maverick economists, called ecological economists, also urge instrumental reasons for protecting nature

and natural environments. A member of this group might argue, for
example, that the barnyard community, in which Wilbur played a major role, provided free but valuable ecosystem services. Charlotte controlled flies – a service for which Zuckerman would otherwise have
to pay an exterminator. Ecological economists contend that environments with the most "existence" value, such as wetlands, rain forests,
and estuaries, also provide crucial ecological services that markets fail
to price. Ecological economists applaud efforts to shadow price or
monetize ethical and aesthetic "benefits," but they also believe that
conventional economists overlook crucial instrumental reasons for
preserving the natural world.

This book argues, on the contrary, that Zuckerman's dilemma arises
all the time with respect to natural objects and environments; indeed,
environmental policy is most characterized by the opposition between
instrumental values and aesthetic and moral judgments and convictions. I shall try to show that these judgments and commitments have
little connection with benefits; they have to do with the intrinsic qualities of actions, objects, and places, not with consequences for welfare.
And I shall suggest that humanity generally must destroy the intrinsic
beauty and character of the natural world to capture and exploit its
services – to maximize net benefit. For example, the once-magnificent
Hetch Hetchy valley does, indeed, provide a water supply for San
Francisco, but only because the valley was dammed, not because its
beauty was preserved.

How can society best resolve dilemmas in which aesthetic and moral
values and commitments pull one way and economic or instrumental
values pull the other? I think that John Muir, in his polemic about
Hetch Hetchy, suggested the right conceptual categories. He condemned those he called "temple destroyers" and "devotees of ravaging
commercialism" and praised those who strove to protect the monuments of the Almighty. I understand these categories – the conflict
between commerce and Creation. What I object to is the penchant of
environmentalists to invoke the vocabulary of commerce – utility, benefit, instrumental value generally – to protect the works of Creation.

Once you accept as inevitable the discourse of environmental economics, once you take on board its mare's nest of tautologies, ambigui-
ties, and confusions, the temptation becomes irresistible to invoke economic arguments to protect the natural world. And environmentalists

like me who question the appropriateness and validity of these plainly pretextual instrumental arguments may be ostracized as traitors to the cause. We seek, rather, to show that economic arguments are in fact less convincing or persuasive than the moral and spiritual convictions that actually ground and justify environmentalism.

In a democracy, the way to work out Zuckerman's dilemma, I believe, is to bring those whom Muir condemned as "temple destroyers" and as "devotees of ravaging commercialism" together with the defenders of temples and the protectors of nature under conditions that are fair to both and have them work out their differences, case by case, so that each side comes away with the most it can. This could involve halving the difference – which is what happened when Hetch Hetchy was flooded but the Yosemite valley was consecrated to preservation. In Chapter 8, I shall offer case studies of negotiations to show how democracy does indeed work.

What I think messes things up is the penchant of the devotees of purity and preservation to adopt and thus endorse the vocabulary, methods, and moral assumptions of the devotees of ravaging commercialism. For example, environmentalists who rightly believe we should protect species because they are part of Creation for decades insisted "that pharmaceutical and other commercial applications of biodiversity should help justify its conservation."[30] When in 1991, Merck bowed to pleas and pressure of environmentalists by investing about $1 million – less than one-tenth of 1 percent of its annual research budget – in taxonomic research in Costa Rica, it reaped a public relations bonanza because environmentalists never wearied of citing and celebrating the project as vindicating the economic value of wild rainforest species. Merck "terminated its landmark bioprospecting contract with Costa Rica in 1999 after producing no commercially viable products."[31] Experts in drug discovery caution, "The idea of exploiting the rain forests to find wonderful drugs is, quite frankly, not credible."[32]

The costs of randomly assaying creatures for their compounds are so great that bioprospecting in wild nature makes no economic sense. Shaman Pharmaceuticals, which followed clues in ethnomedicine, filed for bankruptcy protection in 2001. Pharmaceutical companies develop "drugs based on molecules that scientists can create for themselves in the laboratory, using new combinatorial chemistry techniques."[33] This does not necessarily doom bioprospecting.

Arguably, the mutated organisms that fester in dumps for toxic, hazardous, and radioactive wastes are biologically so active they could provide a blockbuster product. Indeed, although it discovered nothing of economic value in the rainforest, Merck has derived important antibiotics from microorganisms it found in soil samples it gathered near its headquarters in lovely Rahway, New Jersey.

Like other pretextual instrumental arguments, the false hope that wild ecosystems might yield valuable commercial products has led to counterproductive results. "Increasingly, scientists hoping to collect specimens in developing countries rich in flora and fauna are being met with major bureaucratic barriers. Local governments are afraid that their biological riches will be stolen without compensation."[34]

Environmentalists, ecologists, and others who touted the idea that cancer-cures – not just viruses like Ebola and HIV – lurk in the rainforest now find themselves suspected of biopiracy when they come to study what they love. Similarly, environmentalists who extolled the economic value of biodiversity in crops now find themselves "condemning the legal walls that Third World governments are building around seed banks."[35]

We lose sight of the glory and magnificence of nature when we – like the Conquistadors looking for the fountain of youth – regard it as a mine of mythical genetic treasure. That moral principle and aesthetic judgment command us to protect and preserve the last great places, as the Nature Conservancy calls them, is what no one can deny. When instead environmentalists speak of services and resources, their moral compass turns from the Almighty to point to the Almighty Dollar. The rhetoric of environmentalism presents an odd example of the sheep who appears in the wolf's clothing.

A Look Ahead

Here is a road map to the chapters that follow. The second chapter takes up the seminal 1967 essay in which economist John V. Krutilla acknowledged that Robert Solow and others had shown that technology would always and easily substitute between resource flows so that general scarcities of raw materials were not to be feared. Krutilla saw in this finding a challenge to environmental economics because if scarcity was not in the cards – if markets will always find substitutes for any natural resource – then it was no longer clear why a discipline within economics to study the environment is required.

Krutilla brilliantly got the chestnuts of environmental economics out of the fire by arguing that economists who study the environment should turn their attention from material flows to moral, aesthetic, and spiritual values. Krutilla suggested that since market prices fail to capture the amounts devotees of purity and preservation are willing to pay to protect nature, economists must find ways to measure the nonuse or "existence" value of natural environments. Since 1967, mainstream environmental economists have generally accepted Krutilla's assessment that the pricing mechanism will assure the relative abundance of natural resources. These economists have turned, as a result, to the problem of attaching economic measures to the "preferences" of those whose views of environmental policy are at odds with their own.

This second chapter criticizes – and sometimes ridicules – theories and methods economists have perfected over three decades to price ethical principles and aesthetic judgments as "benefits" to be entered into the utility calculus on which they propose social policy should be based. The alternative I defend engages those with ethical and aesthetic knowledge and information in the policy-making process. In other words, what knowledgeable people have to say – not how much they are willing to pay – should inform policy. As an example, the chapter describes the way historians and other Civil War aficionados helped the Park Service to design its new visitors' center at Gettysburg. The successful negotiation among businesspeople, Park Service agents, and concerned citizens balanced historical, moral, aesthetic, and instrumental considerations without attaching "prices" to anyone's moral commitments. A survey of willingness to pay would have bollixed rather than balanced relevant values, commitments, and beliefs.

Chapter 3 argues that attempts by environmental economists to measure the value of environmental goods must take as data the preferences individuals are willing to pay to satisfy. This chapter contends that preferences cannot provide data for economic analysis because they are not visible or observable. Instead, the economist must "observe" behavior. Any example of behavior, however, is open to conflicting interpretations and descriptions. The choices we make are no more observable than the preferences they are said to reveal.

This chapter acknowledges that "preference" may refer in a formal sense to an ordered relation between stipulated alternatives, as in social choice theory. There is nothing wrong with social choice theory as a formal science, but stipulation is not observation. The chapter concludes that preferences – and the choices on the basis of which they are constructed – are unobservable and thus provide no data for economic science. If preferences cannot provide data for economic analysis, economics cannot be a science of valuation, that is, value in use. The prices at which goods are exchanged, in contrast, are directly observable or may be inferred from data. Thus, environmental economists can help society determine not value in use (benefit, utility) but price, that is, value in exchange.

Chapter 4 argues that economists, to estimate the value of non-marketed environmental goods, seek to measure "total" benefit or maximum willingness to pay (WTP). I follow Alfred Marshall in arguing that in competitive markets, where individuals seek to maximize – not equalize – benefit per dollar, maximum WTP cannot be observed. This is true because no matter how much they benefit from having something, people pay the market price or the lowest price they can conveniently find. People also must take into account – and make assumptions about – the prices of complements, in other words, goods needed for the good in question to function, and about the prices of substitutes.

Maximum WTP estimated for one good, moreover, cannot be compared with that of another, for each measurement assumes that the other good trades at market prices. If close substitutes for the good under consideration (e.g., turkey for ham) trade at market prices, then maximum WTP does not reflect benefit because it is capped at the market prices of substitutes. Market prices, I argue, are settled largely by competition among suppliers. If these prices constrain WTP, then WTP, too, is settled largely on the supply side and thus does not measure consumer benefit.

Chapter 5 criticizes the commonplace economic analysis of pollution as representing an "external" or a "social" cost of production. The chapter shows that this standard economic approach to pollution leads to a laissez-faire policy, since individuals (the polluter and the polluted, as it were) will always bargain by themselves to an outcome that maximizes net benefits in view of the costs – including the transaction costs – they confront. Markets take transaction costs like other costs into account; therefore, markets function as perfectly in the presence of transaction costs as in their absence.

Ronald Coase showed that market prices are always "right" because no one occupies a legitimate position to second-guess them. I rely on standard arguments taken from Coase to show that the government would have to pay at least the same information and other transaction costs as private parties to reallocate resources and thus cannot provide a more efficient outcome than would an unregulated market. In fact, the clear result of microeconomic theory after Coase is that markets cannot fail to allocate resources efficiently in view of the greater information and other transaction costs that any other method faces.

After describing the Coasian *reductio* of the economic approach to regulating pollution as a market failure or externality, I offer suggestions about how the government may identify "stopping points" even though it treats pollution as a trespass or assault rather than as a social cost. One appropriate rule, I suggest, may be to regulate to the "knee of the curve," in other words, to the point at which the cost of controlling the next incremental unit of pollution begins to increase rapidly. Society should continually promote pollution-control technology to push the knee of the curve farther out along the control axis.

Chapter 6 takes up the suggestion defended by ecological economists that nature provides services, such as water purification and flood control, that justify its preservation on instrumental grounds. These economists often cite the utility of the Catskills watershed to the citizens of New York City to illustrate how undeveloped, wild ecosystems provide free services that development could only diminish. I argue, on the contrary, that in the example of the Catskills, dams, pipes, chlorination, and the control of wildlife are required to deliver rainwater and keep it potable. Contrary to common assumptions, the Catskill ecosystem does not purify rainwater; rain approximates distilled water and so is fairly pure to begin with. Biodiversity contaminates rainwater as it flows to the city. Economic or instrumental values serve as reasons to dam a river, build a resort, plough a field, alter a genome, kill waterfowl, and so on. Septic systems must be built precisely because nature does not treat sewage. As the Pilgrims found when they died, nature is a place where you cannot get good service.

This chapter concludes by reviewing an attempt by a group of ecological economists to measure the value of nature's services, that is, to determine the price of everything. The laudable and legitimate ethical commitment to protect nature, I argue, should not lead us to grasp at economic sophistries, however meretricious and spurious, that might serve in the battle for preservation. A more credible approach might be to present aesthetic and ethical concerns in their own terms, to argue for environmentalism on the basis of ethical commitment, not economic efficiency.

Chapter 7 takes up the principal argument ecological economists offer to convince us to walk more lightly on the earth. These economists argue that the economy has outgrown the environment, in other words, that people are consuming resources at an unsustainable rate so that we will inevitably – and rather quickly – run out of raw materials and energy. This is the Malthusian view – as Chapter 1 explains – that Krutilla rejects. For mainstream economists such as Krutilla, postindustrial society has moved from a resource to an information economy, so that technology will always find a way to substitute more for less plentiful resource flows to provide the same goods. The debate between the ecological and mainstream environmental economists remains unresolved. What is worrisome is a thesis they appear to agree upon, namely, that the principal argument for protecting and respecting nature is an instrumental and economic one.

Chapter 8 describes the constructive contribution economists may make to environmental policy. Rather than attempting to "price" benefits – I argue throughout this book that economics cannot serve as a science of valuation – economists may assist society by suggesting new institutional arrangements through which people may make the bargains that may now elude them. In theoretical terms, economists can show society how, by redesigning institutions, to lower transaction costs that burden voluntary exchange. The government can design tools, for example, tradable property rights and arrangements of governance that encourage people to acquire and exchange information and reach collaborative agreements. Economists also inform environmental policy by showing how social goals can be achieved in more cost-effective ways.

I know of no better way to explain the useful role of economics in environmental policy than to provide case studies. The "cap-and-trade" strategy that successfully reduced sulfur and lead emissions has been so thoroughly examined in the literature that I shall not discuss it here. Instead, Chapter 8 describes an equally suggestive developing market for grazing rights on the western range. A second case study examines a successful stakeholder negotiation in which industry and environmental groups agreed on a plan to protect visibility in the Grand Canyon from possible impairment by pollution from a nearby coal-fired power plant. This chapter concludes by describing how economic analysis enabled a stakeholder group to work out a Final Project Agreement to regulate two major new plants Intel constructed in Arizona to fabricate microchips.

Chapter 9, the final chapter, describes in detail the most indicative, exemplary, and exciting stakeholder negotiation I have come across, namely, the story of the Quincy Library Group in northern California. This dramatic and continuing negotiation or collaboration illustrates how democracy can respond to Zuckerman's dilemma. On the one side, local environmentalists defended the beauty of the Plumas, Larson, and Tahoe national forests against logging interests and thus made strong enemies in the communities where those environmentalists lived. On the other side, loggers and others with an economic stake in exploiting the resource taunted and hated the environmentalists. Yet both groups came together to endorse a strategy rich in local knowledge and experience needed to manage the forest against the threat of catastrophic fire.

This final chapter illustrates problems that arise when agencies and interest groups, in order to protect their powers and prerogatives, invoke science to defeat rather than to inform political compromise and collaboration. There is hardly a view about the environment so silly, unfounded, and meretricious as to be absent from the peer-reviewed scientific literature. One can always cite an article in a peer-reviewed journal to support an absurdity and then condemn those who disagree as betraying reason and science. Nothing displays self-righteousness in environmental controversies more than the appeal to science. One can always claim that science is on one's side – it is like claiming that God is on one's side – as a reason not to compromise or to work out political solutions.

Once one recognizes that environmental disputes at bottom rest on ethical and aesthetic rather than economic conflicts – differences in principle rather than in preference – one has taken the first step to resolving them. We cannot take this step toward political deliberation and reconciliation as long as we conceive of environmental issues primarily in economic and scientific terms. We should recognize the ethical principles, aesthetic judgments, and spiritual commitments that underlie and justify environmental policy. These beliefs, principles, and judgments unite rather than divide us as a democracy.

2

At the Monument to General Meade *or* On the Difference between Beliefs and Benefits

When you visit Gettysburg National Military Park, you can take a tour that follows the course of the three-day battle. The route ends at the National Cemetery, where, four months after the fighting, Abraham Lincoln gave the 270-word speech that marked the emergence of the United States as one nation.[1] The tour does not cover the entire battlefield, however, because much of it lies outside the park. Retail outlets and restaurants, including a Hardee's and a Howard Johnsons, stand where General Pickett, at two o'clock on a July afternoon in 1863, marched 15,000 Confederate soldiers to their deaths. The Peach Orchard and Wheatfield, where General Longstreet attacked, became the site of a Stuckey's family restaurant.[2] The Cavalry Heights Trailer Park graces fields where General George Custer turned back the final charge of the Confederate cavalry.[3] Over his restaurant, Colonel Sanders, purveyor of fried chicken, smiles with neon jowls upon the monument to George Meade, the victorious Union general.[4] Above this historic servicescape loomed until recently a 310-foot commercial observation tower Civil War buffs called "a wicked blight on the battlefield vista."[5]

One spring day, on my way to give a seminar on "economics and the environment" at Gettysburg College, I drove quickly past the battlefield where 23,000 Union and 28,000 Confederate soldiers fell in three days. I felt guilty speeding by the somber fields, but I had to teach at two o'clock. I checked my watch. I did not want to be late. How do you keep your appointments and still find time to pay homage to history?

My ruminations were soon relieved by a strip of tawdry motels, restaurants, amusement arcades, and gift shops touting plastic soldiers and "original bullets! $6.95 each." At the battlefield entrance, I caught sight of the famous golden arches of the battlefield McDonald's where, on a previous occasion, my then eight-year-old son enjoyed a Happy Meal combo called the "Burger and Cannon." Nearby, a sign for General Pickett's All-You-Can-Eat Buffet beckoned me to a restaurant that marks the spot where rifle and artillery fire had torn apart Pickett's underfed troops. If you have young children, you understand the deep and abiding significance of fast food and convenient restrooms in historic and scenic areas. You may ask yourself, though, how you can have comfort, convenience, and commerce and at the same time respect "hallowed ground."

Are Battlefields Scarce Resources?

I began the seminar at Gettysburg College by describing a National Park Service plan, then under discussion, to build new facilities to absorb the tide of visitors – an increase of 400,000 to 2 million annually – that welled up in response to *Gettysburg*, a movie based on Michael Shaara's blockbuster novel, *The Killer Angels*.[6] Working with a private developer, the Park Service proposed construction of a new $40 million visitor center, including a 500-seat family food court, a 450-seat theater, and a 150-seat "upscale casual" restaurant with "white tablecloth" service, gift shops, parking lots, and a bus terminal not far from the place where Lincoln delivered the Gettysburg Address.[7] Several senators, including then Senate Majority Leader Trent Lott (R-Miss.), objected that the project "commercializes the very ground and principle we strive to preserve."[8]

It is one thing to commercialize the *ground*; it is another to commercialize the *principle* we strive to preserve. Tour buses, fast food, and trinket shops, although they commercialize the ground, express a local entrepreneurial spirit consistent with the freedom, vitality, and mystery of the place. The soldiers probably would have liked such haunts as the National Wax Museum, the Colt Firearms Museum, and the Hall of Presidents. They certainly would have appreciated General Lee's Family Restaurant, which serves great hamburgers practically at the site of Lee's headquarters. Homespun businesses try to tell the story and perpetuate the glory of Gettysburg – and even when they succeed only absurdly, they do so with an innocence and ineptitude that do not intrude on the dignity and drama of the park.

In contrast, the upscale tourist mall envisioned by the initial Park Service plan seemed, at least to Senator Lott, to elevate commercialism into a principle for managing Gettysburg. Rather than stand by the principle of commercialism or consumer sovereignty, however, the Park Service scaled back its plan.[9] In its defense, the Service pointed out that Ziegler's Grove, where its Visitor Center and Cyclorama stood at the time, overlooks the main battle lines. The revised proposal, which received U.S. Department of the Interior approval in November 1999, called for razing these facilities and returning Ziegler's Grove to its 1863 appearance, in order, as one official said, "to honor the valor and sacrifices of those men who fought and died on that ground for their beliefs."[10]

Since the seminar took place in mid-afternoon – siesta time in civilized societies – I had to engage the students. I did so by proposing as my own view a thesis so outrageous and appalling that the students would attack it. I told the class that the value of any environment – or of any of its uses – depends on what people now and in the future are willing to pay for it. Accordingly, the Park Service should have stuck with its original plan, or, even better, it should have auctioned the battlefield to the highest bidder, for example, to Disney Enterprises.[11]

I asked the students to bear with me long enough to consider my proposal in relation to the subject of the seminar, the theory of environmental economics. This theory defends consumer sovereignty as a principle for environmental policy. More specifically, this theory asserts that the goal of environmental policy is to maximize social welfare at least when equity issues – matters involving the distribution of benefits among individuals – are not pressing.[12] Welfare, in turn, is defined and measured by willingness to pay (WTP) for goods and services. According to this theory, environmental policy should allocate goods and services efficiently, that is, to those willing to pay the most for them and who, in that tautological sense, will benefit most from their enjoyment, possession, or use.

In the United States, unlike Europe, I explained, battlefields are scarce resources that, like any scarce environmental asset, should be allocated efficiently. To be sure, the Park Service tries to accommodate tourists. The problem, though, is that the Park Service does not exploit heritage values as efficiently as a competitive market would. Gettysburg is woefully underutilized, or so I argued. Even Dollywood, Dolly Parton's theme park in rural east Tennessee, attracts more visitors.[13] Unlike the managers of Dollywood, the Park Service pursues a principle that is not economic but ethical; it seeks not to maximize welfare but to educate the public and to honor "the valor and sacrifices of those men who fought and died on that ground for their beliefs."[14]

A young lady in the class blurted out, "But that's what the Park Service should do." She acknowledged that the Park Service has to provide visitor services. It should do so, she said, only to the extent that it will not "detract from what they did here," to paraphrase President Lincoln. She understood the significance of "what they did here" in moral and historical rather than in economic terms. The value of hallowed ground has nothing to do with market behavior or with WTP, she said. We should protect Gettysburg because to do so is the only right and honorable course; it would be wrong to sell it to the highest bidder.

I explicated her concern the following way. A private developer, I explained, might not realize in gate receipts at Gettysburg the WTP of those individuals, like herself, who wished to protect an area because of their ethical or aesthetic preferences. I promised to describe to the class the contingent valuation (CV) method economists have developed to determine how much individuals are willing to pay for policies consistent with their disinterested moral beliefs, for example, the belief that the nation has an obligation to honor those who died so that it could live.

This reply, I am afraid, did little more than taunt the student. She asked me, "Do you really believe that the Park Service should manage the battlefield in whatever way would maximize net benefits – even if that means desecrating it?"

I answered, "The goal of environmental policy is to satisfy all wants and preferences on a willingness-to-pay basis to the extent that the resource base allows. The policy maker must remain doggedly neutral among opinions about what is sacred or profane, good or evil, appropriate or inappropriate, so that his or her opinion is not given special weight."

"So, you believe that society should manage the battlefield in a way that maximizes the satisfaction of preferences. I believe, on the contrary, that we should manage the park to honor those who gave their lives so that the nation may live. We have different opinions."

"Yes, we do," I said.

"How much are you willing to pay for your opinion?"

Economists, I explained, are able to express objective, disinterested views – not just personal wants and preferences – about social policy. For example, environmental economists often argue that pollution should be taxed in an amount equal to the costs it imposes on society. An economist may assert this view even though he lives in Maine, where there is little air pollution. The economist will not gain as a result of his recommendation; rather, the prices he pays for goods may increase, while the air he breathes remains the same. In making policy recommendations, economists rise above self-interest to offer objective beliefs. These beliefs have to be judged on their merits; they are not benefits that WTP can measure.[15]

The student replied that she could not understand why the historic, aesthetic, and moral judgments that formed our identity as a nation constituted subjective preferences or "benefits" while the views of welfare economists represent "neutral" objective truths.

"Because economists are social scientists," I explained.

"I rest my case," she said.

Conservation Revisited

To prepare for the seminar, I had asked the students to read *Conservation Reconsidered*,[16] an essay economist John V. Krutilla published in 1967 in response to neoclassical economists who had studied the effects of technological advances on economic growth. Neoclassical macroeconomists such as James Tobin,[17] Robert Solow, and William Nordhaus[18] argued that technological progress would always make more abundant materials do the work of less abundant ones – for example, the way kerosene substituted for whale oil in providing household illumination. Solow, a Nobel laureate in economics, wrote that "[h]igher and rising prices of exhaustible resources lead competing producers to substitute other materials that are more plentiful and therefore cheaper."[19] These economists adopted a model of economic growth that contained two factors: capital (including technology) and the labor to apply it.[20] This model differed from that of classical economists, such as Ricardo and Malthus, because "resources, the third member of the classical triad, have generally been dropped."[21]

In the essay the class read, Krutilla cited studies to show that advancing technology has "compensated quite adequately for the depletion of the higher quality natural resource stocks."[22] He observed that "the traditional concerns of conservation economics – the husbanding of natural resource stocks for the use of future generations – may now be outmoded by advances in technology."[23] Krutilla, along with other environmental economists in the 1970s, rejected the view that the resource base imposes limits on growth.[24] Had they accepted the Malthusian position, they would have risked losing credibility both with their mainstream colleagues and with foundations and institutions, such as the World Bank, that supported their work.[25]

The neoclassical model of growth posed two problems for environmental economists. First, this model, which presupposed that information ("technological capital") could easily, inexpensively, and consistently substitute for resources ("natural capital"), did not sit well with environmentalists, many of whom rejected neoclassical thinking and joined the maverick discipline of ecological economics, which emphasizes traditional Malthusian concerns about resource depletion.[26] I shall discuss ecological economics in a later chapter. Even more important, the neoclassical theory of perpetual resource abundance left mainstream environmental economists no obvious scarcities to study. It suggested that economists could do little more than advise society to privatize resources, to enforce contracts, and otherwise not to worry but just leave markets alone, because nature would not be a limiting factor to economic growth.

The macroeconomic model that became dominant after 1950 could explain, for example, why the extinction of whales would have no significant economic effect. Industry could obtain the same goods, for example, lubricants and fuels, from other, less expensive sources. The economy apparently depends far more on plant and animal breeding and biotechnology – crops bear very little resemblance to their ancient ancestors – than on the preservation of wildlife. For example, the last wild progenitor of cattle went extinct in Poland more than two centuries ago; its demise has been economically irrelevant. Of course, one can hope that pharmaceutical companies or agricultural firms will show some interest in wild biodiversity, and if they do, this would suggest that biodiversity has an economic application. The mainstream macroeconomic view, however, left the economic value of nature to the market. If any wild ecosystem, species, or landscape could be exploited economically, some firm would figure out how to do it. Otherwise, wild places and creatures, having no economic use, would seem to have no economic value.

The Move to Microeconomics

Krutilla and other mainstream environmental economists, to find fertile fields for further research, moved the focus of their science from macroeconomic to microeconomic analysis.[27] Macroeconomists study the principles and conditions of economic growth and prosperity; they are interested in important social concerns such as the business cycle, the balance of trade, inflation, productivity, and employment. Microeconomists study the behavior of individuals and firms as they trade in competitive markets. According to microeconomic theory, when markets fail properly to bring buyers together with sellers, prices at which commodities and services change hands may not reflect the benefits they provide or the costs involved in producing them. Microeconomists try to identify ways to assess costs and benefits that markets fail to price.[28]

Pollution is a standard example used to illustrate microeconomic analysis. If the production of a good, say, an automobile, imposes costs, for example, dirty air, on members of society for which they are not compensated, these individuals unwillingly subsidize the production or consumption of that item. This subsidy distorts markets because it encourages the overproduction of some things (e.g., cars) and the underproduction of other things (e.g., clean air) relative to what people want to buy. The production and use of cars imposes social costs, that is, costs on society that are not reflected in the private costs, prices people pay, to own and drive those cars. This gap between social and private costs, economists reason, justifies regulation.

As early as 1920, welfare economist A. C. Pigou had distinguished between "private" and "social" costs and had characterized pollution as an unpriced "externality" or social cost of production. Pigou had also proposed a solution: to tax the difference between private costs, those reflected in prices, and social costs, those people bear without compensation, so that the prices charged for polluting goods would reflect the full costs, including the pollution costs, that go into providing them.[29]

By the 1960s and 1970s, economists had fully characterized Pigou's argument as what one called "the economic common sense of pollution."[30] In Chapter 5 of this book, I shall argue that the microeconomic analysis of pollution in terms of a divergence between private and social costs fails, first, because no one can measure and respond to the relevant costs or benefits better than those that are affected by them, in other words, the parties to whatever transactions occur or do not occur. Second, pollution-control law relies for its justification on common law principles of nuisance, not on a Pigouvian concept of market failure. Public law regulates pollution, in other words, not as an "externality" to be controlled to the extent that the benefits outweigh the costs, but as an invasion, trespass, or tort.[31] This remains the case even though environmental agencies often and rightly use market incentives, such as "cap and trade" strategies, to improve environmental performance. The "cap" or ceiling under which pollution permits or allowances are traded represents a social decision about safety and health and not a calculation about benefits and costs.

Krutilla and colleagues saw a way, however, to apply the Pigouvian analysis of market failure far, far beyond the problem of pollution. These economists knew that people often make sacrifices, such as by paying dues, to support causes and to vindicate convictions concerning the natural world. These beliefs or commitments surely involve values; values, in the context of economic theory, suggest preferences and, therefore, WTP that market prices may not fully capture.[32] This WTP, if entered into a social cost-benefit analysis, could serve environmentalism by justifying regulation. Krutilla and other economists who worked at Resources for the Future, an influential Washington think tank, and in academic departments saw a way to transform ethical and aesthetic judgments into data for economic analysis. It was to treat these judgments, even though they are disinterested or have little to do with welfare, just like consumer preferences – as subjective wants and desires or as potential "benefits" – that markets failed to price.

The young lady in my seminar, for example, thought the Park Service should restore rather than commercialize the battlefield. If policy went her way, arguably, she would experience a benefit; if not, a cost. This example and many others like it suggest that markets may fail whenever people support principles or judgments they cannot easily vindicate through private exchange. Experts might correct market allocations by measuring WTP for outcomes consistent with political beliefs and moral commitments, thus offering a scientific basis to what might otherwise appear to be partisan politics. Ethical, political, and ideological positions, through the magic of WTP, could be represented as data for economic calculation. This possibility opened a new vista to and offered a raison d'être for environmental economics.

Moral Commitment as Consumer Demand

At about the time neoclassical economics removed resource scarcity as a cause for concern, citizens across the country swelled the rolls of organizations such as the Sierra Club, which sought to preserve pristine places, endangered species, wild rivers, and other natural objects. These environmentalists, Krutilla pointed out, contributed to organizations such as the World Wildlife Fund "in an effort to save exotic species in remote areas of the world which few subscribers to the Fund ever hope to see."[33] Krutilla noted that people "place a value on the mere existence" of resources, such as species, even though they do not intend to consume or own them, as they would ordinary resources.[34]

Krutilla argued that if people value natural objects because they are natural, then technological advance cannot provide substitutes for them.[35] Among the permanently scarce phenomena of nature, Krutilla cited familiar examples, including "the Grand Canyon, a threatened species, or an entire ecosystem or biotic community essential to the survival of the threatened species."[36] On this basis, Krutilla and many colleagues reinvented environmental economics as a "new conservation"[37] that addresses the failure of markets to respond to the "existence" or "nonuse" value of natural objects people want to preserve but may not intend to experience, much less use or consume.

Krutilla was correct, of course, in observing that people often are willing to pay to preserve natural objects such as endangered species.

In the previous chapter, I mentioned one person who said, "We're eliminating God's creatures. All these nonhuman creatures... have a certain intrinsic worth because they are part of God's creation."[38] People who believe species have an intrinsic worth may be willing to pay to protect them. Does this suggest that species have an economic value or utility that market prices fail to reflect?

Krutilla thought so. He reasoned that those who wished to protect natural environments find it difficult to communicate their WTP to those who own them. Given this difficulty, "the private resource owner would not be able to appropriate in gate receipts the entire social value of the resources when used in a manner compatible with preserving the natural state."[39] Krutilla proposed that the analysis Pigou had offered to justify the regulation of pollution might also serve to justify governmental action to protect species, wilderness, and other natural objects. He wrote, "Private and social returns are likely to diverge significantly."[40]

Krutilla's analysis suggests an argument to show that the principle of consumer sovereignty can justify historical preservation at Gettysburg but allow commercial exploitation at Dollywood. At Dolly Parton's theme park, the owners capture in gate and table receipts total WTP for the goods and services the resort provides. Owners who respond to market signals supply just those goods and services the public most wants to buy. The managers of Dollywood, moreover, cover all the costs in labor, materials, and other expenses of their business. The prices they charge, then, will reflect the full social costs involved in producing what they sell.

At Gettysburg, according to this analysis, the same overall principle – to maximize net benefits to individuals – produces a different (and a politically palatable) recommendation. Patriotic Americans, many of whom may never visit the area, may be willing to pay to restore the battlefield or to spare it from commercial exploitation. Private, for-profit owners of Gettysburg would have no incentive to take this WTP into account, however, because they cannot capture it in gate and table receipts. The prices managers charge for attractions, then, will not reflect the full social costs of providing them – particularly the costs to patriotic Americans who would suffer if the battlefield is desecrated. Thus, a Pigouvian argument may provide an economic and, in that sense, scientific rationale for the belief that society should restore Gettysburg to its 1863 condition rather than sell it to Disney to run as a theme park.

This kind of economic argument may appeal to environmentalists because it opposes the privatization of places, such as Gettysburg, that possess intrinsic value. This argument is especially appealing because it rejects privatization on economic grounds – the very sorts of reasons that might be thought to justify it. Since the Pigouvian approach leads to comfortable conclusions, environmentalists might embrace it. Why not agree with economic theory that the goal of social policy is to maximize net benefits with respect to environmental assets, whether in places like Dollywood or in places like Gettysburg? After all, the cost-benefit analysis, once it factors in the WTP of environmentalists, will come out in favor of protecting the environment.

The problem is this: to buy into this argument, one must accept the idea that the same goal or principle – net benefits maximization – applies to Dollywood and Gettysburg.[41] Critics may contend, however, that the approach to valuation appropriate at Daydream Ridge in Dollywood is not appropriate at Cemetery Ridge in Gettysburg. At Daydream Ridge, the goal may be, indeed, to satisfy consumer demand. Dolly Parton has what it takes to do that. At Cemetery Ridge, the goal is to pay homage to those who died that this nation might live.

To say that the nation has a duty to pay homage to those from whom it received the last full measure of devotion is to state a moral fact. You can find other moral facts stated, for example, in the Ten Commandments. The imperative "Thou shalt not murder" should not be understood as a policy preference for which Moses and other like-minded reformers were willing to pay. Rather, like every statement of moral fact, it presents a hypothesis about what we stand for – what we maintain as true and expect others to believe – insofar as we identify ourselves as a moral and a rational community.

Our Constitution puts certain questions, for example, religious belief, beyond the reach of democracy. Other moral questions, for example, over military intervention in conflicts abroad, invite reasoned deliberation in appropriate legislative councils. Environmental controversies, once the issues of resource scarcity are removed from the agenda, turn on the discovery and acceptance of moral and aesthetic judgments as facts. The belief that society should respect the sanctity of Cemetery Ridge states a moral fact so uncontroversial nobody would doubt it. This tells us nothing, however, about a scarcity of battlefields, the inelasticity of hallowed ground, market failure, or the divergence of social and private costs. It suggests only that the principle of consumer sovereignty that economists apply to evaluate management decisions at Dollywood does not apply at Gettysburg or, indeed, wherever the intrinsic value of an environment is at stake.[42]

Are Beliefs Benefits?

By construing intrinsic or existence value as a kind of demand market prices fail to reflect, Krutilla and other environmental economists envisioned a brilliant strategy to respond to the quandary in which neoclassical economic theory had placed them.[43] They kept their credentials as mainstream economists by accepting the neoclassical macroeconomic model with respect to resources the economy uses. They could still be recognized as serious scientists by the World Bank and by their professional colleagues. Yet they could also appeal to the many foundations and groups that espoused environmental causes by quantifying nonuse values, that is, ethical and aesthetic judgments, in economic and scientific terms. As a result, a lot of money flowed from public and private foundations to environmental economists to support their efforts to "green" their science by building up the purported benefits of environmental protection.

Mainstream environmental economists "greened" their science by attributing a general scarcity to "nonuse" resources such as wilderness, species, scenic rivers, historical landmarks, and so on, that many people believe society has a duty to preserve. Indeed, by applying the divergence-of-private-and-social-cost argument not just to pollution but also to every plant, animal, or place that anyone may care about for ethical or cultural reasons, economic theory appealed to environmentalists. Environmentalists now could represent their beliefs as WTP prices failed to reflect.[44] At last, they could claim that economic science was on their side.[45]

Krutilla, who was himself an environmentalist, envisioned "existence" or "nonuse" value as a basis for protecting wild and natural places that the industrial economy had brought everywhere under attack. Like any environmentalist, Krutilla hoped to help preserve the natural world. By introducing the concept of "nonuse" or "existence" value, however, Krutilla and his colleagues also achieved a great deal for the discipline of environmental economics. First, by transforming moral and aesthetic judgments about the environment into preferences for which people are willing to pay – by feeling the pain of environmentalists and finding ways to "price" it – Krutilla and his colleagues created a complex research agenda centering on the measurement of benefits associated with nonuse value.[46] Since 1970, indeed, research in environmental economics has been preoccupied with measuring existence value or nonuse value, that being the benefit people obtain from policies they approve for ethical and other principled reasons and not for the sake of any benefit they obtain.[47]

Second, Krutilla and colleagues created a division of labor between policy scientists and consumers.[48] As policy scientists, economists announce the goal of environmental policy – net benefit maximization – and the methods to achieve it.[49] As policy consumers, citizens serve as locations or channels at which WTP can be found. In this division of labor, citizens play no political role but function as the sources of data about WTP. They regard themselves as receptacles for utility rather than as participants in a deliberative democratic process.

Economists announce *ex cathedra* that the goal of social policy is welfare maximization – whether at Dollywood or at Gettysburg. Edith Stokey and Richard Zeckhauser summarize that "public policy should promote the welfare of society."[50] A. Myrick Freeman III explains, "The basic premises of welfare economics are that the purpose of economic activity is to increase the well-being of the individuals who make up the society."[51] In a widely used textbook, Eban Goodstein states, "Economic analysts are concerned with human welfare or well-being. From the economic perspective, the environment should be protected for the material benefit of humanity and not for strictly moral or ethical reasons."[52]

In announcing this view and in offering their services to society in pursuing it, environmental economists tout their neutrality among values and preferences. Economists reiterate that "each individual is the best judge of how well off he or she is in a given situation."[53] Henry Ford is reputed to have said that people could have automobiles "in any color so long as it's black."[54] Individuals can make any social judgment they wish, as long as it concerns the extent to which policy outcomes harm or benefit them.[55] When they adopt the welfare-economic framework, environmentalists surrender their identity as moral and political agents and accept an identity as policy consumers. As policy consumers, they make judgments about what is good for them – judgments good only as far as their WTP extends.[56]

Third, environmental economists made a very attractive offer to environmentalists to adopt the cost-benefit conceptual framework. An endangered butterfly, for example, may be worth millions if every American is willing to pay a dime for its survival. Economists may offer a ceremonial bow in the direction of markets, but they quickly and predictably tell a story of market failure and then call for a scientifically based outcome justified by cost-benefit analysis.[57] As soon as all the WTP for the protection of places like Gettysburg or a species like a butterfly is toted up, the efficiency of protecting hallowed ground or endangered creatures will be obvious. Environmental groups, who associated economists with the enemy, now saw that economic science could be their friend.[58] Environmentalists, who might have complained that industry groups had "numbers," could now come up with numbers, too.[59]

By adopting the conceptual framework welfare economists offered them, environmentalists surrendered their ethical convictions and aesthetic judgments. In exchange, they received the great promise that economic science would justify their goals on scientific grounds. And since WTP adds up quickly when aggregated over all the members of society, environmentalists could be sure that every cost-benefit analysis, properly implemented, would come out "right."

Is Existence Value a Kind of Economic Value?

To establish a connection between existence value and economic value, economists have to explain in what sense people benefit from the existence of goods they may neither experience nor use. To be sure, individuals are willing to pay to protect wonders of nature they may never expect to see. That they are willing to pay for them, however, does not show that they expect to benefit from them. Generally speaking, just because a person's preferences are his or her own does not show that the satisfaction of those preferences improves his or her well-being. The students in my class were willing to pay to protect hallowed ground at Gettysburg. They did so, however, largely from a sense of moral obligation and not in any way or manner because they thought they would be better off personally if the battlefield were preserved.

I wrote the following syllogism on the blackboard.

Major premise: The terms "economic value" and "welfare change" are equivalent.

Minor premise: Existence value has no clear relation to welfare change.

Conclusion: Therefore, existence value has no clear relation to economic value.

The major premise, which equates economic value with welfare, explains the sense in which economic value is *valuable*. Unless "economic value" referred to some intrinsic good, such as welfare change construed, for example, as felt happiness or satisfaction, one would be hard-pressed to explain the sense in which environmental economics can be a normative science.[60]

According to Freeman, "[T]he terms 'economic value' and 'welfare change' can be used interchangeably."[61] He adds, "Society should make changes in environmental and resource allocations only if the results are worth more in terms of individuals' welfare than what is given up by diverting resources and inputs from other uses."[62] Economists generally "define value as the well-being, or utility, derived from the consumption of a good or service."[63] If there is "non-consumption" or "existence" value, it, too, must correlate with well-being or welfare.

To establish the minor premise, I argued that the statement "society ought to do *x* and I will contribute to its cost" does not entail "I shall benefit from *x*." When behavior is motivated by aesthetic judgment or by ethical concerns, it may lack a meaningful connection with well-being or welfare. Accordingly, economist Paul Milgrom concedes that for existence value to be considered a kind of economic value, "it would be necessary for people's individual existence values to reflect only their own personal economic motives and not altruistic motives, or sense of duty, or moral obligation."[64]

To escape the conclusion that existence value has no relation to economic value, an economist may challenge either the major or minor premise. The major premise seems to be indispensable, however, if economics is to rest on a consequentialist moral theory such as utilitarianism. The reference to welfare explains why the benefits with which economists are concerned are *benefits*. The minor premise may be more vulnerable. This premise appears false if individuals make choices only in response to their beliefs about what will benefit them. Why not suppose, then, that people (other than economists) judge policy outcomes only on the basis of their personal self-interest? This assumption would connect preference with well-being for the ordinary citizen.

The students pointed out to me that Krutilla adopts this very position. In the essay the class read, he proposed that individuals who wish to protect the wonders of nature do so to increase their own psychological satisfaction.[65] Krutilla wrote:

These would be the spiritual descendants of John Muir, the present members of the Sierra Club, the Wilderness Society, National Wildlife Federation, Audubon Society and others to whom the loss of a species or the disfigurement of a scenic area causes acute distress and a sense of genuine relative impoverishment.[66]

The reference to "distress and a sense of genuine relative impoverishment" is crucial, of course, because these factors link existence value with economic value by connecting it with expected changes in welfare. Krutilla continued, "There are many persons who obtain satisfaction from mere knowledge that part of wilderness North America remains even though they would be appalled by the prospect of being exposed to it."[67] The reference to "satisfaction" connects the "is" of WTP to the "ought" of economic value and valuation.[68]

Contingent Valuation

During the past thirty years, economists have developed the method of contingent valuation (CV) to assess existence or "nonuse" values.[69] The CV method, as one authority writes, "is based on asking an individual to state his or her willingness to pay to bring about an environmental improvement, such as improved visibility from lessened air pollution, the protection of an endangered species, or the preservation of a wilderness area."[70] The CV method "asks people what they are willing to pay for an environmental benefit."[71] The authors of a textbook see this method as "uniquely suited to address non-use values."[72]

Contrary to what textbooks say, the CV questionnaire never asks people what they are willing to pay for an environmental *benefit*. It asks respondents to state their WTP for a particular *policy* or *outcome*, for example, the protection of a rare butterfly. Economists interpret the stated WTP for the policy as if it were WTP for a benefit the respondent expects that policy to afford her or him. Yet a person who believes that society ought to protect a butterfly may have no expectation at all that he or she will benefit as a result. Indeed, as Tom Tietenberg observes, people who do not expect to benefit in any way from an environmental good may still be committed to its preservation.[73] He notes that "people reveal strong support for environmental resources even when those resources provide no direct or even indirect benefit."[74]

Empirical research shows that responses to CV questionnaires reflect moral commitments rather than concerns about personal welfare. In one example, a careful study showed that ethical considerations dominate economic ones in responses to CV surveys.[75] "Our results provide an assessment of the frequency and seriousness of these considerations in our sample: they are frequent and they are significant determinants of WTP responses."[76] In another study, researchers found that existence value "is almost entirely driven by ethical considerations precisely because it is disinterested value."[77]

Some economists acknowledge that "existence value has been argued to involve a moral 'commitment' which is not in any way at all self-interested."[78] They explain, "Commitment can be defined in terms of a person choosing an act that he believes will yield a lower level of personal welfare to him than an alternative that is also available to him." If "existence" value lowers welfare, on which side of the cost-benefit equation should it be entered? The individual does not want less welfare per se, but "adherence to one's moral commitments will be as important as personal economic welfare maximization and may conflict with it."[79]

Responses to CV questions reflect disinterested views about policy, not welfare-related judgments. Reviewing several CV protocols, economists concluded that "responses to CV questions concerning environmental preservation are dominated by citizen judgments concerning desirable social goals rather than by consumer preferences."[80] Two commentators noted that the CV method asks people to "comment, without very much opportunity for thought, on a hard issue of public policy. In short, they most likely are exhibiting offhand opinions on the same policy issue to which the cost-benefit analyst purports to give his own answer, not private preferences that might be reflected in their own market transactions."[81]

We should not confuse WTP to protect a battlefield with WTP to provide a benefit. Battlefields and benefits constitute different goods that can be produced and should be measured separately. If economists cared to measure the benefits of alternative outcomes, the CV questionnaire should ask respondents to state their WTP for the welfare change they associate with an environmental policy. Here is an imaginary protocol I suggested to the class:

> Many people believe society should respect the "hallowed ground" at Gettysburg for moral, cultural, or other disinterested reasons. This questionnaire asks you to set aside all such disinterested values; it asks you not to consider what is right or wrong or good or bad. In responding to this survey, consider only the benefit you believe you will experience, that is, the personal satisfaction, if the battlefield is preserved. Please state your WTP simply for the welfare change you expect, not your WTP for the protection of the battlefield itself.

This question addresses benefits. Since CV questionnaires in fact ask nothing about benefits, responses to them tell us nothing relevant to economic valuation. Yet CV methodology, which economists have been developing for decades, has become the principal technique policy makers use to measure "nonmarket benefits based primarily on existence value" of assets such as old-growth forests and endangered species.

As philosopher Ronald Dworkin points out, many of us recognize an obligation to places and objects that reflects a moral judgment about what society should do, not a subjective expectation about what may benefit us.[82] He writes that many of us seek to protect objects or events for reasons that have nothing to do with our well-being. Many of us "think we should admire and protect them because they are important in themselves, and not just if or because we or others want or enjoy them."[83] The idea of intrinsic worth depends on deeply held moral convictions and religious beliefs that underlie social policy. Dworkin observes:

> Much of what we think about knowledge, experience, art, and nature, for example, presupposes that in different ways these are valuable in themselves

and not just for their utility or for the pleasure or satisfaction they bring us. The idea of intrinsic value is commonplace, and it has a central place in our shared scheme of values and opinions.[84]

Beliefs are not benefits. If economists believe that society should tax pollution or allocate resources to maximize welfare, they do not necessarily think this because they will be better off as a result. They are not simply trying to increase demand for their services. Similarly, people who believe that society should protect endangered species or old-growth forests do not necessarily think that this will improve their well-being.[85] A person who wants the Park Service to respect hallowed ground may consider that policy justified by the qualities of the battlefield itself and not by welfare consequences for her or him. It is hard to understand, then, how CV measures the nonmarket benefits of environmental goods.[86] If responses to CV surveys are based on moral beliefs or commitments, there would seem to be no relevant benefits to measure.

Does WTP Measure Welfare?

A young man in the class referred back to the syllogism that remained on the blackboard. He asked whether the syllogism still would be sound if the term "existence value" were replaced by "willingness to pay." He reasoned that if existence value, when based on moral commitment rather than self-interest, has no necessary relation to welfare, this would be true of WTP as well. He asked what WTP measures and why economists believe that WTP relates to or measures well-being and thus economic value.

A full answer to this question will be found in Chapter 4. To respond to the student, however, I reminded the class of what economic value consists in, namely, something akin to human happiness. As R. Kerry Turner explains, "Positive economic value – a benefit – arises when people feel better off, and negative economic value – a cost – arises when they feel worse off."[87] As Goodstein points out, the "moral foundation underlying economic analysis, which has as its goal human happiness or utility, is known as utilitarianism."[88] Happiness, contentment, and feelings of satisfaction are psychological states that, arguably, have intrinsic value.[89] Insofar as economic value is "valuable," its value lies in or refers to subjective well-being or experienced happiness.

Does WTP measure, correlate with, or have anything to do with happiness, well-being, or contentment? We can answer this question empirically by using income as a surrogate measure for WTP; after all, people with more money can obtain more of the things they want to buy. We can use perceived happiness or subjective well-being to measure how well off people are. To determine whether WTP relates to well-being, we can find out whether people who have more money are happier than those who have less. A great deal of evidence exists in relation to this empirical question.[90]

Empirical research overwhelmingly shows that after basic needs are met, no correlation whatsoever holds between rising income and perceived happiness.[91] Researchers consistently find there is very little difference in the levels of reported happiness found in rich and very poor countries.[92] Although the buying power of Americans has doubled since the 1950s, reported happiness has remained almost unchanged.[93] Absolute levels of income seem not to affect happiness, although relative levels do. People do not like to earn less than their peers.[94]

A great many reasons explain why no empirical relation holds between what people are willing to pay for something and the happiness they derive or expect to derive from it. Happiness seems to depend on the things money cannot buy, such as love, friendship, and faith, not on the extent of one's possessions.[95] The literature contains studies in which people report they become *less* happy as their income and purchasing power increase.[96] Studies relating wealth to perceived happiness find that "rising prosperity in the USA since 1957 has been accompanied by a falling level of satisfaction. Studies of satisfaction and changing economic conditions have found overall no stable relationship at all."[97] One major survey states, "None of the respondents believed that money is a major source of happiness."[98] That money does not buy happiness may be one of the best-established findings of social science research.[99]

Although economists invoke utilitarianism as a moral foundation, WTP and therefore economic value has no clear relation to happiness and, therefore, no basis in utilitarianism. As Richard Posner wrote, the "most important thing to bear in mind about the concept of value [in the economist's sense] is that it is based on what people are willing to pay for something rather than the happiness they would derive from having it."[100] If economic value is a function of what people are willing to pay for something rather than the happiness they would derive from having it, it is not surprising that those willing to pay the most for goods derive the most economic value from them. The term "economic value" simply coincides with "WTP" and has no empirically demonstrated connection to anything else.

I asked the class how we get from "people are willing to pay more for *A* than *B*" to "*A* is better than *B*." To answer this question, I referred to the syllogism on the board, which now read:

Major premise: The terms "economic value" and "welfare change" are equivalent.

Minor premise: WTP has no meaningful demonstrated relation to welfare change.

Conclusion: Therefore, WTP value has no demonstrated relation to economic value.

Environmental economists escape this syllogism, I proposed, by ingeniously defining "welfare change" or "benefit" in terms of willingness to pay. Freeman describes this crucial step. He explains that economic theory defines "the benefit of an environmental improvement as the sum of the monetary values assigned to these effects by all individuals directly or indirectly affected by that action."[101] Tietenberg analyzes the connection between WTP and benefits in the same way. "Total willingness to pay is the concept we shall use to define total benefits," he explains.[102] Economic theory defines "benefit" or "welfare change" in terms of willingness to pay. The statement that WTP measures or correlates with well-being states a tautology and means nothing more than the empty identity, "*A* is equivalent to *A*."

The central argument of environmental economics, then, comes to the trivial assertion that resources should go to those willing to pay the most for them because they are willing to pay the most for those resources. In this tautology, the terms "welfare" or "well-being" simply drop out. They function as stand-ins or as proxies for WTP and cannot be distinguished from it. The measuring rod of money correlates with or measures nothing but itself. The stipulated and thus specious identity of welfare and WTP constitutes the normative foundation of welfare economics.

Environmental economics fails as a normative science because it cannot tell us why or in what sense an efficient allocation is better than a less efficient one. Lacking all normative content, terms like "utility," "well-being," or "welfare" fail to move environmental economics from the "is" of WTP to the "ought" of value or valuation.

Naked Preferences

A young man in the class wondered aloud if this critique of environmental economics had gone too far. The CV method, after all, attributes enormous economic value to so-called "useless" species and to remote places that few people may visit. Instead of rejecting this technique, he suggested, we should be grateful for it. "To the extent that people are willing to pay for existence value – whether the protection of species and habitats, the functioning of ecosystems, or the dignity of Gettysburg – these intangibles are appropriately included in the overall calculus of benefit," he said. The young man argued that WTP is an appropriate measure of value even if it does not correlate with any independently defined or substantive conception of well-being or welfare. He added that the CV method, because it aggregates WTP for policy preferences, provides valuable information to policy makers. This is true whether preferences reflect judgments about social goals or about personal benefits.

The student suggested, then, that even if WTP and economic value are logically equivalent, environmental economics retains its usefulness as a policy science. He conceded that references to "welfare," "well-being," or "happiness" could be dismissed as window-dressing. We need only WTP itself as an expression of preference. Preferences still matter regardless of whether they are based on self-interest or on moral or political judgment.

This view is one many economists share. "The modern theory of social choice," writes W. Michael Hanemann, "considers it immaterial whether preferences reflect selfish interest or moral judgment."[103] This view goes back at least to Kenneth Arrow's observation: "It is not assumed here that an individual's attitude toward different social states is determined exclusively by commodity bundles which accrue to his lot under each. . . . [T]he individual orders all social states by whatever standards he deems relevant."[104]

Let us drop the reference to welfare or well-being from the fundamental thesis of environmental economics. We are left, then, with the idea that preference, weighed or ranked by WTP, should be satisfied insofar as the resource base allows. "In this framework, preferences are treated as data of the most fundamental kind," writes economist Alan Randall.[105] "Value, in the economic sense, is ultimately derived from individual preferences."[106]

What sort of value can be derived from preferences? If we no longer refer to welfare or well-being, it is hard to understand why the satisfaction of preferences, weighed by WTP, matters. Plainly, individuals should have the greatest freedom possible, consistent with the like freedom of others, to try to satisfy their preferences and vindicate their values both in markets and through political processes. The statement that people should be free to pursue their own goals through social institutions that are equitable and open expresses a piety nobody denies.[107]

The thesis that social policy should aim at satisfying people's preferences, in contrast, expresses a dogma of welfare economics for which no good argument can be given. Having a preference may give the individual a reason to try to satisfy it, and he or she should have the greatest freedom to do so consistent with the like freedom of others. Absent a reference to a meaningful social goal such as happiness, the provision of basic needs, or the pursuit of justice, however, what reason has society to try to satisfy that preference?

The idea that preferences should be satisfied just because or insofar as people are willing to pay to satisfy them creates two problems for economists.[108] First, economists must explain why their own policy preferences, such as for pollution taxes, should not be assessed or evaluated on the same WTP basis as the judgments or beliefs of others. Economists would also have to show why the satisfaction of preferences, even those preferences having no relation to happiness or any other substantive good, is a good thing. Why should preferences count on a WTP basis rather than, say, in relation to the reasons or purposes that underlie them or in relation to the consequences, for example, for happiness or pleasure, of their satisfaction?

Consider, first, the way society evaluates policy proposals put forward by economists. Economists expect public officials to consider these proposals on their merits. Why should public officials treat the views economists defend any differently from those put forward by other citizens? If society uses WTP to evaluate the views or judgments of some citizens, it should apply the same measure to all. A CV study of how much economists are willing to pay for efficiency in the allocation of resources might be needed to assess the validity of this proposal or principle on the same basis as that of any other policy preference.

Consider, second, the idea that it is a good thing that people's preferences be satisfied on a WTP basis, no matter how they are formed or what is gained by satisfying them. To test this theory, let us suppose that a visitor to Gettysburg suggests that the Park Service rebuild the Stuckey's restaurant with its parking lots in the middle of the area where Longstreet attacked. This citizen might argue that since Longstreet himself may have dined there, the restaurant should be restored with the original battlefield.

Odd notions of this sort are not uncommon. One visitor to Gettysburg expressed amazement "that so many important battles had occurred on Park Service land." Another visitor questioned a guide's description of the fierce fighting because "there are no bullet marks on the monuments."[109] Silly ideas may lead people to propose silly policies. If the satisfaction of preference ranked by WTP is all that matters, then these ridiculous proposals would be just as valid as those offered by Civil War historians. The WTP of those ignorant of history would be every bit as good as, possibly greater than, the WTP of those steeped in the lore of Gettysburg.

The idea that society use WTP as the standard by which to judge the merit of policy proposals defies common sense. We do not measure the worthiness of political candidates and their positions by toting up the campaign contributions they attract. A recent survey revealed that about "half of young adults believe that separation of races is acceptable."[110] That individuals are willing to pay to segregate schools by race or to exclude non-Christians from office would not make those policies any better. It would only make those individuals worse.

The point of political deliberation in a democracy is to separate, on the basis of argument and evidence, more reasonable from less reasonable policy proposals. The Park Service held public meetings (but did not commission CV studies) to reevaluate its plan for Gettysburg. It sought out the opinions of those who knew the history of the place. As a result, it located the new facility in an area where no soldier had fallen.[111] The outcome of political deliberation depends less on the addition of individual utilities than on the force of the better argument.[112]

Designing for Dilemmas

The students who attended the seminar cared about the environment. One student opined that society has an obligation to save old-growth forests, which he thought intrinsically valuable. Another mentioned pollution in the Grand Canyon. She said we have a responsibility to keep the area pristine no matter who benefits from it. Another argued that even if a species had no economic use, it is wrong to cause its extinction. Another student proposed that the government should promote prosperity and try to give everyone an opportunity to share in a booming economy. She understood the importance of macroeconomic goals but saw no reason to apply microeconomic theory to social policy.

I framed this thought for the students in the following way. If an environmental agency pursues an ethical goal, for example, to minimize pollution as a moral trespass, it has to design for a particular kind of dilemma. (This is the Zuckerman's dilemma I described in the previous chapter.) The agency must pursue its mission in ways that allow the economy to prosper.[113] The agency would have to balance morally based environmental convictions with economic growth as measured by macroeconomic indicators such as levels of employment. Full employment, unlike the microeconomic efficiencies about which environmental economists theorize, does affect human welfare and happiness in the substantive sense of these terms.[114]

How might an agency balance its zeal to control pollution with its need to accommodate economic prosperity? To suggest an answer, I drew a graph in which the x-axis represented incremental pollution reduction and the y-axis represented the "misery index," that is, the product of unemployment and inflation rates. One may argue that statutes like the Clean Air Act mandate pollution control to the "knee of the curve."[115] This is the area where the curve begins to go asymptotic because further reductions in pollution cost so much that they cause rapidly increasing increases in unemployment and inflation.[116]

The authors of the Clean Air Act may have hoped that technological innovation would continually push the "knee of the curve" farther out along the pollution-control axis.[117] On this reading, the statute requires the EPA to minimize pollution (as a form of coercion), rather than to optimize it (as an external cost). The EPA may adopt the "knee of the curve" as a moral principle to balance two intrinsically valuable but competing goals. One is to make the environment cleaner; the other is to allow the economy to expand.[118]

Environmental agencies can and should pursue their moral missions and avoid the unhelpful tautologies of welfare economics. The Park Service, for example, did not commission a cost-benefit analysis to plan for Gettysburg. It assumed it had a duty to design the Visitor Center in a way that respects hallowed ground; within that mandate, it also has to provide for the education and basic needs of visitors. Similarly, the U.S. Fish and Wildlife Service has to collaborate with landowners to design Habitat Conservation Plans that protect species while allowing economic development to take place.[119] Sometimes, a collaborative group can find an inexpensive technical "fix," for example, by relocating the endangered creature to another habitat where it can live in peace.[120] A deliberative body representing "stakeholders" can often deal with a particular problem better than a governmental agency located in Washington.[121] The Clinton administration called for initiatives to "reinvent regulation" by devolving power to such groups.[122]

The statutes under which environmental agencies operate, such as the Clean Air Act, tend to be so aspirational that they offer little or no guidance to an agency that has to answer the hard questions, such as how safe or clean or natural is enough.[123] The agency, in the absence of a clear political mandate, has to find some way to give its decisions legitimacy. It may therefore cloak its ethical determinations in the language of science. Environmental scientists, in their eagerness to speak truth to power, may encourage this reliance on their disciplines.

The problem, however, is that science has no moral truth to speak; it cannot say how safe, clean, or natural is safe, clean, or natural enough. Nevertheless, agencies defend decisions with arguments to the effect that, "The science made me do it."[124] This may explain the attempt to develop economics as a science of valuation – an attempt, as I argue in this book, that is as hopeless and futile as the effort to square a circle, although it employs a lot more people. Environmental agencies, though they must adopt regulations that are ethical at bottom, rarely, if ever, offer a moral argument or principle for Congress to review and citizens to consider and debate. Instead, agencies tend to look to economic and other sciences to answer moral and political questions these sciences cannot possibly answer. And the environmental sciences – strained in this way well beyond their limits – lose credibility as a result.[125]

Retreat from Gettysburg

After the seminar, I chose a route out of Gettysburg that avoided the battlefield and, with it, the ghosts of the past. But my path was full of portents of the future. At a 110-acre site southeast of the battleground, which had served as a staging area for Union troops, I saw equipment gathered to construct the massive mall the Park Service had decided not to build. The developer, the Boyle Group of Malvern, Pennsylvania, according to its promotional literature, promises to erect an "authentic village" containing seventy outlet stores, an eighty-room country inn, and a large restaurant. According to the flyer, visitors to Gettysburg will find the village a refuge from the drudgery of touring the battlefield and learning its history. "History is about the only thing these millions of tourists take home," the promo states. "That's because there is no serious shopping in Gettysburg."[126]

Society can count on firms such as the Boyle Group to provide shopping as serious as anyone could want at Gettysburg and everywhere else. The nation does not have to elevate shopping and, with it, the allocation of goods and services to those willing to pay the most for them, to the status of legislation. Environmental laws state general moral principles or set overall goals that reflect choices we have made together. These principles and goals do not include the empty and futile redundancy of environmental economics – the rule that society should allocate resources to those willing to pay the most for them because they are willing to pay the most for those resources.

An agency, such as the Park Service, may engage in public deliberation to determine which rule to apply in the circumstances. The principle economists tout – the satisfaction of preferences weighed by WTP – is rarely if ever relevant or appropriate to environmental policy.

In the next chapter, I shall argue that preference, as environmental economists deploy this notion, is itself an empty and useless theoretical term that cannot be observed or measured. It represents an artifact of assumption, a construction of confusion, an intellectual will-o'-the-wisp.

The surest way to approach environmental law is to recognize that it is based on moral and aesthetic judgment – on principle, not preference. At Gettysburg, the principle speaks for itself. "What gives meaning to the place is the land on which the battle was fought and the men who died there," as longtime Gettysburg preservationist Robert Moore has said. "Keeping the place the same holy place, that's what's important."[127]

3

Should Preferences Count?

Of the many jokes economists tell about themselves, this is my favorite. Two graduate students overtook Professor Paul Samuelson as he walked. "There's a beggar at the corner," they told him, "who, when offered the choice between fifty cents and a dollar, always takes the fifty cents." Samuelson replied, "He's irrational or it's impossible." When reassured that the beggar had his wits about him, Samuelson decided to see for himself. "In my left hand, I have fifty cents; in my right, one dollar; you may have whichever one you prefer," Samuelson said to the beggar.

"I'll take the fifty cents," the man answered without hesitation.

After giving him the two quarters, Samuelson asked, "Don't you understand that a dollar is worth twice as much as fifty cents?"

"Of course I do."

"Then why did you take the fifty cents?"

"Had I taken the dollar," the beggar replied, "economists wouldn't troop down here every day to offer me the choice."

Welfare economics rests on "one fundamental ethical postulate," namely, that the preferences of individuals are to count in the allocation of resources.[1] This approach to social policy assumes that, for any social decision, preferences are already given and "that the role of the social decision process is just to follow them."[2] In this framework, "preferences are treated as data of the most fundamental kind. Value, in the economic sense, is ultimately derived from individual preferences."[3]

The beggar chooses fifty cents over a dollar. Does this show that he prefers fifty cents to a dollar? Does it show fifty cents benefits him more than a dollar? Does it show that the value of fifty cents is greater than that of a dollar? What relationships hold between choice, preference, and value? That strong connections link these concepts constitutes the bedrock requirement of the theory of welfare economics. This chapter argues, on the contrary, that the only general relations that hold among these terms are stipulated – constructed as tautologies within the theory and otherwise without merit or application.

Three Conceptions of Preference

In the last chapter, I argued that the correlation between preference satisfaction and economic value is either tautologically true or empirically false. Value in the economic sense – welfare or well-being – cannot be derived from preference satisfaction except trivially by definition. I shall summarize that argument later. In this chapter, I argue that preferences do not provide data for the valuation of environmental goods.

My argument has the following form. The term "preference" can be used in three different senses; in none of these three senses do preferences provide data for economic analysis. First, the term "preference" can be used in a psychological sense to refer to a subjective mental entity or state. A simple appetite or desire would count as such a preference, but so would an overall strategy or goal. Second, the term "preference" may be used in a conceptual sense to refer to a theoretical construct inferred from a description of behavior. If Samuelson described the beggar's action as "choosing fifty cents rather than a dollar," he might infer that the beggar preferred fifty cents to a dollar. Preference in the psychological sense precedes choice as a cause precedes its effect. Preference in the conceptual sense follows choice because it is constructed on the basis of a description of observed behavior.

Third, the term "preference" may be used in a formal sense – as it generally is used in social choice theory – to refer to a logical relation between *stated* or *given* alternatives. The choice the individual makes is then construed in relation to predetermined options – as choosing fifty cents or choosing a dollar, for example – no matter what the individual believes he or she does or how the individual understands the alternatives he or she confronts. Preference is given – in that sense it is a datum – but it is not observed. It is given by fiat, stipulation, or presupposition. Preference is "given" because it is assumed in the way behavior is interpreted or described.

In which of these three senses do preferences constitute "data of the most fundamental kind" for economic theory and valuation? Preferences in the psychological sense, as I shall argue, do not constitute data of any kind; as private mental states, they cannot be observed. I am not suggesting that preferences in the sense of mental entities do not exist; I imagine they do. I note only that economics as a rather positivistic science has little faith in its ability to describe entities as shadowy and as private as are mental states.

Preferences in the conceptual sense – theoretical constructs inferred from descriptions of behavior – do not constitute data either. Rather, the behavior itself is thought to provide data on the basis of which preferences are constructed. However, whatever behavior is observed – such as the beggar's asking for fifty cents – invites any number of plausible but conflicting accounts. The observer implicitly decides how to describe a bit of behavior as a choice by divining in some mysterious way the alternatives that confront the individual, as Samuelson attributed an "opportunity set" to the beggar. Likewise, anyone who observes a person's behavior – I will provide examples later in this chapter – will be at a loss to know which alternatives frame the choice that person makes. The observer comes up with an ad hoc story to describe what the agent does.

Preference in the third sense – stipulated preference – can be read mechanically from a person's behavior, in the way a Scantron may read a punched ballot. Preference in this sense is not a private mental state. It is not, like preference in the second sense, a conceptual construct inferred from ad hoc descriptions of behavior – descriptions ginned up by the observer presumably on the basis of empathy. Rather, preference in this sense is logically derived from what the agent does in view of alternatives that are explicitly stated in advance. In this context, both the agent and the observer have the same information about the options that formally frame the choice. This differs from the situation in which the observer, like Samuelson, in an attempt to interpret behavior, makes assumptions about the opportunity set to which the agent responds.

Theories of social and consumer choice apply most easily in situations, such as a list of candidates on a ballot, in which the individual, whatever his views or values, is assumed to choose between alternatives that are stipulated in advance. That people have all kinds of different values and preferences that lead them to mark their ballots as they do is irrelevant to the formal description of what they do, that is, vote for candidate *a* or *b*. If one voter took a bribe, if another followed the suggestion of his or her spouse, and if another simply checked the first box, their behavior would be interpreted to represent the same preference as long as they marked the ballot the same way. One does not refer to anything the individual thinks or wants to determine the relevant preference; rather, one mechanically reads the ballot as indicating a preference between stipulated options. If the alternatives are not stipulated exogenously – if the agent exercises autonomy in sizing up a situation and the observer has to divine the opportunities to which the agent responds – choice would not reveal preference and could not provide data for economic analysis.

Preference in the Psychological Sense

To say that a person likes ice cream more than cottage cheese or favors beef over fish may be to attribute to that person a psychological state such as an inclination or taste. Appetites and desires of this commonplace sort conflict all too often with more general or longer-term goals or interests, such as losing weight or remaining healthy. Analysts distinguish between "intrinsic" and "overall" preferences.[4] As an intrinsic preference, the beggar probably valued a dollar over fifty cents. His overall preference, which motivated his choice, was to keep a steady income by gulling economists.

Intrinsic preferences comprise wants and desires; Kant called these "inclinations" and did not think much of them. "If I had my druthers..." introduces a statement about one's preferences of this sort; it is in the subjunctive mood. That is the way it is with the ordinary wants and desires we take pleasure in satisfying. We rarely get to act on our "druthers" because other reasons, motives, and circumstances tend to take precedence over them. As we get older, overall preferences (general goals and commitments) crowd out our inclinations, though I am not sure whether we leave our vices or they leave us. Often we just do what is required in the situation as we see it. As cartoonist Jules Feiffer has said: "I've discovered that the best decisions are the ones that are forced on you, and if you had been given your druthers, your life would have been far more miserable."[5]

Neither intrinsic nor overall preferences conceived as states of mind can be "treated as data of the most fundamental kind" because they are not data of any kind. As a private mental state, preference in the psychological sense – this is true for both intrinsic and overall preference – cannot in principle be perceived or observed. In the case of "overall" preference, moreover, the individual does not respond to the "given" situation but reconstructs or reinvents it by reflecting on what he or she has reason to want.[6] David McNaughton has written that to choose is not necessarily to find in one's mind a preexisting desire between given alternatives but often to deliberate about or to feel through a complex situation – to organize "competing conceptions of a situation in an overall picture in which the various considerations find their proper place."[7]

Preference in the psychological sense (a mental state of favoring) seems to be neither a necessary nor sufficient condition of choice. That it is not a sufficient condition is obvious. As a resident of Maryland, for example, I prefer that the local baseball team, the Orioles, win the pennant. Not even God Almighty can choose that outcome, however, given the fecklessness of the Orioles' bullpen. Just as I may prefer what I do not choose, so I may choose what I do not prefer. Daniel Hausman has written, "What agents choose is not necessarily what they prefer ... because their choices may be dictated by factors ordinarily distinguished from preference, such as moral principle."[8] Ian Little wrote, "The verb 'to prefer' can mean either 'to choose' or 'to like better,' and these two senses are often confused in economic literature. The fact that an individual chooses A rather than B is far from conclusive evidence that he likes A better."[9]

A recent dinner party I attended illustrates Little's point. Although I was tired and would rather have stayed home, I went to the dinner since I had accepted the invitation. It was a principle – that I ought to keep the promise I made in accepting the invitation – not a preference that got me out of the house.[10] In saying this, I assume that to act on a principle (deontological commitment) is fundamentally different than to act on a desire (self-interest, pleasure, or personal goals). Thus, I chose to go to the dinner party, but as a matter of preference – psychological "liking better" – I would have gone to bed.

Economists themselves say that preference in the psychological sense cannot provide data for economic analysis. John Hicks wrote that economics studies human beings "only as entities having certain patterns of market behavior; it makes no claim, no pretense, to be able to see inside their heads."[11] Little similarly discouraged reference to private mental entities. He wrote that "if an individual's behavior is consistent, then it must be possible to explain the behavior without reference to anything other than behavior."[12] According to Daniel Hausman, Samuelson held that "the economic task of determining the empirical consequences of utility theory was wedded to a philosophical project of eschewing all reference to subjective (and hence unobservable) states."[13] Alexander Rosenberg adds that theorists typically "deny any economic commitment to psychologically represented preferences."[14] Economists recognize that choice is not determined by psychological "tastes."[15] Preferences in the psychological sense may exist, but they do not provide data that economic analysts may study.

Preference in the Conceptual Sense

"The individual guinea-pig," Paul Samuelson wrote in 1938, "reveals his preference pattern – if there is such a consistent pattern" in his or her behavior.[16] For example, if an observer notices that a person consistently chooses x over y when both are available, the observer can conclude that the individual prefers x to y. Preference derived in this way must be understood as a conceptual construct based on a description of a person's behavior on some assumption about the alternatives that confront her or him. Preference in the psychological sense precedes the behavior; preference in the constructed sense follows it. Amartya Sen described this obvious difference as follows: "From the point of view of introspection of the person in question, the process runs from the preference to the choice, but from the point of view of the scientific observer the arrow runs in the opposite direction: choices are observed first and preferences are then presumed from these observations."[17]

Many economists follow Samuelson in regarding observed behavior rather than subjective preference as providing the data of economic valuation. Economists must then interpret the behavior they observe as enacting or representing a choice. This in turn requires that they know the alternatives, *a, b, c,* among which the individual chooses or believes he or she chooses. Anyone who knows the alternatives the agent chooses among – his "opportunity set" – may be able to construct his preference from his behavior. For example, if one knows that the beggar confronts two alternatives – fifty cents or a dollar – one can infer from his behavior a preference for fifty cents. If one assumes a different opportunity set – one that includes the strategy of "gaming economists" as an option – one can describe the behavior differently and infer a different preference.

Economists may not see any particular difficulty in identifying the opportunity set or the set of alternatives that frame and give meaning to any instance of behavior that represents a choice. "In economics," Raymond Kopp writes, "introspection goes a long way toward causal verification of a theory. I know, for example, that I prefer coffee to tea, silver cars to black cars, and hiking to fishing."[18] Kopp appears to argue that the economist can reflect in his own mind the minds of other people to discern how they sort out complex situations. The telepathic power Kopp ascribes to economists – the mental reenactment of the actions of others – is supposed to provide "causal verification."

One can imagine, for example, that Kopp may have been present at the dinner party I attended. Would he be able to tell by introspection that I would rather have been at home? My behavior was polite. How would Kopp or anyone else know that I acted not on a preference to attend the party but on a principle not to break a promise? Perhaps half the people there – it was an older crowd – would rather have gone to bed. If so, half the crowd differed in its motives and values from the other half. I hope observation would not reveal – especially to the host – which half was which.

To rely on empathetic introspection to derive the fundamental data of economic evaluation, as Kopp recommends, is not to escape, as microeconomic theory wishes, from a reliance on subjective, private, mental states in determining preference orderings. Introspection simply replaces the mental states of the observer for those of the agent. Moreover, empirical studies have questioned the idea that economists are particularly sympathetic with or insightful about the feelings of others.[19] No matter how deeply sensitive economists may be, they may nevertheless disagree about how to interpret the behavior they observe. There are a lot of ways introspectively to read the mind of the beggar, to dope out the motives of a dinner companion, and so on – and mental telepathy of the sort Kopp relies upon is unlikely to settle the matter.

Economic theory fails to distinguish *describing* a choice from *observing* it. Anyone can offer a description of the choice the beggar makes; his behavior invites any number of plausible interpretations. No one can observe, however, which of these many plausible descriptions may be correct, that is, which preferences the beggar acts upon. Preferences, of course, are unobservable. What is sometimes ignored is that choices, from which preferences are supposed to be inferred, are unobservable as well.

Girl Scout Cookies and the Price of Fish

An ordinary market transaction I completed recently illustrates the difficulty anyone may experience in figuring out the opportunity set that governs even a simple exchange. Several weeks ago, you might have observed a child knock on my door and, after a conversation, exchange pieces of paper with me. I gave her a check for $20; she gave me a receipt promising the delivery of eight boxes of Girl Scout cookies, mostly Thin Mints and Samoas®. I am not sure how I sized up the situation – although I was acutely aware that this was my neighbor's daughter and that my wife would be irked if I had turned the girl away. I challenge the reader on the basis of the observed exchange to identify the set of alternatives this commonplace and ordinary transaction represents.

Your empathetic mind's-eye reenactment might suggest that I valued Thin Mints and Samoas to the tune of at least $2.50 a box. You would be wrong: I forgot about them, and when they were delivered, I took them to the office. If you knew that the nine-year-old girl was my neighbor's daughter, you might surmise that what I valued was good will around the neighborhood. If you learned I had a nine-year-old daughter as well, a friend of the Scout, you might guess I was trying to maintain peace in my family. Another possibility is that I am just a soft touch and would not turn down a sweet little girl who had to make her cookie quota. Another suggestion would be that I valued the scouting experience and wanted to support the Girl Scouts. All I know is that it had nothing to do with cookies; my office mates ate them. I am sure something about what my wife would approve went through my head. How many boxes would show that I am not cheap but also not a spendthrift? Why do people order Girl Scout cookies? Do any two people who place the same order have the same reasons or preferences?

Let me offer another example to test the thesis that economists can observe consumer behavior well enough to identify the alternatives in terms of which individuals frame the choices they make. Before 1966, demand for fish in Boston remained strong, and for that reason, fish prices were high. In 1966, however, demand collapsed, and fish prices plummeted as a result.[20] This happened abruptly, and fish prices did not recover for a long time. How would an economist describe the observable behavior – that is, the fact that a large number of people switched from fish to meat? What choice and therefore preference did the observed drop in demand for fish reveal?

A little market research would show that Catholics in Boston bought most of the fish, especially toward the end of the week. Any economist could use introspection to explain these facts. He or she might say that until 1966, Catholics preferred fish to meat and paid high prices for it, especially for family dinners over the weekend. Then one day in 1966, their tastes suddenly changed, and they preferred and therefore purchased meat rather than fish. Perhaps an advertising campaign by the Beef Council made the difference. Introspection may suggest that better or leaner beef became available.

Empathetic introspection could suggest another reason to explain the menus of Catholics in Boston. Perhaps Catholics wanted to go easy on fish to save the seas. Empathetic observation of consumer behavior in Boston, however, would not discover an event in Rome. In 1966, the pope lifted the ban on eating meat on Fridays. This fact – rather than any change in preference – might account for the change in demand for fish among Catholics. Who knows? Nothing an economist or anyone else could observe about the market behavior of Catholics suggests anything about papal decrees. All one can observe is that Catholics bought much less fish and as a result fish prices dropped.

Now, once one knows about the papal decree, it is the work of a minute to construct a preference ordering that includes adherence to the pope's wishes as an argument in the opportunity set. The individual chooses among

1. Eating meat with papal consent.
2. Eating fish with papal consent.
3. Eating meat without papal consent.

One can say that the Catholics preferred 1 to 2 and 2 to 3. To get to this preference ordering, one has to stipulate its elements or arguments. Given the set of alternatives among which a person is said to choose, one can handily construct a preference ordering to explain the choice. The alternatives among which the agent chooses, however, are not in the least revealed by his or her behavior. One can study consumer behavior at the fishmonger's and at the butcher shop – one can know everything about price changes – without finding out anything about the pope.

A textbook in microeconomics states that "in real life, preferences are not directly observable: we have to discover people's preferences from observing their behavior."[21] To describe that behavior as a choice, however, one must already have decided whether to include factors like papal decrees – and therefore one must have in effect already attributed a set of preferences to the individual.[22] For many of us – those who purchase Girl Scout cookies included – the relevant preference set is inscrutable. The "discovery" of preference, then, is a matter of imputation or interpretation. Preference in this sense is an artifact of what the observer may or may not know and therefore an artifact of how he or she interprets behavior.

Preference in the Formal Sense

Social choice theory, insofar as it is a mathematical discipline, employs a formal conception of preference that has no psychological referents and does not require the interpretation of behavior. Rather, social choice theory begins by positing a set of individuals $(i_1, i_2, i_3 \ldots i_n)$ and a set of alternative social states $(s_1, s_2, s_3 \ldots s_n)$. It then defines for any individual i_i a preference ranking or ordering for alternatives s_1 through s_n. As an essentially uninterpreted ranking relation logically

defined upon a stipulated set of alternative states, the term "preference" has logical syntax but not semantics. In other words, social choice
theory concerns logical relations among formal terms and has nothing
to say about how to observe or identify the referents of those terms in
the world.

From the perspective of social choice theory, any object makes rational choices if it behaves in a way that is consistent with the axioms
of the theory. One might in this way construct the "preference schedules" of inanimate objects. The sun "prefers" to rise in the east, for
example, and a penny, when tossed, is "indifferent" between landing
heads or tails. The behavior of the letter "i" reveals its preference,
first, not to follow immediately after "c" and, second, to come immediately before "e." The first preference "dominates" the second. A
social choice theorist might ask whether words sounding like *a*, such
as "neighbor" and "weigh," present anomalies – instances, perhaps, of
irrational preference-reversal – or whether they might be considered
instances of rational behavior in view of a reconceived version of "i"'s
behavior and a reconstructed preference ordering.

The point here is that microeconomics – unlike social choice
theory – requires data. If microeconomists studied pennies rather than
people, they would be able to obtain data by observation because there
are so few ways to describe the behavior of pennies. They land "heads"
or "tails." With people, it is different. The behavior of an individual
purchasing Girl Scout cookies, for example, can be described in terms
of any of a hundred preferences ranging from supporting the Scouts
to avoiding the ill will of neighbors. With a formal science, such as
social choice theory, the data are stipulated; opportunity sets are explicitly defined. With an empirical science, the data have to come from
some source other than the scientist. Insofar as microeconomics takes
preferences as its data, it is not an empirical science. Preferences as
mental states exist outside the scientist, but they cannot be observed.
Preferences as constructs inferred from behavior are artifacts of the scientist's own introspective assumptions and thus are not independently
sourced.

Even if micro- and welfare economists have no data, however, they
can develop the formal, mathematical side of their science. Like social
choice theorists, they may begin with "given" because stipulated descriptions of alternative social states and then construct preference

schedules, maps, or orderings as rankings among these stipulated state-descriptions. If microeconomics is to be considered an empirical rather than a formal science, however, it cannot stipulate but must be able to tell in fact what people do and why they do it. The economist must be able – as no one is able – to tell by observing my purchase of Girl Scout cookies what preference or preferences that purchase reveals.

If welfare economics and its subdisciplines, such as environmental economics, take preferences as data, they are formal sciences, like social choice theory and perhaps indistinguishable from it. Valuation must remain an abstract exercise practiced on stipulated preference sets. Absent a method for the observer to choose among the myriad plausible ways to describe a given piece of behavior, each description "revealing" a different choice, microeconomics lacks data and cannot be seen as an empirical science.

Epistemological versus Psychological Programs

Experimental psychologists have engaged in experiments to determine how well human behavior in the laboratory conforms to axioms adduced by social choice theory. Psychologists who seek to elicit and test preference maps in laboratory settings have found that the axioms of rationality do not apply to the choices people actually make. Experiments have found that the preferences people "reveal" given plausible descriptions of their behavior in laboratory settings are not always transitive or antisymmetrical.[23] An individual may choose *a* over *b* and then *b* over *a*, for example, if these alternatives are described in logically equivalent but emotionally different terms.

Theorists concerned with the relation between individual values and collective choice, however, have nothing to fear from empirical psychological research. They may point out that theirs is not a psychological but an epistemological theory. They are not trying to account for behavior in an empirical way, as psychologists do; rather, they are trying to understand the logical or formal structure of rational decision-making. It is one thing to describe the causes of human behavior – to ask why people act as they do. It is another to explore logical frameworks or models – to explain how the concept of rationality might apply logically or formally to individual and collective choice.[24]

Thus, social choice theorists do not use "preference" in a psychological sense to refer to some sort of "private" mental episode or event. Nor do they try to construct the preferences that cause behavior on the basis of ad hoc descriptions of it. Rather, they employ the term "preference" as a theoretical variable with stipulated values that is useful in explaining the logical or formal structure of rational individual and collective choice. In the context of this attempt to identify logical structures rather than psychological factors, social choice theory deserves the admiration it has received.

Philosophers will find the distinction between psychological and epistemological programs familiar. Rudolf Carnap and Nelson Goodman, in describing the logical structure of appearance, for example, found it useful to speak of "qualia" or sense-data.[25] They attempted to show how complex relationships – such as the idea that object *b* lies between *a* and *c* – might be built formally or logically out of these simple conceptual units. These philosophers understood the difference between an epistemological program of clarifying the logical structure of perception and a psychological program of identifying its causes. They did not pretend that "qualia" exist as mental states we "see"; they did not do psychology. Similarly, social choice theorists may acknowledge that the formal enterprise of clarifying the logical structure of rational choice may have nothing to do with the *sturm und drang* of empirical psychology.

The distinction between logical and psychological programs, while it defends the work of formal social choice theorists against refutation by psychologists, does not similarly serve the interests of welfare economists. Unlike social choice theory, welfare economics does not self-consciously confine itself to an epistemological or a formal enterprise. Rather, welfare economists believe they are writing equations – or describing logical relations – among actual items, that is, preferences, in the world. The syntax is thought to have a semantics; the logical relations among preferences economists study are supposed to represent something about behavior that can be observed.

The term "preference" in the context of social choice theory refers to an argument (or element) in an ordering that is "given" because it is stipulated. The term "preference" in the context of empirical psychology refers to a mental state that is "given" in that it exists independently and is not stipulated. The term "preference" as it occurs in microeconomics casually combines both elements – both the idea of a stipulated value of a variable in an epistemological program and the idea of a psychological spring, motive, or trigger for action. Welfare economists move carelessly and thoughtlessly between the logical analyses of rationality and psychological claims about well-being. This macaronic element in welfare economics – its cavalier mix-up of epistemological and psychological "givens" – is what makes the theory impossible to test and ultimately even to understand.

The Description of Behavior

I have now argued that preference, insofar as it is supposed to serve as an empirical datum of economic analysis and valuation, rests on little more than "just so" stories used to describe behavior. Preference in this context is an epiphenomenon, an artifact of description, a conceptual will o' the wisp. There is nothing new about my argument. Empirical psychologists – B. F. Skinner is an example – have for at least fifty years dismissed the concept of preference as it occurs in economics as a conceptual artifice that has no empirical basis. Skinner disparaged preference-based explanations of behavior not only because preferences, as mental states, are unobservable but also because explanations based on them are ad hoc. He argued that mental states such as preferences are "invented on the spot to provide spurious explanations" for behavior.[26]

Critics lined up to lodge the same charge against Skinner's invocation of reinforcing events as explanatory causes of what he called operant behavior.[27] These critics pointed out that Skinner was able to explain and predict the behavior of laboratory rats because there was so little of it. Two psychologists watching the behavior of a laboratory rat would agree in their description of the reinforcing event (a food pellet), the stimulus (a flashing light), and the behavior (treadle pushing) they observe. In situations this well controlled, scientific inquiry can succeed whether or not it invokes "mental" states. What is crucial is that the behavior to be explained (treadle pushing) is identifiable apart from the conditions that are supposed to explain it (food pellets) – that the cause does not vary with (and is not determined by) the way we happen to describe the effect.

In contrast to the limited number of ways we may describe behavior in laboratory rats (or the behavior of pennies), there are many ways to characterize the behavior of Professor Samuelson's beggar – or, indeed, any human behavior. The graduate student who accompanied Samuelson, for example, might describe the beggar's behavior as "choosing two quarters rather than a dollar." This would make sense to the graduate student who, unlike Samuelson, had no reserved parking space and often needed coins to feed the meter. The beggar preferred and therefore chose coins over paper money.

Since this event may have transpired decades ago when Samuelson was in his prime, quarters would have been made from silver. If the encounter took place the year the Hunt brothers cornered the silver market, two quarters (melted) really were worth more than a dollar. If the encounter happened today, the coins would carry images of the states; perhaps the beggar was collecting the set. Perhaps the beggar skipped quarters across a lake and made lots of money wagering on the number of skips. Since he could use each quarter only once, he needed more. Who knows? According to Kopp, economists have an ability of introspection that allows them to plumb the depths of human consciousness. This is an ability that I do not possess. When I was a kid, I listened to a radio program that told me, "The Shadow knows." Only the Shadow can do what welfare economists attempt – to see into the hearts and souls of men.

Economic theory assures us that while preferences are unobservable, they can be "inferred (constructed) by analysis of the choices people make."[28] The problem with this position, however, is that choices are themselves unobservable and must be inferred from assumptions the observer makes about opportunity sets and, therefore, preferences. If the agent exercises any autonomy in sizing up the situation and discovering the opportunities it offers, the observer cannot infer from observed behavior what the preferences are. It seems to be a chicken-and-egg situation. If preferences are not observable and must be derived from choices that are also unobservable, in what sense are preferences exogenously given? Preferences represent theoretical constructs inferred from stipulated or ad hoc descriptions of behavior. To describe behavior is already to make assumptions about how the individual sizes up the situation. How, then, can preferences constitute data "of the most fundamental kind"?

Microeconomics as a Postmodern Science

The science of microeconomics can be usefully contrasted with the science of phrenology. Phrenology asserted a correlation between two variables: (1) bumps on the head and (2) human behavior. By examining one variable, cranial bumps, phrenologists drew inferences about the other variable – human behavior. Phrenologists thought that they could assess "the relative strengths, weaknesses, proclivities, and abilities of an individual's behavior from measurement of the contours of one's head."[29]

The science of microeconomics, including environmental economics, asserts a correlation between two variables, those being (1) preferences and (2) human behavior. While phrenologists associated behavior with the bumps on people's heads, microeconomists associate behavior – at least market behavior – with the preferences that exist, if at all, inside those heads. Why did phrenology fall into disrepute as a science, while disciplines based in microeconomics and welfare economics have flourished?

The answer – the reason that phrenology failed while microeconomics flourishes – is that phrenology had data, while microeconomics has none. The bumps on people's heads are observable; the preferences inside are not. The availability of empirical data doomed phrenology. The fatal problem was that the variables phrenology studied – bumps and behavior – are logically independent. One could observe or measure a person's cranial bumps without assuming anything about his or her behavior. This made phrenology vulnerable to empirical falsification – and the science did not survive.

Economists do not have this problem because the variables they study – preferences and behavior – are conceptual and theoretical constructs that are logically related. These emerge together from introspective reenactments or empathetic insights that take place within the scientific observer. The observer tells a "just so" story – he or she makes up a plausible explanation to explain the motions, that is, the behavior in question; then he or she infers the relevant preferences from that story. The way the behavior is interpreted or described is logically related to the preferences that it is then said to represent. Unlike phrenology, which works with independently observable objects, such as bumps and behavior, microeconomics works with logically related conceptual constructs, namely, choices and preferences. Microeconomics, therefore, will never have to meet the fate of phrenology.

Phrenology failed as a science because it referred not just to logically interrelated conceptual constructs, such as preferences and choices, but to observable things, such as cranial contours. For example, the founder of phrenology, Franz Josef Gall, proposed that the quality of "amativeness" or lust was associated with the prominence of the occipital bone. Critics sorted out subjects by the extent of their sexual activity and found no correlation between amativeness and the prominence of this bone. Hypotheses in phrenology could be tested empirically, and the science was eventually abandoned as a result.

With microeconomics it is different. One can measure the extent of a person's amorous activity without knowing anything about the extent of his occipital bone. One cannot describe or "observe" a person's choice, for example, to obey the pope, however, without presupposing a commitment to obey the pope in the relevant preference set that explains the observed behavior, which in this case is purchasing fish. One must first describe the choice in terms of a set of alternatives, for example, a set that includes religious duties, in order to "observe" that the action responds to one of those alternatives. One can infer a given preference from a choice only by initially describing the choice in a way that refers to that preference. Choice does not reveal preference; rather, assumptions about preference reveal choice.

If preferences are supposed to provide the data for microeconomics, then microeconomics has no data. As long as it has no data, it will perpetually flourish as a science. Blissfully unshackled to any data on which to test assertions and to assess recommendations, microeconomists are free to work forever on the mathematical consequences of their assumptions. They can endlessly address in well-funded research the paradoxes and conundrums – the problems of methodology and technique – the absence of data creates.

By addressing mathematical perplexities and technical difficulties, microeconomists attract funding and build academic reputations. Nothing shows this better than the tens of millions of dollars society has wasted in supporting fruitless research into benefits estimation and transfer, for example, on how to structure Contingent Valuation (CV) questionnaires – how to frame them, what sort of information to include, and how to interpret the response. Microeconomists need not fear the problem that defeated phrenology – the ghastly prospect of testable empirical hypotheses. The massive research funding for improving CV methodology shows that the science of environmental economics has reached the apex of the postmodern; it results only in grant proposals, litigation, debates over methodology, and calls for further study.

An economist may reply that in spite of my animadversions, microeconomics and, in particular, environmental economics provide the only scientific approach we have for identifying human values, making trade-offs, and justifying environmental decisions. Rather than cavil about the limitations of environmental economics, according to this response, I should try to buttress its strengths, because there is no other scientific basis for balancing values and allocating resources efficiently in environmental policy.

I propose, on the contrary, that economic and political institutions, such as markets and elected legislatures, provide the legitimate bases for making tradeoffs – entering contracts, working out conflicts, arranging bargains, and so on – and that no policy science is required. I agree with middle-of-the-road Libertarians who think that public policy should seek primarily to improve the institutional arrangements – courts of common law, markets, and political processes – to make them more effective and transparent instruments of individual and collective choice. As Robert Sugden has written, the principal role of social policy may not be "to maximize the social good, but rather to maintain a framework of rules within which individuals are left to pursue their own ends."[30]

The challenge society faces in resolving conflicts is not typically one of making tradeoffs scientifically; it is one of classifying problems, identifying the principles appropriate to solving them, and assembling information about how to apply those principles in cost-effective ways. Communists once argued that society ought not to trust the vagaries of democracy and the imperfections of markets because social science – by understanding the principles and laws of behavior – offers a surer path to social progress. The fundamental choice, as always, lies between the institutions of a free society and the pretensions of social science. That is the big trade-off.

A Review of the Argument So Far

Let me pause now to review the argument this book has offered.

That the satisfaction of the preferences of individuals (and its collective product, social welfare) should be a goal of social policy – indeed, the principal goal when equity issues are not paramount – is the thesis of welfare economics and its subdisciplines, such as environmental economics. Edith Stokey and Richard Zeckhauser, for example, assert "that individual welfare is all that counts in making policy choices."[31] A. M. Freeman III concurs, "Society should make changes...only if the results are worth more in terms of individuals' welfare than what is given up by diverting resources and inputs from other uses."[32]

I asked why preference – as distinct, for example, from belief, argument, reason, or opinion – should count in social decision-making. Why is it a good thing, all else being equal, that preferences be satisfied – preferences taken as they come, on a willingness-to-pay (WTP) basis, constrained by income and bounded by indifference between alternatives? Having a preference gives the individual a reason to try to satisfy it – and he or she should be free to attempt to do so in ways consistent with the like liberty of others. But does society have a reason to try to satisfy that preference – along with the preferences of all other individuals – to the extent the resource base allows? Does the theory of welfare economics have it right when it proposes that preference satisfaction and with it the welfare of individuals should count as a principal goal of social policy?

Welfare economists contend that people are better off – their welfare increases at least in their own estimation – insofar as their preferences are satisfied. If we regard this thesis as expressing an empirical proposition, how may we test it? We might ask if individuals form preferences with their welfare or well-being in mind. If they do, then they may be better off in their own estimation to the extent that their preferences are satisfied.

As I emphasized in the last chapter, however, people often base preferences on concerns other than personal well-being. Two economists have written, "Preferences may have all kinds of motives, including a concern for others, for future generations, for different species, etc. This has been consistently shown in existing valuation studies that have investigated the motives behind stated WTP."[33]

The previous chapter noted that those who have studied the motives behind WTP for environmental goods consistently have found that people base their behavior not only on what they believe will benefit them but also on what they judge is good in itself, meets certain norms, suits the identity or character of their community, or conforms with principles appropriate to the circumstances.[34] Amartya Sen describes disinterested and principled concerns as "commitment" values. "One way of defining commitment is in terms of a person choosing an act that he believes will yield a lower level of personal welfare to him than an alternative that is also available to him."[35] The extent to which judgments about environmental policy reflect commitment values casts into doubt any empirical connection that might be thought to hold between preference and welfare.

Empirical studies demonstrate, as the previous chapter noted, that after basic needs are met, people do not as a rule become better off, even in their own estimation, as their incomes rise and they are able to satisfy more of their preferences.[36] In the theory of welfare economics, however, it is true *by definition* that the benefit an outcome confers on a person varies with the extent to which the individual prefers and is therefore willing to pay for it. By "welfare," economists mean the satisfaction of preference; the thesis that the satisfaction of preference correlates with welfare thus expresses an empty tautology. Terms such as "well-being," "welfare," or "benefit" serve as synonyms, stand-ins, or proxies for preference satisfaction; accordingly they cannot justify preference satisfaction as a goal of environmental or of social policy.

Environmental economists also base an argument for preference satisfaction on a supposed connection between preference and choice. The idea is that choices satisfy preexisting preferences. "For microeconomists," Raymond Kopp and Katherine Pease write, "the study of choice is the raison d'être and from the study of choice, economic values can be defined and empirically constructed." These economists explain: "A choice implies that an individual is confronted with a selection of alternatives . . . Contemporary economic theory . . . suggests what is chosen must be at least as desirable, from the perspective of the individual making the choice, as the alternatives that were not chosen."[37]

If economists could identify these alternatives, then they could discover data they need to allocate resources scientifically. In the present chapter, I have shown that economists cannot identify the alternatives that individuals confront. Choice is at best a conceptual construct inferred from ad hoc descriptions of behavior – descriptions that themselves presuppose beliefs about available options and therefore about preferences.

To be sure, one could interview a person – the beggar, for example – to gather other information on which to base hypotheses about the choice that person made. Yet two obvious difficulties confront the suggestion that economists might interview people to determine preference schedules and opportunity sets. First, the costs of identifying preferences are likely to be far greater than the costs of satisfying them, especially if industry, environmental, and other groups, each having done its own interviews, enter into litigation with each other about their findings. Economists can absorb any amount of funding to work on methodologies to identify preferences.[38] A vast amount of research on CV and other methods has resulted – and can result – only in more conundrums and calls for more funding for more research.

Second, one can hardly say that preferences are data of the most fundamental kind if they must be inferred from interview and other investigative techniques. If preferences do not comprise data for economic valuation, where are data to come from and how are they to be verified? If economists cannot answer this question – if they do not know how to obtain data for discerning preferences – this is a good reason to abandon the enterprise of economic valuation. The question of how to determine preferences is not one for further research – enough money has been thrown away already trying to answer it. If benefits assessment requires preferences as data, it is a groundless effort. After forty years of struggling with CV and other methodologies, economists still have no reliable way of observing or discerning preferences. It is time to give up.

Conclusion

This chapter has asked if preferences should count in social policy. Why is it a good thing, all else being equal, that preferences are satisfied – preferences taken as they come, measured by WTP, constrained by income, and bounded by indifference between "given" alternatives? Everyone agrees that individuals should be free to attempt to satisfy their own preferences in ways consistent with the like liberty of others. One may also agree that economists can serve society by suggesting ways to improve or to design institutions and processes for social decision-making. I discuss this useful application of microeconomic theory in Chapter 8. There seems to be a broad social consensus that certain kinds of preferences, including basic needs such as health care and meritorious interests in science and art, deserve social recognition. Has society a reason, however, to try to satisfy preferences taken as they come, whatever they may be? Does the theory of welfare economics have it right when it proposes preference satisfaction as the principal goal of social policy?

To show the theory is wrong, I have argued that preference satisfaction as a policy goal cannot be justified either in terms of welfare or in terms of choice. That people prefer many objects and outcomes – especially social outcomes – for reasons other than their own well-being drives a wedge between preference and welfare. Empirical studies show, moreover, that to satisfy a preference in the sense of meeting or fulfilling it – the sense in which an equation or condition is "satisfied" – is not to satisfy the individual who has that preference, that is, to make him or her happier or more content. The relation economists assert between preference satisfaction and concepts such as "welfare" or "well-being" is at best an empty, trivial, frivolous, fatuous, specious, and tautological one.

The attempt to justify as a policy goal preference satisfaction in terms of choice likewise represents a vacuous and meretricious exercise. If "preference" refers to psychological wants, dispositions, or desires, then they are neither necessary nor sufficient conditions of the choices we make. Sometimes we give in to our desires, so that they causally determine the choices we make, but more often we act according to social norms, moral principles, or other reasons and responsibilities instead. Both we and society are better off as a result. In either case, no one refers to "preference" in the psychological sense as a possible source of data for economic analysis. Preferences as psychological states are private mental entities and cannot be observed.

If "preference" refers to a construct of economic theory inferred from "observed" choices, then it simply is not true that the individual makes "choices on the basis of his or her preferences, choosing that state which is most preferred."[39] The individual does not base his or her choices on theoretical entities or on the conceptual constructs of economic theory. The ways analysts choose to describe behavior, in which bits of activity are characterized in relation to a presupposed set of alternatives, represent conjectures that are not usually or easily tested against alternative interpretations. The choice the individual makes – like the preference or opportunity schedule supposed to occasion it – is unobservable and dramatically underdetermined by empirical evidence. The relation between the terms "preference" and "choice" in economic theory appears as tautological as that between "preference" and "well-being" or "welfare."

Preference in the sense economists give to the term has no meaningful, nontrivial relation either to well-being or to choice. There is no reason to think that preference as economists understand the term provides data for economic valuation or that the satisfaction of preference constitutes a plausible or practicable goal of social policy. The concept of preference – and the goal of satisfying preference – can offer nothing other than confusion to environmental and social decisions. Insofar as economic theory depends on the concept of preference – or takes preferences as its fundamental data – it has no reliable contribution to make to public policy.

4

Value in Use and in Exchange *or* What Does Willingness to Pay Measure?

The story is told of an accountant, a physicist, and an economist who took a refresher course in mathematics. To gauge the sophistication of the class, the instructor asked, "What is the value of *pi*?" The accountant answered without hesitation, "The value is three, as rounded to the nearest integer." The physicist replied with equal assurance: "The value equals 3.1415926, taken to seven decimal places." The economist chuckled at the naiveté of his classmates. With Olympian condescension, he answered, "The value of *pi* depends on how much people are willing to pay for it."

Environmental economists define value in terms of preference and measure the relative significance of preferences in terms of willingness to pay (WTP). In Chapter 2, I argued that WTP does not correlate with or measure any substantive conception of the good, such as happiness. In Chapter 3, I tried to show that preferences, in any case, are inscrutable and unobservable. The behavior one can observe – I used the example of my purchase of several packages of Girl Scout cookies – is consistent with any number of different preferences. By paying for several boxes of cookies, I bought or tried to buy something else, for example, the good feeling that I had acted decently, that I had supported the Scouts, that I had not shamed my family, or the like. Every object one buys comprises myriad qualities and relationships, only some of which one may desire and few of which may be visible to others. Accordingly, even if WTP measures value, the question arises, "which value?" or "the value of what?" This can be a most difficult question, and it is not clear that even the buyer of Girl Scout cookies can answer it.

The Argument of This Chapter

In the present chapter, I complete the argument that shows that WTP fails to correlate with or measure value or benefit. To do this, I shall distinguish between two concepts. First, the *market price* of the next unit of a good is the amount the consumer actually pays for it in a competitive market. Market prices are easily observed, say, in advertisements. Second, the *marginal benefit* of a good to a person can be expressed as the most a person is willing to pay for another unit of that good. Thus, I want to distinguish between (1) the price a person pays for an item and (2) the maximum amount he would pay for it if its market price increased. For example, if you get an infection, you need an antibiotic, which may be inexpensive. The price you pay, then, may be less than you would be willing to pay, given the great benefit you may receive from the pills.

Price is a function of supply and demand (benefit), just as the area of a field is a function of its length and its width. The price of a good tells one almost nothing about the demand for it – or the benefit it provides – just as the area of a field tells one next to nothing about its length. One could define the "marginal field" as the field in which area expands to equal length. For such a field, by definition, area and length are equal – but this, of course, is impossible. Similarly, one can define a "marginal consumer" as the one for whom benefit equals price. I believe such a construct is equally unrealistic. Suppose a consumer can spend a dollar either on a life-saving antibiotic, from which he will gain a huge benefit, or on a candy bar, the benefit of which equals just a dollar. The rational individual will always spend the dollar on the good that provides the greater benefit. Accordingly, price and benefit are nearly as unlikely to align as the area of a field and its length.

With these two concepts – market price and maximum WTP – in mind, I want to argue for two propositions. First, I shall argue that market price does not vary with, correspond to, or usefully reflect or measure benefit. Rather, market price is generally settled on the supply side by competition. It is more likely to reflect or vary with producer cost than consumer demand. This hypothesis makes intuitive sense.

When you need something – for example, if you get a flat tire – you do not ask yourself, "What is the maximum I am willing to pay for another tire of a suitable quality?" Rather, you ask "What is the minimum I have to pay for that additional tire?" The consumer, in other words, does not seek out a high price that will equal or reflect the benefit he or she obtains from obtaining a new tire to replace one that is flat. Rather, the consumer looks for a low price so that he or she will then have money left to buy other things.

Second, I shall argue that in general people do not know, need to know, want to know, or have any context or basis for knowing or, indeed, caring how much more they would pay for a good – or how much less they would buy – if its price shot up a lot higher. Ask a person how much he or she is willing to pay for a tube of toothpaste, for example, and the individual will reply in terms of the amount he or she usually pays for it. As long as people can pay and are used to paying competitive market prices, they will not be willing to pay and they do not have to worry about paying far higher prices. With respect to ordinary goods, people judge only whether they want or need an item, whether the market price is worth paying, whether it is fair, and whether they can make the same purchase for less elsewhere. We are all so used to benchmarking our WTP on market prices that we rarely have any idea what we would do in the face of dramatically higher ones. We generally manage our budgets by paying the lowest prices we can conveniently find; we do not have to know the highest ones we are willing to pay.

On the basis of these two propositions, I shall argue that economists cannot determine or measure the value or benefit associated with the purchase or consumption of a typical consumer good. The argument has the form of a dilemma. To measure benefit, economists must rely on either (1) market prices or (2) measures of maximum WTP. First, market prices provide no evidence that can be used to estimate the benefit people obtain from the goods they purchase. The "next," "marginal," or "incremental" drink of water can generally be obtained free of charge in public places. This provides no indication of the benefit it provides. Second, no one has – or can be bothered to have – the foggiest idea of what he or she might do in the context of price shocks, that is, situations in which the price of toothpaste, for example, shoots up. Thus, even if maximum WTP correlated in some way with benefit or utility, it cannot be measured. Nobody but the destitute needs to know his or her maximum WTP for the next tube of toothpaste or any other run-of-the-mill consumer item.

Maximum WTP refers to a conceptual will-o'-the-wisp that is generally invisible and incomprehensible to everyone including the consumer. There may be exceptions. A destitute person might be able to consume so little that the amount he or she pays for an item correlates with the benefit he or she obtains. In a concentration camp or in similarly dire circumstances in which competitive prices do not exist, the individual may deal with a discriminating monopolist who ingeniously gouges the most each prisoner is willing to pay for the good the monopolist controls. In a competitive market, however, people seek out the lowest price they have to pay for the item they want to buy. They do not undertake the extensive research needed to come to some idea about the highest amount they would be willing to pay, for example, if they had to deal with a discriminating monopolist in a concentration camp. Thus, people do not know, need to know, or have the basis or information for knowing their maximum WTP for most things.

In recent times, especially in the field of environmental economics, economists have sought to extend their science to measure the benefit or utility that goods provide.[1] According to this view, "total willingness to pay ... represents the total value or total benefit associated," for example, with environmental improvements.[2] I shall argue that the purpose for which society might employ economic analysis, asset allocation, requires only market prices and not estimates of total utility or maximum WTP. Margins, I shall argue, are good for allocating, but not for valuing. Market prices – actual or "shadow" – are all one knows that is relevant to efficient allocation, and all one needs to know.[3]

Value in Use and Value in Exchange

Although Adam Smith is usually credited with the distinction, Aristotle had noted about 2,000 years earlier that objects may be valuable either for the benefit they provide (utility) or for what they can buy (price). Aristotle wrote, "Of everything which we possess, there are two uses; for example, a shoe is used for wear and it is used for exchange."[4] A thing is valuable because of the benefits, that is, the "wear," that it provides. In the other sense, a thing is valuable because of what may be obtained in exchange for it.

Adam Smith restated Aristotle's view that benefit or utility (value in use) and market price (value in exchange) do not rise and fall together; in fact, they seem to be independent. Smith stated this observation as follows:

> The word VALUE, it is to be observed, has two different meanings, and sometimes expresses the utility of some particular object, and sometimes the power of purchasing other goods... The one may be called "value in use"; the other, "value in exchange." The things which have the greatest value in use have frequently little or no value in exchange; and on the contrary, those which have the greatest value in exchange have frequently little or no value in use.[5]

Classical economists such as Adam Smith believed that the principal goal of economic theory lies in understanding the conditions that explain the prices at which goods are exchanged. "What are the rules which men naturally observe in exchanging them either for money or for one another, I shall now proceed to examine,"[6] Smith wrote. He did not think that economic theory could measure the benefit or utility people obtain or expect to obtain from the goods they purchase. Nor did Smith believe economics had any reason to try to measure benefit or utility. Smith hoped only to analyze the conditions or rules that "determine what may be called the relative or exchangeable value of goods."

Smith argued that the market price of a good will eventually settle near the cost of producing it. If gloves are scarce and shoes abundant, for example, gloves will sell temporarily for more than they cost to produce; however, manufacturers will quickly divert resources from making shoes to making gloves. The price of a good "tends in the long run to correspond to its cost of production."[7] Insofar as competition among suppliers drives prices down to production costs, people will have to spend less money than they otherwise would pay for things they want or need. They will then have money left to buy other things. A competitive, efficient economy – one that pays attention to price signals – produces more of the things people want and asks lower prices for them than a less efficient economy, or so Smith thought. As technology improves, production costs decrease, causing prices to fall. The market provides more things and better things at lower prices.

Unlike Adam Smith, environmental economists today set out to measure the "value in use" – that is, the utility – associated with policies that protect or provide a good such as greater visibility in national parks, wildlife, and so on. David Pearce summarizes, "Economic value is measured in terms of willingness to pay."[8] Eban Goodstein reiterates "that one can measure the benefits of environmental improvements simply by determining people's willingness to pay (WTP) for such improvement and adding up the results... An alternative approach would be to ask an individual their minimum willingness to accept (WTA) compensation in exchange for a degradation in environmental quality."[9] According to another text, "*Benefits are the sums of the maximum amounts that people would be willing to pay to gain outcomes that they view as desirable.*"[10]

The attempt to measure maximum WTP confronts two initial problems. First, for an economy to function efficiently, market price, that is, knowledge about value in exchange, provides the appropriate signal. Cost-benefit analysis, for example, is usually defined on market prices. It is not clear, then, why economists would mix information about market prices with information about maximum WTP or about any measure of benefit or utility. What besides confusion could result? Smith obtained remarkable clarity about the way a competitive economy functions by distinguishing between value in exchange (price) and value in use (benefit, utility) and focusing entirely on value in exchange. We give up that clarity when we take the value of some things at market price and of other things at maximum WTP. The reason to break ranks with classical economists in order to measure value in use, then, is not obvious, to say the least.

Second, as I shall argue presently, maximum WTP, as a concept, belongs in the same category as the maximum number of angels that can dance on the head of a pin – a lovely pretext for academic and mathematical speculation but without empirical content or context. To inquire about the maximum one would pay for consumer goods such as milk and toothpaste is to ask a question that may arise in concentration camps or in other horrible circumstances in which purchasers have to deal with hideous scarcity and therefore pay monopoly rents. This is not the sort of thing, fortunately, that we often need to think about in the context of a competitive market. Except in special cases, the consideration of maximum WTP for ordinary goods – how much more than the given price the consumer might disgorge – is otiose and irrelevant.

The Price-Equals-Marginal-Benefit Rule

Consider the syllogism:

> The market price of a good does not vary with or reflect the benefit that good provides;
> The amount people pay and expect to pay for a good is its market price.
> Therefore, the amount people pay and expect to pay for a good does not vary with or reflect the benefit that good provides.

I want to defend this syllogism. It appears to be unexceptionable. It says that however much you need an item – let's say you are about to run out of toothpaste, milk, bread, paper, lightbulbs, or any other typical consumer good – you "take" the price you find, say, at Wal-Mart, Target, or wherever you shop. You look for the lowest price you can conveniently pay for the item your need. You do not try to find a price so much higher that it reflects your need. No matter how much one needs the good – and no matter what different levels of utility different purchasers obtain from it – the price one pays is roughly the same and is exogenously given, largely as a result of competition among suppliers for customers.

That there is no preestablished equality between price and benefit may seem obvious, yet this intuitively plausible premise contradicts a standard assumption of neoclassical economics – an assumption that defies ordinary experience and common sense. This is the view that the consumer expands his or her consumption of every good just to the point that the value of the next unit – the next orange, gallon of milk, etc. – equals its market price. Thus the price you pay, for example, for an antibiotic, which could be as little as a dollar, equals and must equal the life-saving benefit it provides. This sort of absurdity is what the price-equals-marginal-benefit rule implies.

Charles Kolstad, in his introductory text on environmental economics, provides a representative example of the only argument that is ever given to prove the rule that marginal benefit (or the maximum one is willing to pay for the next unit of a good) equals and must equal the price one does pay. To demonstrate this rule, Kolstad writes that when a consumer needs to fill his car with gasoline priced at $1 a liter,

the consumer expands the amount desired first to 10 liters, then to 20 liters, all the while asking if the next liter of gasoline is worth more than the $1 price. This process stops when the value of one more liter is exactly the price, $1. The result of this experiment is for a consumer buying a good in a market, the value of one more unit of the good is exactly the price.[11]

Now, it is plain that Kolstad never ran this experiment. If he had, he would have seen that the consumer buys 20 liters and stops because that is how much his tank holds. He fills up his tank at the given price – after he has determined that he cannot conveniently find a lower one. The consumer has a certain routine, for example, commuting to work, and needs a given amount of gas, which is the amount he purchases. Typically, consumption of gasoline is not particularly elastic with respect to the prices that are usually charged for it – and this is true of most of the ordinary things we buy. We budget for what we need in view of fairly stable prices.

Textbooks in microeconomics routinely "prove" the price-equals-marginal-benefit rule by invoking declining marginal utility to show that the consumer has accumulated just the amount or number of oranges, bottles of milk, cakes, pies, and so on, such that the utility of the next unit purchased would equal the price. However, nobody expands his or her purchases of these goods to the point at which marginal utility equals market price. We do not have room in our refrigerators.

Arguments to Show that Price Does Not Equal Marginal Benefit

The idea that the benefit a person expects from – or his or her maximum WTP for – the next or incremental unit of a good equals the price paid is so counterintuitive, implausible, and absurd that no one would ever think of it, except that it is a foundational principle of neoclassical microeconomics. There is no argument for this fallacy other than the kind of silly story Kolstad tells. But since this kind of story embellishes virtually every text in microeconomics, it may be useful here to provide, say, five arguments to show that Aristotle, Adam Smith, John Stuart Mill, and other such authorities were correct in thinking that even with respect to the incremental or marginal purchase – the "next" gallon of gas you buy – value in use (benefit) does not vary with, equal, or reflect value in exchange (price).

First, one may define the "marginal consumer" as the consumer who has expanded his or her consumption of each and every good to the point at which the price he or she pays for the "next" unit equals his or her marginal benefit. By analogy, the "marginal producer" is defined as the firm whose cost of production for the next or "marginal" good equals its market price. The "marginal consumer" and the "marginal producer," however, are conceptual constructs or theoretical entities that have never been shown to exist in fact and certainly bear no obvious similarity to consumers or producers generally. In other words, empirical research has not shown that these conceptual constructs apply to people in the real world. The typical consumer, like the thirsty person who drinks at a public fountain, may obtain a vastly greater benefit from a good than is reflected in the price he pays for it. Likewise, the typical producer, let us hope, makes a profit.

Second, people who make their initial purchase of a good – those who buy their first car, computer, refrigerator – pay roughly the same price as those who buy their second, third, and so on. If the principle of declining marginal utility is correct, then the initial purchase corresponds to a greater benefit and WTP than would subsequent purchases. Yet the prices paid are the same – namely, the ones charged by Wal-Mart or Best Buy, for example – for either an initial or a subsequent unit. If benefit differs while price is constant, benefit cannot equal price.

Third, it is simply not true that people expand their consumption to the point at which marginal utility equals price. Rather, people respond to market opportunities by purchasing novel, fashionable, or better goods while discarding those they have. For example, a few years ago, I paid $2,000 for a Pentium I computer. Recently, I bought for half that price a far more powerful machine with many more features. Question: even though the "next" or "incremental" computer I purchased was far more powerful and fancy than the one I owned, why did I pay less for it? Answer: Because I could. The lower price I paid for the incremental computer had nothing to do with Menger's law of decreasing marginal utility, that is, with the idea that I valued the second computer less because I already had the use of the first. I tossed out the old one. The lower price is explained by Moore's

Law of increasing technological ability, according to which the cost of computing power declines by one half every eighteen months. People benefit more from the additional but more powerful computer, car, or other item that replaces the clunker – even though they pay less for it – because technology halves what it costs to produce. Thus, we know that the lower price of the "next" or "marginal" unit does not reflect a smaller benefit but a lower production cost.

Fourth, there are many goods the need for which arises because of contingent circumstances, for example, because you get sick, experience a flat tire, need a drink, or receive a hot tip and have to reach your bookie right away. You pay the price you have to pay for the medicine, tire, martini, or phone call. The price is determined independently from the benefit. Goods like milk, eggs, toothpaste, toilet paper, and many other consumer items, moreover, are the sorts of things that you run out of and have to replenish. Which of us hasn't had to make a trip to the store because we used up the last tube, box, or roll? The principle of decreasing marginal utility is largely irrelevant. You fill up the car when it is near empty – not when the marginal benefit equals the price.

Fifth, one could conduct an experiment to see if people who benefit differently from consuming the "next" unit of a good – and thus whose marginal WTP differs – in fact pay different prices. One could gather people who have just completed a fast together with others who have eaten normally; then at dinner time, one could take them all to the same restaurant, say, one with a buffet. If they all pay the same price – the one the restaurant advertises – then benefit cannot correspond to price. If the hungrier people insist on paying more, however, that would provide evidence for the odd notion that the benefit of the meal corresponds to its price.

I think five arguments are enough – though any number can be provided – to debunk the misconception that everyone expands his or her consumption of each and every good just to the point at which the benefit of the next, incremental, or marginal unit equals the price. Price in fact has no relation to benefit; value in exchange does not vary with value in use. Prices provide the information society needs to allocate assets efficiently, but they do not indicate anything about the value of those assets. Margins are good for allocation but not for valuation. Prices do not provide information about maximum WTP or benefit.

Price Shocks

An advocate of standard utility theory might reply that maximum
WTP – the kind that represents utility – becomes visible during price
shocks. As the market price of a good rises, according to this reply,
some people will buy less, some none at all, until no more units are
sold. One could theoretically ascertain these purchasing decisions and
thus trace a demand curve above the current market price. While this
may be true in theory, it is hard to see how in practice a person could
know – or would care to know – his or her demand curve in the area
much above market price. Only when the price of a good actually increases will people have an incentive to determine how much more
they will pay or how much less they will buy given the prices of goods
that would do instead. Only when price shocks occur do people have
a reason to gather the information they need to determine how much
less of the good to purchase and how much higher a price to pay.

The absence of significant price shocks in the United States since
World War II is a remarkable fact. When I entered "price shock" as
the keyword in a computer search of the economic literature, I found
hundreds of mathematical discussions of the concept, but very few
empirical studies. Most of the empirical papers examine price reductions, such as brand-switching patterns in response to promotions.[12]
Economists have begun to study consumer response to rapidly falling
telecommunication prices.[13] Nearly all the empirical studies of price
increases address the oil price shocks of 1973, 1979–80, and 1990–
91. These papers typically find that the "price elasticity of demand
depends on consumer preferences but more importantly on the technology of energy use."[14] Since the technology of energy use – more
efficient engines, for example – constantly changes, so do consumer
decisions about whether to invest in new technology or to pay higher
prices for gasoline instead. What is more, the oil shocks were driven
by political problems – such as the Arab boycott to protest support for
Israel – for which consumers may prefer political and military rather
than market responses.

To think about how to respond to higher market prices, consumers
want to know whether the price increase is fair – whether it results
from the higher cost of supply or from market manipulation.[15] Fairness
realized by actual price competition provides a necessary condition for
WTP.[16] Where monopolies exist, society regulates them, setting rates

at levels deemed to be reasonable given costs.[17] The enforcement of antitrust laws indicates our unwillingness as a society to tolerate prices that are not set either by competition or by regulation. Prices set by competition or by regulation, however, generally reflect producer costs and possibly profit but not consumer benefit. Accordingly, it follows logically that as a society we are unwilling to tolerate and therefore unwilling to pay prices that reflect consumer benefit, except in special and unusual instances, for example, the instance of the "marginal" consumer who wants the product the least, but still enough to purchase it at the lowest price.

Price shocks occur too seldom and involve too many confounding factors to provide opportunities for people to work out the utility schedules economists attribute to them. Since commodity prices have declined over the past decades and centuries while incomes have risen, people have some idea of the shapes of their demand curves in the area beneath market prices. They have far less experience with determining how much more to pay or less to buy in response to price increases. In California, for example, consumers initially paid steeply higher energy prices but later learned that the price increases resulted from market manipulation. They then determined that they were not willing but were coerced to pay higher prices. The government demanded refunds and arrested suspected manipulators.[18]

The literature of experimental psychology has long argued "that people do not maximize a precomputed preference order, but construct their choice in light of available options."[19] Consumers "do not have well-defined existing preferences, but construct them using a variety of strategies contingent on task demands."[20] Rather than having preexisting utility schedules or demand curves, people construct their WTP ad hoc in the context of market conditions. People look for bargains to obtain the greatest benefit per dollar. Buyers do not in fact bid up market prices to demand values. Rather, if you go to Best Buy, Target, Wal-Mart, and other discounters, you will see, in fact, that competition has driven prices down to production costs.

Price Dispersal and Price Discrimination

According to Alfred Marshall, "the more nearly perfect a market is, the stronger is the tendency for the same price to be paid for the same thing at the same time in all parts of the market."[21] The "marginal" consumer – the one who wants the good the least and so drives the hardest bargain – establishes the lowest price at which a good is sold. Everyone else – no matter how much greater his or her desire, need, or utility than that of the marginal consumer – demands and pays the same low price. The lowest price caps the maximum price the consumer expects to pay – otherwise, why would there be bargain hunting? – and this does not vary with or represent a measure of utility.

An advocate of standard utility theory might object that people do in fact pay different prices for the same things. Price dispersal does exist; the same goods may sell at somewhat different prices even at neighboring stores. What is more, suppliers are able to discriminate among consumers by charging higher prices to those who want a good more. As a result, seats on the same airplane, for example, are often sold at quite different prices. The existence of price dispersal and discrimination suggests that people pay more who expect to benefit more from the items they buy.

The literature that studies price dispersal, however, does not support the idea that people who benefit more are willing to pay more for a good. Rather, this literature attributes price dispersion to search costs.[22] Studies suggest that people pay a little more for inexpensive items to avoid the bother of finding a bargain, but they look hard for the best deal on big-ticket items. Lach found that while some price dispersion exists for chicken, flour, and coffee, there is much less for refrigerators.[23] "Dispersion is low for goods which are expensive, are bought frequently, constitute a large portion of household expenditures, and in markets characterized by intensive search for the best price."[24]

If people who benefit more from an item often paid a proportionately higher price for it, then sellers would price discriminate, in other words, they would sell the first unit of a good at a high price corresponding to its demand value to the consumer who wants it the most, the next unit to the next most desirous client, and so on, with the last unit sold at marginal cost to the marginal consumer, that is, the one who benefits from the object the least but still enough to purchase it. If the second premise of my syllogism is correct, then price discrimination would not exist. The marginal consumer would set the lowest price and all other consumers, limited only by information costs, would seek and get that price. If, on the contrary, people in general pay prices that correspond to their different utilities, price discrimination would often characterize consumer markets.

Price discrimination of one kind or another can sometimes be found in retail markets. Examples include gasoline prices that vary by location, cents-off coupons, special hotel rates for seniors and students, airline fare discounts based on nonrefundable purchases, and premiums for new movies, fashions, technologies, books (as hard covers), and other novelties that will be marked down later (as paperbacks). These different prices arguably reflect different levels of WTP and thus different utilities.

Economists who have studied price discrimination have found, however, that different people pay different prices for a good because of factors other than the different levels of utility they associate with that item. Narasimhan and Howell observed unsurprisingly that consumers who redeem coupons do not place a lower value on the products they buy – and so insist on paying less – than those who pay the shelf price.[25] Rather, they put a lower value on the time they must spend collecting and organizing coupons.

Studies suggest that those with higher incomes or who subjectively value their time more will pay higher retail gas prices rather than go to the bother of finding a lower one.[26] Premiums paid for being the "first on the block" to read the latest novel or install the newest gadget may not represent greater utility associated with the product itself but rather are side payments for a different good, such as the status of owning it first or the convenience of not having to wait. People who are the most eager to fly – and thus who might be willing to pay higher prices – routinely obtain the lowest fares because they reserve seats the earliest, that is, they are first to the market. Airlines plainly charge different prices for seats on the same plane – but their strategy is to fill the marginal seat, in other words, to fill the plane, more than to extract the marginal dollar from those who most want to fly. Thus, what little price dispersal or discrimination occurs does not necessarily indicate differences in WTP that correlate with differences in benefits. Price dispersal and discrimination can be accounted for in other ways.[27]

I have now defended the premises of the syllogism – first, that price does not vary with or reflect benefit; second, that people benchmark WTP on price. The conclusion follows that WTP does not vary with or reflect benefit. At a time when the Federal Reserve speaks darkly of deflation, it is hard for sellers to drive prices above bargain levels. The discovery that people pay prices that reflect benefits rather than bargains would certainly come as news to firms that have not seen a profit for years. "Nothing without a deal is getting looked at," said Bruce Rzentkowski, a Chrysler dealer in Milwaukee, according to a *Wall Street Journal* report.[28] "It's about the deal more than it is about the product these days."

The Demand Curve and Consumer Surplus

While value in exchange is visible in market prices, how can we observe value in use, that is, utility or benefit? To make utility or benefit somehow visible and to show how it relates to WTP, economists may describe hypothetical situations in which the price of a given good rises incrementally. In these hypothetical scenarios, as they confront price increases, consumers purchase incrementally fewer units of a good and finally none at all. In the counterfactual context in which price competition is assumed not to exist and consumers do not switch to a substitute whenever they can save a few pennies, one can draw a "demand curve" and write a number at the top. The number, which is usually stipulated, is then said to represent the greatest WTP of the most ardent consumer for an initial unit of the good. At incrementally lower prices, incrementally more units are bought. Benefit or utility is then said to correspond to the entire area under this demand curve.

In a representative textbook, Barry Field defines the concept of "total WTP." Field writes, "The total willingness to pay for a given consumption level refers to the total amount that a person would be willing to pay to attain that consumption level rather than go without the good entirely." He illustrates this definition with a demand curve. "Suppose the person is consuming at a level of three units; her total willingness to pay for consuming this quantity is $81 . . . ($38 for the first plus $26 for the second and $17 for the third)."[29]

The question arises how Field could know that the individual is willing to pay $38 for the first unit "rather than go without the good entirely." A consumer will be observed to pay the market price for each unit, first or third, unless she can get it for less.

Where do numbers that indicate a higher WTP – $38 and $26 – come from? Field has made up these figures to illustrate the concept. How else but by stipulation – by making up numbers – could one project the demand curve well above market price? If prices increased a lot, one could obtain data about consumer WTP in amounts above current levels, as long as the prices of substitutes increased as well, while the prices of complementary goods remained stable. Absent price shocks for whole categories of goods – absent general scarcities that fortunately do not occur – where are the data to come from?

This critique of the concept of maximum WTP follows Alfred Marshall in his discussion of consumer surplus. He wrote "that we cannot guess at all accurately how much of anything people would buy at prices very different from those they are accustomed to pay for it: or, in other words, what the demand prices would be for amounts very different from those which are commonly sold."[30] Marshall anticipated the concepts of Hicksian Equivalent and Compensating Variation by remarking that we have good information about such changes in consumption "as would accompany changes in the price of the commodity in question in the neighborhood of the customary price." He called attempts to measure demand prices "liable to large error" and "highly conjectural except in the neighborhood of the customary price."

When Marshall described measurement of demand price or total WTP as "highly conjectural," he did not deny that demand curves generally point downward and to the right. He did not deny, in other words, that people buy more of an item as its price falls. He did suggest that the ability of economists to measure demand prices ends with that simple observation about downward slope. Marshall argued, moreover, that even if there were some way to get at demand or scarcity prices – well above market prices – these estimates would be useless because they could not be aggregated or compared with each other. He wrote "that the demand prices of each commodity, on which our estimates of its total utility and consumers' surplus are based, assume that *other things remain equal*, while its price rises to scarcity value." Values thus estimated cannot be aggregated or compared with other values similarly derived because each hypothetical valuation assumes that all other goods trade at customary prices. "[W]e cannot say that the total utility . . . is equal to the sum . . . of each separately."

I do not deny that demand curves slope downward. Becker has shown this would be the case even if people made purchases randomly, since budget constraints limit the sale of expensive items.[31] I am proposing that wherever a person stands on the demand curve and no matter what one assumes about his utility function, he will benchmark his maximum WTP on market prices. Bargain days indicate how many more units of an item people will buy as its price declines. This kind of evidence fills out the demand curve under the market price. There are few if any data to fill in demand curves above market prices for ordinary commodities. In a competitive market – especially given increasing technological prowess – prices drift down with production costs. If WTP is benchmarked on market prices, it correlates with producer cost more than with consumer benefit.

A Constructive Suggestion

To cope with the absence of market prices for public environmental goods, economists have developed methods of Contingent Valuation (CV) on the premise that "if you wish to know the value people place on something (a view, clean air, etc.), just ask them."[32] A representative text introduces the stated preference or CV method in the context of market prices:

When we want to measure peoples' willingness to pay for potatoes, we can actually station ourselves at stores and see them choosing in real situations. But when there are no markets for something, like an environmental quality characteristic, we can only ask them to tell us how they would choose *if* they were placed in certain situations; that is, *if* they were faced with a market for these characteristics.[33]

The textbook follows with a description of the goal of a CV questionnaire. "The central purpose of the questionnaire is to elicit from respondents their estimate of what the environmental feature is worth to them." The text equates this "worth" with maximum WTP. "In economic terms, this means getting them to reveal the maximum amount they would be willing to pay rather than go without the amenity in question."

If people were faced with a market for the good in question, however, they would not reveal the maximum they would pay rather than go without it. Taking into account the prices of substitutes and complements, they would pay prices settled by competition among suppliers. The prices people pay for potatoes, for example, are well honed by competition. The textbook confutes the kind of minimum have-to-pay that is captured in market prices with the kind of maximum WTP that is supposed to reflect benefit or utility.

The central difficulty with CV as an attempt to measure utility or benefit is not that it presupposes a hypothetical rather than an actual market. The problem is that it does not presuppose a market at all. In a market, competition drives prices down to costs. To use Field's example, the prices people pay for potatoes are low, since supply vastly and chronically exceeds effective demand. Year after year, farmers plow potatoes under because they cannot get rid of them.[34] If consumers were faced with a market for environmental amenities, they would discover prices that reflect what these amenities cost to produce or to protect. Economists do not measure maximum or total WTP for potatoes – a truly worthless, pointless, and hopeless task. Why do this for environmental goods, many or most of which could as easily be traded in marginal or incremental amounts?

Consider the protection of endangered species. Some cost more than others to protect; some ways of preserving them are more expensive than others. It may be enormously expensive to protect a given endangered beetle, for example, in its current habitat, where a highway may be planned, but inexpensive to move it elsewhere. Another beetle may cost more to protect or be impossible to move. Each beetle may have different characteristics. For example, the endangered American burying beetle, a nocturnal, social creature, uses keen chemoreceptors in its antennae to find carrion, usually birds and mice. The beetle inters the carrion by digging "a roughly circular subterranean chamber where the adults remain to care for their brood and protect the carrion from raids by other beetles. That kind of parental care is common only among social insects, like bees."[35] The female lays eggs nearby, and the hatched larvae "beg for regurgitated food just like baby birds." The life history of this beetle shows its intelligence and sociality.

In a CV survey, respondents might read about this beetle and thirty other endangered insects, including endangered beetles that are a lot less charismatic and a lot more expensive to protect. They might be

told that the Fish and Wildlife Service (FWS) would have to pay about
$10,000 to reestablish a viable population for burying beetles on part
of its former range. It would cost $100 million to reroute the highway
planned for its current habitat. Respondents might be offered a menu
of beetles and insects that need protection and decide given the costs
and characteristics of each which to protect within some budget constraint, as they do for other kinds of goods. Respondents could then
pick from many endangered creatures those they are willing to pay to
preserve under different scenarios at prices set to reflect the actual
costs of preserving them. They could anchor WTP in production costs
within an overall budget – as in a normal market.

Research into production cost, I believe, could lend some legitimacy
to CV surveys. If the FWS has a certain budget allocated to saving
species, it is useful to know how much each species costs to protect.
Respondents to a survey given this information could say how they
would allocate the given budget among different "competing" species
at their respective costs. This would not differ very much from the
sort of mental accounting people undertake when they decide how to
allocate their budget for groceries, for vacations, for housing, and so
on.[36] Questions of marginal allocation can be answered without having
to deal with the conjectures and conundrums that bedevil attempts –
altogether unnecessary – to estimate maximum WTP as a measure of
utility.

If the intention of CV is to impute market prices to nonmarketed
environmental goods, the outlook may be promising. A CV survey may
concede the point of the argument offered here, namely, that in competitive markets, people are not willing to pay much more than what
an item reasonably costs. A survey may allow respondents to compare
the good in question with others like it that might also be provided at
comparable or different prices. Such an experiment could determine
the choices people would make between competing public goods at
their production costs. This may be more manageable and useful than
attempting to measure total WTP or utility for each good separately
and in a series as if one could aggregate or compare the results.

It is conceivable that some environmental goods may be so "lumpy" –
that is, amenable only to all-or-nothing purchase – and so lacking in
substitutes that market price could not be based on competition. I have
looked through the literature, however, and found little argument to

show that environmental goods are lumpier than are other kinds of commodities and services, although it is often jauntily assumed that as a rule they are. Even a good as lumpy as the ozone layer may be said to have substitutes – sunblock and parasols, for example. I concede, however, that if economists could clearly establish that an environmental good cannot be produced and sold in incremental amounts and has no substitutes or closely competing goods – a tall order – maximum WTP could colorably be relevant to public decisions.

Economists may have refrained from incorporating in CV instruments information about production costs because they knew that respondents would benchmark their WTP on those costs just as they do in competitive markets – where, indeed, they drive prices down to them. In this way, economists have avoided finding out anything about shadow or surrogate market prices. They therefore have avoided finding out anything relevant to cost-benefit analysis or to an investment decision. Instead, analysts typically have sought to elicit total WTP as a measure of benefit or utility – an endeavor that is equally fruitless and needless with respect to goods that are and those that are not marketed.

Conclusion

In this chapter, I have dwelt on the well-known distinction between value in exchange and value in use. Value in exchange (price) can be observed and measured but does not vary with or reflect benefit. Value in use (taken as total WTP) varies with or reflects benefit but cannot often be observed or measured. People benchmark WTP on market prices. These provide an excellent basis on which to maximize benefits across all transactions – but no basis on which to assess the benefit offered by any one transaction. Margins are good for allocating, not valuing. One does not know, need to know, or even care to know one's maximum WTP for anything. One needs to decide only if an item is worth buying at its market price given the prices of complements and substitutes.

Economists use the terms "total WTP" and "benefit" to refer to what Smith called "value in use." Value in use, unlike value in exchange, cannot be measured. It cannot be observed in a competitive market, where consumers are willing to pay one supplier no more than the price a competitor charges. Small differences in quality will produce tiny cross-elasticities around market prices for substitutable goods. These Hicksian variations near market prices, however, may indicate little or nothing about total WTP or benefit.

This chapter has argued that WTP cannot measure the value of anything. If WTP is construed as equal to market price, it is determined largely by competition among suppliers rather than by demand among consumers. If WTP is construed as equal to benefit, it cannot be measured or observed even with respect to marketed goods, much less nonmarketed ones. The attempt to elicit maximum WTP as a measure of benefit or utility appears to be a snare and a delusion of no use to environmental policy, even if it is a central concept or concern in textbooks of environmental economics.

5

The Philosophical Common Sense of Pollution

In an account of parental responsibilities, Clovis, the pampered pro-
tagonist of many of Saki's stories, said that his mother taught him "the
difference between right and wrong; there is some difference, you
know, but I've forgotten what it is." He explained that his mother had
also introduced him "to at least four different ways of cooking lobster,"
and one cannot remember everything.[1]

Because one cannot remember everything, I shall pause here to review the three ways I have so far described of cooking the lobster of environmental and welfare economics. The present chapter adds a fourth
general argument against the conceptual framework economists use
to attach value to environmental assets. In later chapters I shall say
something about the democratic alternatives to economic analysis –
where I shall offer reasons to remember the difference between right
and wrong, in other words, to consider arguments of principle, even
if economists would have us consider only preferences.

The Argument So Far

So far, I have presented three general arguments. First, I have proposed
that the concept of "welfare" to which economists appeal to provide
a normative basis for their science in fact has no normative content
or substance. Economists suppose that the satisfaction of preferences
taken as they come on a willingness-to-pay (WTP) basis bounded by
indifference curves is a good thing – but why is it good? To explain

why preference-satisfaction is a good thing, microeconomists assert a relation between preference and welfare. According to this theory, since welfare is a good thing, and since preference-satisfaction is a means of obtaining it, preference-satisfaction is a good thing. On this basis, environmental economics presents itself as a normative science.

On the contrary, as I have argued, two empirical findings show that no significant relation connects welfare and the satisfaction of preference. First, researchers consistently find that the reasons people give for preferring environmental outcomes often have nothing to do with what they believe will make them better off. Rather, people cite principled views, moral commitments, or political convictions instead. This shows that a substantive connection between preference and welfare (well-being, utility, benefit, etc.) does not exist even in the minds or the expectations of those whose preferences they are.

Second, virtually all of the empirical evidence that has been gathered on the topic shows that no correlation holds between the satisfaction of preferences and perceived happiness or well-being, after basic needs are met. Accordingly, economists cannot look for justification to utilitarian theory and to its assertion of happiness as a basic value or purpose. There is nothing terribly wrong with happiness, I suppose, but the goal of preference-satisfaction, which economists endorse, has no known relationship with it.

The idea that people should be free to try to satisfy their preferences, whatever they are, through fair and efficient institutional arrangements open to all expresses a platitude nobody denies. The idea that the society is obliged to try to satisfy those preferences – not just basic needs or meritorious desires but each and any preference taken as it comes – is the bedrock assumption of welfare economics. There is no justification whatever for this assumption. Welfare economists genially define welfare or utility as the satisfaction of preference. In other words, they assume the very relation between preference and welfare that has to be demonstrated. By positing what has to be proved, economists reduce their theory to triviality. "The method of 'postulating' what we want has many advantages; they are the same as the advantages of theft over honest toil."[2]

The second cooking lesson concerned the inability of environmental economists to find meaningful empirical data that would allow researchers to describe or identify the preferences individuals hold about environmental outcomes, goods, or services. Since preferences as states of mind cannot be observed, they cannot provide data for normative analysis. Preferences might be inferred from the choices people make, if these choices were themselves observable. However, the choices that people make in ordinary consumer markets – I used as an example my purchase of Girl Scout cookies – are not observable. People have all kinds of reasons for doing what they do – and exactly the same visible behavior can plausibly be explained or described in any number of ways, each supposing a different set of preferences. The behavior one can observe is open to interpretation, consistent with multiple descriptions, and inscrutable with respect to the preference it represents. It provides no clear data for determining the values that underlie it.

A third method of cooking the lobster questions the concept of willingness to pay. To provide a way to measure benefit, environmental economists assert that the value of a good to a person can be gauged by his or her WTP for it. I argued, on the contrary, that ordinary observation, common sense, and the theory of rational consumer choice all demonstrate that people will not pay – and therefore that they are not willing to pay – a price much higher than that at which a good is sold competitively. It is obvious that WTP is benchmarked on or anchored to market prices, that is, roughly the lowest prices people can conveniently find for commodities and services they want to buy. Since competition drives these prices down to production costs, WTP is settled more on the supply side than on the demand side; it does not measure benefit in typical markets.

One might suppose that WTP could correlate with benefit in a co-ercive situation in which a discriminating monopolist controls a given good and drives up its price, while all other goods trade competitively. Even in this weird context, however, WTP for the good in question would reflect not the benefit of that good to the individual but the prices of near substitutes and the costs involved in obtaining complements. What is more, people generally respond to monopolies by regulating them and setting prices at some margin over costs. As of this writing, the people of California are sending to jail those convicted of manipulating markets for electricity. It would be news to these convicts that Californians were willing to pay higher than fair and competitive energy prices.

Arguably, economists could speculate about WTP for lumpy goods for which no substitutes exist, but there is little reason to suppose that environmental assets are often of this sort. Protecting species, for example, does not involve a single lumpy purchase but a choice among many candidates, and the same thing might be said of vistas, forests, wildlife, and so on. If environmental economists believe that environmental assets are not the sorts of things that can be priced competitively but can be ordered only in lumpy amounts at demand prices, they should explain why this is the case. No such explanation or demonstration adorns the literature.

So far, then, I have argued – indeed, I believe I have shown – that environmental economics, insofar as it sets the satisfaction of preference as a normative foundation, fails as a policy science. It fails because it offers no reason to believe that the satisfaction of preference is a good thing. It fails because it provides no plausible source of data for identifying preferences. It fails because the measure of value it provides – WTP – has no clear connection with anything but market prices. These are better indicators of production costs than of consumer benefits. The conceptual edifice of environmental economics constitutes a network of confusions, presuppositions, contrivances, and dogmas so interrelated and entrenched that one may find them overwhelming. It is a house of cards, however, that collapses in the light of conceptual clarity and at the touch of criticism.

The Fourth Lobster Pot

This chapter seeks to add a fourth argument against the conceptual framework of environmental economics – an argument that suggests a constructive alternative. In this chapter, I question the coherence and applicability of the concept of market failure particularly in the context of policy for controlling pollution. I shall contend that almost any outcome anyone does not like can be described as a market failure, that is, in terms of some good markets do not price. The concept of market failure, in other words, provides a pretext for overriding in the name of efficiency whatever actual markets may do and thus moves policy away from free markets to centralized planning.

Welfare economists often contend that if markets functioned well, people could be left to pursue their own ends. A problem arises, economists say, because markets in fact pervasively fail to allocate resources – especially environmental resources, which comprise many public goods – to those willing to pay the most for them. Accordingly, Herman B. Leonard and Richard Zeckhauser assert, "A centralized decision process should try to achieve outcomes like those generated by full private consent in private markets."[3] On this view, it is fine for individuals to pursue their own ends in ideal markets where they extract the full benefits of exchange. Social policy based on scientific management is justified, however, because markets ubiquitously and woefully fail to meet this ideal.

Environmental economists make perfunctory obeisance toward markets only to reject them as inadequate to the task of allocating environmental goods. By the late 1960s, as economists Alan Kneese and Blair Bower of Resources for the Future observed, it had become clear to them and to their colleagues that market failures are so pervasive, at least with respect to environmental assets, that "the pure private property concept applies satisfactorily to a progressively narrowing range of natural resources and economic activities." Bower and Kneese called for governmental agencies with trained economists like themselves at the helm to manage scientifically the allocation of environmental goods and services. "Private property and market exchange," Kneese and Bower concluded, "have little applicability to their allocation, development, and conservation."[4]

I shall offer an argument to show that whatever outcomes markets reach must be assumed, on the contrary, to be more efficient than the allocations centralized planners and scientific managers would prescribe instead. This is true because market players are as able as anyone to deal with the information, transaction, and other costs that confront them. In other words, I shall argue that markets never fail to allocate resources efficiently because there is no basis on which to say what would be a more efficient allocation. To be sure, one can always hire experts to write a cost-benefit analysis to show that one's preferred outcome is the efficient one but, as I shall show by example in a later chapter, there is no way to settle the question between dueling cost-benefit analyses. Indeed, I suppose society could transfer its entire economic product to committees of experts to find out what allocations are needed to overcome market failures. The result would be that everything is allocated in the name of efficiency to the scientific planners themselves.

Two Concepts of Pollution

The literature of economics proposes that pollution is a bad thing because or insofar as it represents a cost of production that markets fail to price – a cost people bear without receiving compensation. According to this view, society should permit just those emissions that "pay their way," in other words, those that would still occur even if polluters had to pay for the resulting harm or damage. Accordingly, pollution is acceptable if it results from economic activity the benefits of which outweigh the costs, including all the costs associated with pollution. Many economists, following a suggestion Arthur Pigou put forward in the 1920s, have proposed to tax polluters at an amount equal to the marginal cost or damage per unit of the wastes they emit into the water or air. Such a tax would give polluters an incentive to control pollution to the point at which they would have to pay more to reduce emissions by the next unit than society would benefit from that unit of reduction. This yields an "optimal input mix because the waste disposal services provided by the environment" will be priced along with all other resources.[5]

A second and more intuitive approach regards pollution not as an economic cost to be optimized but as a public harm to be minimized. Environmental statutes seek to minimize or eliminate the harm pollution causes, particularly to our health. The Clean Air Act, for example, directs the Environmental Protection Agency (EPA) to set those "ambient air quality standards . . . which, in the judgment of the Administrator . . . and allowing an adequate margin of safety, are requisite to protect the public health."[6] The Occupational Safety and Health (OSH) Act directs the secretary of labor to regulate toxic materials in the workplace to ensure to the extent feasible "that no employee will suffer material impairment of health" even if that employee is regularly exposed to that hazard.[7]

The purpose of this chapter is to review criticisms of the Pigouvian suggestion that calls for a tax or some other method for "internalizing" the costs of pollution into the prices of goods that pollute. The chapter then considers the idea of regulating pollution as a moral wrong like trespass or assault. The chapter then asks the inevitable question – how safe is safe enough? – and it argues that although this is ultimately a political issue, economic analysis has something to contribute to the way society may answer it.

The Economic Common Sense of Pollution

In 1970, Larry E. Ruff, then an economist at EPA, wrote that pollution is "an economic problem, which must be understood in economic terms."[8] From this standard economic perspective, pollution is to be managed as a misallocation of resources – a failure of the market to allocate resources to those who are willing to pay the most for them and thus (tautologically) a failure to maximize social welfare.

This commonplace conception of pollution as an "external" cost of production rests on a straightforward analysis. Let us suppose that a coal-fired electric power plant emits a plume of pollution that makes life miserable for people in a neighboring town. In effect, the neighbors, by absorbing the costs of pollution without compensation, subsidize the power plant. To speak more technically, the amount the utility pays for labor, coal, administration – its private costs – will be less than the overall social costs of the power it produces. As a result, the users of electric power "will make decisions based on market prices which do not reflect true social costs."[9] From the perspective of society, coal-fired electric power will be underpriced and therefore overproduced relative, say, to conservation, clean air, and other goods society also wants to buy.

According to this familiar Pigouvian analysis, an appropriate emissions tax will make the price of a polluting good, such as electricity, increase. People will buy less of it relative to other goods they want. This will eliminate the overproduction of the polluting good and the relative underproduction of other commodities. In general, consumers will obtain the optimal mix of the goods they want if polluters are required by taxation or fees to "internalize" (i.e., pay for) all the costs involved in production, including pollution costs they would otherwise pass on or "externalize" to their neighbors or to the public.

"This divergence between private and social costs is the fundamental cause of pollution of all types," Ruff summarized, stating the wisdom of the time.[10] There is "a very simple way," he explained, to bring private costs in line with social costs. "Put a price on pollution."[11] According to Ruff, a Pollution Control Board (PCB) should place a tax on emissions. "Under such a system, anyone could emit any amount of pollution so long as he pays the price which the PCB sets to approximate the marginal social cost of pollution."[12] This "polluter pays" principle appealed to environmentalists. It seemed to enlist economic theory – which they might have assumed to be unfriendly – on their side.

The Pigouvian Illusion

It may be costly to measure what people would pay to avoid – or ask to accept – a given unit of pollution. As Ruff acknowledged, the taxes or fees imposed, if they reflect the damage emissions cause, "should vary with the geographical location, season of the year, direction of the wind, and even the day of the week."[13] "In theory and in practice, the most difficult part of an economic approach to pollution," Ruff conceded, "is the measurement of the costs and benefits of its abatement."[14] As Tom Tietenberg noted, "the information burden imposed by the design of efficient taxes was unrealistically high."[15]

To measure the costs and benefits of pollution abatement, economists would seek information about WTP and willingness to accept (WTA), which includes amounts individuals would pay to reduce pollution and demand to tolerate it. If this information were easily available, however, individuals themselves would act on it to make their own bargains. Suppose, for example, that a factory pollutes a neighborhood. Suppose that both the residents and the factory owner know that a device costing $100,000 could eliminate pollution that the residents are willing to pay $200,000 to avoid. That information would surely lead the factory owner and the residents to a bargain in which the neighbors would pay to install the device or the polluter would install it rather than compensate them for their losses.[16] If adequate information about WTP and WTA were easily available, the affected individuals would act upon it, and the "externality" would not exist.

By the 1980s, economists generally agreed that the enormous complexity of pollution problems – the vast number of affected parties, the synergistic effects, the uncertain science, the powerful economic and ideological interests, and so on – made the process of direct negotiation and agreement unmanageable.[17] Yet, public officials found themselves no better situated than private actors to gather and process the information needed to set "optimal" levels of pollution. Private agents have only to satisfy each other, but public agents must get approval up the bureaucratic chain for their estimates of what things are worth; these estimates must withstand litigation. It is conceivable that

the factory owner and the residents, in the previous example, if acting with good will and in good faith, could figure out how to resolve
the conflict between them at least in simple cases. It is not so clear,
however, that bureaucrats, who are subject to political lobbying, legal
challenge, and so on, could get the same information needed to reach
the same outcome.

The government may confront prohibitive costs when it seeks to
measure the environmental losses caused by even a single episode of
pollution. In the early 1990s, the government spent $30 million to
commission experts to assess damages associated with the discharge
of DDT (an insecticide) and PCBs (industrial pollutants) into the Los
Angeles Harbor.[18] About $10 million was paid for a Contingent Valua-
tion (CV) study of the "nonuse" value of losses in the populations of two
species of fish and birds.[19] The study, which took thirty-six months to
complete, was rejected by a court because of faulty assumptions about
the losses that occurred. In an even more expensive CV study, some
of the same economists estimated damages associated with the EXXON
Valdez oil spill. EXXON spent untold amounts to commission Nobel laureates and other famous economists to debunk the method.[20] No CV
study, however expensive, has ever stood up as credible evidence in
litigation.[21]

Economist A. Myrick Freeman III has written, "It is the failure of
the market system to allocate and price resource and environmental services correctly that creates the need for economic measures of
values to guide policymaking."[22] Even if we accept the idea that pollution represents a failure of the market system, it does not follow
that policy makers need "economic measures of values." Rather, they
might try to make markets work better, for example, by establishing
missing property rights or otherwise facilitating negotiation, collaboration, and exchange among the affected parties. It may make more
sense to improve the existing market than to replace it with scientific
management or centralized planning. Expert assessments of costs and
benefits, in the context of policy formation, become themselves goods
that contending interests may be willing to pay for. Different interest
groups may well hire economists to provide different "economic measures," so that policy failure takes over where market failure left off.

No objective standard can be found against which to test differing
ways of measuring the value of a given resource – for example, an otter

killed by an oil spill. All one can do is pay experts for their opinions. Is it any wonder that the experts favor this approach? Expert opinions, once bought and paid for, if they bear upon decisions that have significant political and economic consequences, may become as hotly contested and litigated as the decisions themselves.

The Pigouvian approach simply transfers to the government the costs of gathering information that market players otherwise would bear. Joseph Stiglitz has summarized this point. Since "the government faces the same information and transactions costs that confront the private sector – then there is nothing the government can do that the private sector cannot do."[23] Charles Perrings wrote, "The implication is that if neither the state nor any other nonmarket agency can do it better, then there is no difference between private and social cost and no cause for believing an external effect to exist."[24] The conception of pollution as a market failure, then, may rationally lead the government to do nothing.

Socialism and the Invisible Foot

The idea that the bureaucrats can arrange an outcome economically superior to free markets is precisely the mistake economists attribute to socialism. Thus, Fred Smith, among others, characterized the Pigouvian approach as centralized planning. "In a world of pervasive externalities – that is, a world where all economic decisions have environmental effects – this analysis demands that all economic decisions be politically managed."[25] Two economists agreed, "To counter market failures centralized planning is seen as a way of aggregating information about social benefits in order to maximize the value of natural resources. Decisions based on this aggregated information are to be made by disinterested resource managers whose goal is to maximize social welfare."[26]

E. K. Hunt argued more radically that the Pigouvian or "market failure" approach is worse than nothing because it gives every person an incentive to create as many externalities as he or she can. The government would have to determine how much the person is willing to accept to stop his annoying but legal antisocial activity. Hunt explains:

[T]he vast majority of productive and consumptive acts . . . will involve externalities. Our table manners in a restaurant, the general appearance of our house, our yard or our person, our personal hygiene, the route we pick for a joy ride, the time of day we mow our lawn, or nearly any one of a thousand ordinary daily acts, all affect, to some degree, the pleasures or happiness of others. The fact is . . . externalities are totally pervasive.[27]

Given the pervasiveness of externalities, "each man will soon discover that . . . he can impose external diseconomies on other men, knowing that the bargaining within the new market that will be established will surely make him better off."[28] Hunt concluded:

The more significant the social cost imposed upon his neighbor, the greater will be his reward in the bargaining process. It follows from the orthodox assumption of maximizing man that each man will create a maximum of social costs he can impose on others. . . . The economy, of course, is efficient but only in providing misery.[29]

Economists have acknowledged that the "shortcomings of the market failure concept have been known for some time, but with little consequence, since its use continues to be widespread."[30] An economist wrote that the concept of an externality is "a vacuous and entirely unhelpful term."[31] Yet: "The concept of market failure seems entrenched in the conventional wisdom of economics, if the conventional wisdom is most clearly revealed by what respected economists tell undergraduate students and policymakers."[32]

The existence of a market failure cannot be a sufficient condition for regulation since externalities are ubiquitous. To "correct" market failures, the government would have to control everything. It cannot be a necessary condition, moreover, because the government has perfectly good reasons for protecting public safety and health – as in the common law of nuisance – without invoking the doctrine of market failure. The invocation of market failure now serves as a mantra or shibboleth; it is a ceremonial incantation that provides a formal but empty blessing – a scientific pretext – for any action one might wish the government to take.

The Coasian Turn in Economics

In the writing of Ronald Coase, particularly "The Problem of Social Cost"[33] published in 1960, economists found a conceptual basis far better than that of Pigou for analyzing pollution-control policy. Coase inspired a destructive and a constructive argument. The destructive argument, which I shall now describe, formulates the reasons that the Pigouvian analysis of pollution fails. The constructive argument, with which I shall conclude this chapter, suggests a better economic basis for pollution-control policy.

In his critique of the Pigouvian approach, Coase emphasized the reciprocal nature of harm, for example, that harm arises not simply because of the emissions of a power plant but also because of the presence of the neighbors who are injured. Coase also explained that the operators of a source of pollution, such as a power plant, will negotiate with those they harm to reach an optimal outcome if they can manage the transaction costs – the costs of getting information about WTP and WTA as well as processing and implementing contracts based on that information. This resolution might require the plant to install scrubbers or the people to move away. The parties will agree on the cheapest solution; the direction in which compensation is paid will differ from case to case depending on the initial distribution of property rights.

A recent incident illustrates this analysis. American Electric Power, a utility with over $60 billion in annual revenues, emitted blue smoke that made life miserable in Cheshire, Ohio, a small town downwind of it. The residents threatened to sue to force the plant to cease the nuisance. The plant then had to choose between closing, purchasing enormously expensive control equipment, or simply paying off the neighbors. The plant bought the whole town for $20 million. "Over the next few months, all 221 residents will pack up and leave," the *New York Times* reported. In negotiating with the townspeople, the plant determined how much they would accept for their property. According to the *Times*, "most residents appear happy to go, no questions asked."[34]

Of course, the number of parties in this example was small and the costs of negotiating the bargain (lawyers, the *Times* reports, charged over $5 million for arranging it) were manageable. For the most part, however, the number of polluters and the number of people they affect is very large. In the many-person case, as two economists point out, "the process of direct negotiation and agreement will generally be unmanageable."[35]

How should the government determine the "optimal" outcome – or the "appropriate" emissions tax – in the many-person case? The task does not become manageable simply because the government tries to do it. Bureaucrats might identify the relevant WTP and WTA of thousands of polluters and those they affect with respect to each incremental amount of each kind of pollution, in view of its synergistic effects, opportunities for pollution abatement, costs of avoidance, and so on. Why would people be willing to fund government agencies to gather and process information they have determined is too expensive for them to gather and process themselves? Ruff acknowledged, "The amount of information needed by the PCB is staggering: to do the job right, the PCB would have to know as much about each plant as the operators of the plant themselves."[36]

If people do not trade to change the status quo, the present allocation must be an optimal one in view of the costs involved in changing it, including the transaction costs. To second-guess the decisions of market players in extracting benefits from trade, bureaucrats would have to know more than entrepreneurs. "The conclusion, unpalatable to many economists," C. J. Dahlman observed, is that any outcome that exists "must be optimal, and if it does not exist it is because it is too costly, so that is optimal too."[37]

Why Markets Cannot Fail

Coase demonstrated that in the absence of transaction costs, markets automatically reach an optimal allocation without government intervention. No further reallocation could make any individual better off without harming someone else; in other words, the status quo will always represent a Pareto Frontier. Markets without transaction costs, moreover, meet the Kaldor-Hicks efficiency test, because the "winners" (those who are better off as a result of any change) will in fact compensate the "losers" (those who would be made worse off), if the winners could still benefit from that change. Since all such changes would be costless, we must assume they have already taken place.

In a market with transaction costs, the status quo similarly marks a Pareto Frontier and passes the Kaldor-Hicks test. "In order to carry out a market transaction," Coase wrote, "it is necessary to discover who it is one wishes to deal with, to inform people that one wishes to deal and on what terms, to conduct negotiations leading up to a bargain, to draw up a contract, ... and so on."[38] People have to pay transaction costs as they do any other kind of costs – labor costs, materials costs, transportation costs, to name a few. If any of these costs is so great that the project results in a loss, the agents will not undertake it. Transaction costs, in other words, are ordinary costs of doing business. C. J. Dahlman has written, "It is difficult to see in what significant way . . . transaction costs differ from regular costs of production."[39]

An analogy with transportation costs (as Dahlman suggested) illustrates the point. The presence of transportation costs prevents the market from achieving the allocation it would have achieved in their absence. Pineapples, for example, are more expensive in Russia than in Costa Rica, where they are grown. The government can correct this market "failure" either by defraying the costs of transportation directly or by subsidizing pineapples so that they sell at a price not affected by transportation costs. Why should the government spend a lot of money to reallocate resources around transaction but not around transportation costs? Why stop there? The government could reallocate resources to achieve the outcome markets would have reached but for labor costs, material costs, intellectual property costs, and so on. The resulting allocation would truly be optimal because the government would absorb all the costs – and everything would be free!

According to Coase, "the costs involved in governmental action make it desirable that the 'externality' should continue to exist and that no government intervention should be undertaken to eliminate it."[40] Another commentator pointed out that state agencies, to reallocate around transaction costs, would be "obliged to carry out factual investigations of mind-boggling complexity, followed by a series of regulatory measures that would be both hard to enforce and valid only for a particular, brief constellation of economic forces."[41] Accordingly, Coase showed that "state interference was unnecessary without transaction costs, and technically impracticable with them."[42]

If transaction costs (like transportation costs) are worth paying, the affected parties will pay them and the situation will change. If they are not worth paying, the benefits of making the change are not worth the costs, including the costs of arranging the transaction. Whether the costs are or are not worth paying, voluntary action always achieves an optimal result. Individuals will always extract the benefits of trade until the costs – including the transaction costs – exceed the benefits. Every market is perfectly efficient given resource limitations. Private and social costs always coincide.

Thus, the theory of "market failure" vindicates the status quo automatically in view of the costs involved in changing it. This shows the theory is worthless. Plainly, society has good reasons to regulate pollution; not all emissions are acceptable. The argument I have offered (following Coase) shows only that economic theory – or the theory of externality or market failure – offers no reason to "correct" the price of environmental goods. Microeconomic theory, when its logical implications are understood, calls for no environmental policy. The price of everything is always right.

Why Regulate Pollution?

So far, I have elaborated on the argument from which Coase concluded that in view of the costs of governmental intervention "most 'externalities' should be allowed to continue if the value of production is to be maximized." Coase added, "This conclusion is strengthened if we assume that the government is not like Pigou's ideal but is . . . ignorant, subject to pressure, and corrupt."[43] Since the opinions of experts provide the only basis for measures of the economic damages a unit of pollution causes, and since experts are for hire on either side of any such question, it seems likely that even if a government agency could come up with a schedule of effluent taxes or charges, legal and political wrangling over them ("rent-seeking") will absorb any possible welfare gains. When regulatory actions respond to cost-benefit analyses and interest groups have a lot at stake, payments to expert witnesses, to scientific review panels, and to blue-ribbon committees, to lawyers, and to lobbyists provide ample empirical evidence that Coase was correct.

Does this mean that society should just give up and not regulate pollution? Yes, if we agree with Ruff that pollution is "an economic problem, which must be understood in economic terms."[44] No, if we believe that pollution is a moral problem – a kind of assault or trespass, rather than an external cost. Pollution and the harms it causes are intrinsically bad; government intervention to control pollution is more sensibly justified in ethical than in economic terms. The moral principle that pollution constitutes a kind of invasion – or that people should not be forced to sell polluters easements on their lungs, livers, or property – justifies the traditional societal response to pollution, which is not primarily to make the polluter pay compensation but to make him cease the nuisance.[45]

Libertarians maintain the most radical position among those who believe that pollution should be enjoined as a violation of personal and property rights rather than optimized as a failure of markets to exchange those entitlements. Philosopher Tibor Machan points out that the morally appropriate approach "requires that pollution be punished as a legal offense that violates individual rights."[46] Libertarian economist Murray Rothbard agrees: "The remedy is simply to enjoin anyone from injecting pollutants into the air, and thereby invading the rights of persons and property."[47] The Libertarian position is consistent with legislation that requires "industry to do the best job it can . . . and to keep making progress without incurring such massive costs that economic chaos would result."[48] As Martin Anderson of the Hoover Institute put this point, "Just as one does not have the right to drop a bag of garbage on his neighbor's lawn, so one does not have the right to place any garbage in the air or the water or the earth, if it in any way violates the property rights of others."[49]

The problem with the Libertarian view is that the government, to implement it thoroughly, would have to close the economy down. "The doctrine enunciated by Anderson," as political theorist Jeffrey Friedman observes, "would require prohibiting all involuntary interpersonal physical contact; the final effect of this prohibition would be to limit the planet to one human occupant."[50] The moral condemnation of pollution may appeal to our intuitions, but it must be self-limiting if it is to appeal to our reason. The government has to determine some stopping point, some way of knowing when the public is safe enough, or of knowing which battles to leave to another day. Otherwise, the best will become an implacable enemy of the good and incremental progress toward pollution control will be rejected in view of an ideal of total purity that can never be achieved.[51]

The Agony of Aspiration

In the 1970s, when politicians discovered that being in favor of the environment won votes, the U.S. Congress enacted, among other statutes, the Clean Air Act of 1970, the Occupational Safety and Health Act of

1970, the Clean Water Act of 1972, the Endangered Species Act of 1972, the Safe Drinking Water Act of 1974, the Toxic Substances Control Act of 1976, and the Resource Conservation and Recovery Act of 1976. These laws were aspirational – one might say, demagogic – because they set lofty but utterly vague and often unrealistic goals, calling, for example, for a workplace free of all risks from toxic substances and for "safe" thresholds for air pollutants for which no such thresholds exist. The Clean Water Act required the restoration and maintenance of the "chemical, physical, and biological integrity of the Nation's waters." The Ocean Dumping Act of 1972 prohibited ocean dumping – but did not say where the wastes must go instead.

While Congress trumpeted the good news that everything would be pure, clean, and safe, EPA and other agencies had to announce the bad news that this could not be done except at prohibitive cost. When EPA managed to wring concessions from industry – reasonable progress, not full compliance – it was sued by environmentalists for abrogating the law. When these suits were successful – as in a famous instance when a court ordered EPA to cut off gasoline sales in California – Congress weakened the statute, extended deadlines, or created exceptions.[52] Statutory requirements soon became fictions as deadlines passed, violations were not monitored or prosecuted, and the agencies fought uphill political and legal battles to make what gains they could, given limited means.[53] Whatever improvements the agency managed to work out politically were challenged by irate environmental groups as falling woefully short of the mandate of the law, as they often did.

The aspirational and draconian goals of environmental statutes by now may be seen as cynical: by promising environmentalists the moon, these statutes ensured that little will be done on earth.[54] The Occupational Safety and Health Administration has regulated at a rate of about one hazardous substance a year, while many new substances are introduced. The enforcement of statutes protecting wetlands – Section 404 of the Clean Water Act, for example – was possible only because of the ability and flexibility of officials to determine what and where a "wetland" is. The U.S. Fish and Wildlife Service avoided the drastic effects of the Endangered Species Act by failing to list species and by approving inadequate plans to protect those that were listed. This was often as much as was politically possible given the intense opposition of those who would rather "shoot, shovel, and shut up" than to dedicate their property to zoological ideals.

The late and unlamented Delaney clause of the Food, Drug and Cosmetic Act, which applied to processed food, illustrates the false promise of aspirational legislation. For decades, the statute prohibited in prepared food any trace of a pesticide that can be shown to induce cancer in animals at any dosage, but it was rarely enforced. Few pesticides have been removed from the market, and pesticide uses and their residues remain ubiquitous. Methods of detecting trace amounts of pesticides and other chemicals and of testing their toxicity showed that every box, bottle, or can of food contains a trace of some substance that induces cancer when given in massive doses to laboratory animals. This being so, the Food and Drug Administration and EPA, which are responsible for setting permissible levels of pesticide residues, had either to close down the food industry or to engage in various dodges and stratagems, such as a *de minimis* risk exemption, to flout the letter of the law. The law was honored more in the breach than in the observance.

The Brief Resurrection of the Non-Delegation Doctrine

Environmental groups, of course, continually sued EPA and other agencies for failing to enforce "no risk" statutes such as the Delaney clause. Environmentalists could point to the text of the statute to show that "Congress intended the EPA to prohibit all additives that are carcinogens, regardless of the degree of risk involved."[55] In 1992, the Ninth Circuit Court became fed up with helping EPA to skirt the law. The Court in *Les v. Riley* determined that food must be completely free of chemical additives, such as pesticide residues, even if as a result no food could be produced or sold in the United States.

Congress responded by repealing the Delaney clause and enacting a more flexible policy, the Food Quality Protection Act of 1996, in its place. This result whet the appetite of industry groups who hoped that if environmental groups prevailed in other suits, Congress might have to repeal the CAA, the OSH Act, and other aspirational statutes.[56] Industry lawyers introduced into briefs the argument that the CAA, for example, either prohibits all air pollution – and thus nearly all economic activity – or the statute delegates the entire burden of law-making to executive agencies and derivatively to the courts. The law, if not taken all the way, merely tells the regulatory agency to do the right thing.

Indeed, Justice Rehnquist, in a concurring opinion concerning permissible levels of benzene in the workplace, had argued in the 1980s that the OSH Act gave "absolutely no indication where on the continuum of relative safety [the Secretary of Labor] should draw his line."[57] Rehnquist added that, "in the light of the importance of the interests at stake, I have no doubt that the provision at issue, standing alone, would violate the doctrine against uncanalized delegations of legislative power," referring to the constitutional requirement that Congress not delegate its basic lawmaking duties to others.[58] Future Justice Antonin Scalia, at the time a law professor, cheered the invocation of the nondelegation doctrine. "[E]ven with all its Frankenstein-like warts, knobs, and (concededly) dangers, the unconstitutional delegation doctrine is worth hewing from the ice. The alternative appears to be a continuation of the widely felt trend toward government by bureaucracy or (what is no better) government by courts."[59]

In 1997, EPA tightened air quality standards for two air pollutants, particulate matter and ozone, in response to evidence of risks described, for example, in an Abt Associates study.[60] Industry groups promptly challenged the new standards before a panel of the D.C. Circuit Court. In *American Trucking Association v. EPA* (1998), the Court remanded the regulation to EPA partly on the grounds that neither the statute nor EPA's interpretation of it provided an "intelligible principle" necessary to channel the authority Congress delegated to the executive agencies. Judge Stephen Williams hypothesized that the statute was vague enough to allow EPA to promulgate a standard that prohibited all emissions as easily as one that set levels just below those associated with London's "Killer Fog" of 1952. Since Congress was unlikely to enact any more-specific requirements, the judges instructed EPA to articulate the principle it used in determining a "stopping point" for regulation, that is, a point at which emissions were safe enough.[61]

It was clear to the D.C. Circuit Court panel that regulatory agencies, if they were faithfully to implement basic environmental statutes such as the CAA, could not permit very much economic activity to go on. If the agencies were to allow any risks or hazards, however small, they must follow some principle other than the aspirational mandate of the law. Rather than void the statute for vagueness, the panel asked EPA to articulate such a principle. It was not clear, however, that EPA could or should say what the law is.

The U.S. Supreme Court, to no one's surprise, reversed the Circuit Court panel's ruling by finding that the CAA did not overdelegate legislative authority to EPA. Even if it had, the agency could not make up for the overdelegation by adopting on its own a principle to limit its actions.[62] The Court's decision gave the impression that it would be a good idea if EPA did articulate the theory it used to decide how far to strengthen standards for pollutants for which no known safe "threshold" level exists.[63] By reversing the Circuit Court panel, however, the Supreme Court ended twenty years of judicial flirtation with the idea that environmental laws – since they set out no "stopping point" for regulation – might be voided for vagueness or overturned for delegating too much lawmaking authority to others, in other words, for creating legislators rather than legislation. Justice Scalia, writing for the Court, kept the monster of the nondelegation doctrine buried in the ice.

The Coasian Turn in Environmental Policy

The final decision in *American Trucking* is consistent with the view that regulatory agencies, such as EPA, may regard themselves as Coasian bargainers in the business of reducing pollution and improving environmental quality. Agencies may supplement or even replace conventional rulemaking with contractual or quasi-contractual arrangements to which regulated firms agree and actually comply, given the alternative – the horrendous transaction costs and uncertain outcomes of conventional "command-and-control" policies.[64] According to Richard Stewart, a particularly cogent analyst, "These arrangements, which can be viewed as 'negotiated command and control,' follow an entirely different logic than 'top down' measures," such as cost-benefit analysis, for rationalizing regulation.[65] "Negotiation follows an entirely different conception of rationality – the rationality of consensus – based on Coasian principles."[66]

William F. Pedersen, who for many years served as Assistant General Counsel at EPA, has written that the regulatory contract approach adapts "the mechanism of mutual adjustment that makes competitive markets such a dynamic form of social organization."[67] Both the regulated and the regulator seek out the least costly means to achieve improvements in air or water quality – giving firms an incentive to break ranks with competitors "by disclosing new and more effective ways to achieve social cost reductions, just as low prices are encouraged by competitive bidding for contracts." According to Pedersen, regulatory contracts "enlist the cooperation of the regulated in designing improved regulations, make agency decisionmaking less cumbersome, make agencies less passive," and improve the efficiency of regulation by allowing much greater inventiveness and flexibility with respect to the means but not the ends of regulation.[68]

The relation between means and ends exemplifies the "entirely different conception of rationality" that distinguishes Coasian bargaining from a "command-and-control" approach. The command-and-control approach turns every means into an end in itself, so that firms find themselves bound to a particular rule, a control technology, or whatever, rather than free to find better ways to reach regulatory endpoints. "This allows any change in regulatory instruments to be depicted as a change in ends" that requires a new social consensus.[69] Bruce Ackerman and William Hassler, in their splendid book on the use of scrubbers in coal-fired power plants, wrote what is probably the most devastating and most influential attack on governmental dictation of the means polluters must use to reduce emissions.[70] A series of analyses that followed demonstrated that industry could achieve far greater emissions reductions – and goals could be set proportionately – if it was given more flexibility in devising its own ways to achieve them.[71]

In Chapter 8, I shall present examples of Coasian bargaining in which a regulatory agency elicits the cooperation of the regulated firm in devising ways to improve environmental quality. The agency may set a target for effluent or emissions reduction, for example, one that "benchmarks" performance on the best practices elsewhere, requiring that the polluter reduce emissions per unit economic output to levels achieved by its most pollution-efficient competitors.[72] In some circumstances, the agency may reward (and thus provide incentives for) better-than-required improvements by allowing a firm to sell the difference as a pollution "allowance" to firms that cannot make emission reductions as cheaply. (In the well-known "bubble" strategy, the firm may take credit for "excess" pollution reductions achieved at one place to offset reductions it would find more difficult to achieve at another.) The agency offers the firm flexibility in finding ways to control emissions in exchange for its active effort to control them.

To avoid suspicion that it will be "captured" by the regulated industry, the agency brings into the contractual negotiation environmental groups and other "stakeholders" who – were they not to "buy in" to the regulatory contract during negotiation – could be expected to defeat or hobble it later by litigation or political action. A consensus contract between opposing parties, say, major environmental groups and polluting firms, lends legitimacy to policies that otherwise would die, for example, at the hands of industry flacks at OMB or environmental lawyers in court.[73] In fact, environmentalists and industry representatives, when both weary of agency inaction or indecision, may cut their own deal without governmental supervision. Among many examples of such environmental entrepreneurism – in which private parties who usually sue each other instead work with each other to resolve environmental disputes – the Quincy Library Agreement, the subject of a later chapter, may be the most spectacular.

The Contracting State

"The modern administrative state may aptly be dubbed 'the contracting state,'" writes law Professor Jody Freeman.[74] As she points out, even "in a command-and-control system, the regulatory process is deeply, if informally, contractual."[75] Freeman alludes to the penchant of the regulated entity to fight the agency at every turn – through litigation, lobbying, tactics of delay, and even fraudulent reporting – if it does not want to cooperate or thinks a regulation is too onerous. Accordingly, in the old command-and-control system, the agency often had to enforce its will through consent decrees – "half-way" covenants – in which the firm contracts to meet negotiated requirements. A regulatory contract starts with the idea that both sides have more to gain through cooperation than contention. It may bow to the inevitable and make a virtue of necessity.[76]

The large literature on regulatory contracting at EPA centers on Project XL, a program that seeks to increase environmental protection and lower costs by negotiating site-specific regulatory contracts.[77] The regulated firm contracts to achieve an overall environmental result better than existing regulations require by means other than those the regulation may call for. The government then waives the regulation. EPA must be assured that the regulatory contract has broad stakeholder support; community representatives and environmental groups may be given funds to monitor compliance. According to one commentator, Project XL "essentially allows private parties to 'contract around' inefficient government regulations by substituting a more efficient alternative for achieving an equivalent level of environmental performance."[78] The same approach had been used to negotiate wetland mitigation under the Clean Water Act,[79] habitat conservation plans under the Endangered Species Act,[80] and workplace safety under the OSH Act.[81]

What makes regulatory contracts work is their openness to a variety of solutions tailored to a diversity of circumstances. For example, a firm in a rural area may be allowed to emit compounds that are regulated because they cause smog in cities but have no ill effect in its environment. In return, the company would reduce well below requirements emissions that contribute to a loss of visibility in a nearby national park.[82] Even in their variety, however, regulatory contracts generally look to technology – and to programs that improve technology – to solve pollution problems. Rather than argue about what levels of pollution are safe, cost-beneficial, or whatever, the agency and the polluter try to find out what technologies will reduce emissions at the lowest cost.

As a rule of thumb, it is fair to say that the incremental costs of pollution control generally increase. For any firm or industry, in other words, the first reductions per unit of emissions will be the least expensive; after the easy initial gains, control becomes more and more difficult. With this in mind, regulatory agencies may require any firm to reduce pollution at least up to the "knee" of the cost curve – that is, to the point at which the costs of controlling the "next" unit begin to go asymptotic or increase exponentially. Agencies may also encourage industries – by incentives and subsidies as well as by regulatory fiats – to develop technology in order to move the knee of the curve continually out along the pollution-control axis.[83] Stakeholders who once litigated and lobbied against each other about whether an effluent limit is "safe" or "efficient" could work together to find the most cost-effective ways to reduce that effluent. When stakeholders invest in engineers rather than in lawyers and lobbyists – when they look for ways to reduce effluents and emissions rather than ways to measure their costs and benefits – society can make progress toward realizing even the aspirational aspects of environmental law.

The Difference between Transaction Costs and Production Costs

Earlier in this chapter, I followed Dahlman in proposing that transaction costs do not differ from production costs in the sense that both constitute costs of doing business that have to be paid. As Dahlman and other economists might point out, however, these two kinds of costs nevertheless differ in a crucial respect. Production costs have to do with the price of labor, materials, and technology and may be the same no matter how well or poorly the processes of exchange are arranged. Transaction costs depend on the structure of institutions and vary with the way that exchange is managed.[84] As Kenneth Arrow has written, "the distinction between transaction costs and production costs is that the former can be varied by a change in the mode of resource allocation, while the latter depend only on the technology and tastes, and would be the same in all economic systems."[85]

While the government confronts basically the same production costs as everyone else, it stands in a special relation to transaction costs. It can rearrange or reform institutions to make it less costly for people to obtain the benefits of trade. The most obvious way the government does this is by establishing property rights in environmental goods and services that individuals could not otherwise exchange.[86] In several successful and well-known examples of the "cap-and-trade" approach, the government has established an overall limit or "cap" on the effluents or emissions a firm or an industry can vent into the air or water but then allows firms to trade pollution allowances under this "cap." Every firm is required to hold a permit for each unit of effluent, but if it emits less than its permits allow, it can sell the unused permits to others. Environmentalists may thus "retire" permits and thus directly engage with industry to clean the air.

Under Title IV of the Clean Air Act, EPA began in early 1995 to require coal-fired power plants – the big polluters in the electric industry – to hold one allowance per ton per year of emitted sulfur dioxide (a cause of acid rain and smog) under a "cap" of total allowances that represented a major overall reduction – about 50 percent – as required by legislation.[87] When they fought regulation, electric utilities contended that the cost of reducing emissions would be prohibitive – thousands of dollars per ton. Now that industry could sell "excess" allowances to competitors, firms found it was much less expensive than they thought – even less than the $750 per ton EPA estimated – to reduce sulfur dioxide emissions. In fact, by 1997, one-ton-per-year emission allowances sold for less than $100.[88] Environmentalists who wanted to reduce pollution could buy up permits. Gridlock – litigation, lobbying, paralysis by analysis, and the exhaustion of resources in fees for experts – gave way to progress because the institutional structure changed. Funds went into producing clean air rather than into paying lawyers, experts, and lobbyists, and defraying other transaction costs.[89]

The idea behind tradable emissions allowances and regulatory contracts is that the government should do all it can to bring down the transaction costs that keep people from making the arrangements or reaching the agreements that will benefit them. By changing the structure of institutions, the government can provide incentives for stakeholders to try to accommodate each other and to abandon the zero-sum jockeying that characterizes environmental conflicts. By refashioning institutions to lower transaction costs, the government helps to protect public safety and health and reduces emissions and effluents. Rather than find the optimal allocation through scientific cost-benefit analysis, the government must engage stakeholders themselves to resolve environmental disputes.

6

On the Value of Wild Ecosystems

Mr. Douglas Tomkins, founder of two clothing companies, North Face and Esprit, says he "made way too much money" in these businesses. "Before I was a businessman, I was a mountaineer, and I came to know and love some of the world's wildest, most beautiful remaining places." In 1990, he says, "I sold all my business interests, immersed myself in the literature of deep ecology[,] ... and have for the last twelve years spent virtually all my resources – time and money – to protect wild nature."[1]

Tomkins has purchased about 800,000 acres of land in Chile to form a nature reserve protecting, among many other natural wonders, about 35 percent of Chile's remaining *alerce*, a gigantic tree that can live for four thousand years. The wilderness forests could have been harvested for pulp. Some of the land, once clear-cut, might have been farmed to provide fresh produce for winter consumption in the United States. Fjords there might have served as sites for salmon aquaculture. According to Adriana Delpiano, Chile's Minister of National Property, "Chile already has 2.5 million acres of national parks, and we don't need any more." She and others complain that Tomkin's nature reserve ties up too much resource-rich "land that could be used for development."[2]

An Economic Rationale for Preservation

In the United States, the conflict between preservation and development is an old story. For more than a century, preservationists have offered ethical and spiritual rather than economic arguments for protecting natural areas. John Muir, for example, sought to protect nature in spite of instrumental values, not because of them. Muir condemned the "temple destroyers, devotees of ravaging commercialism" who "instead of lifting their eyes to the God of the mountains, lift them to the Almighty dollar."[3]

A century ago, the battle over the damming of Hetch Hetchy, a spectacular valley carved from the Sierras by glaciers and the Tuolumne River, pitted those, like Muir, who loved nature for its intrinsic qualities against those, like Gifford Pinchot, who valued it at least as much for the uses to which it could be put. Pinchot, who had headed the U.S. Forest Service, would dedicate even Hetch Hetchy for human benefit – in this instance, by turning it into a watering hole for San Francisco. Pinchot argued it would be irrational to keep the valley "untouched for the benefit of a very small number of well-to-do to whom it would be accessible."[4] Muir countered with a moral conviction, not an economic calculation. Society had a moral and religious duty to respect so sacred and spectacular a monument. "Dam Hetch Hetchy! As well dam for water-tanks the people's cathedrals and churches, for no holier temple has ever been consecrated by the heart of man."[5]

Traditionally, those like Pinchot who have favored economic development have argued that technological intervention is usually required to obtain "services" from ecosystems, the way the construction of a dam realized the potential of Hetch Hetchy to serve as a water tank. To get the benefit of nature's services is often to plow a field, dig a canal, build a road, drill a well, or alter a genome. To turn on a light switch, to purchase fresh produce year-round, to drive a car, or to dwell in a house is to depend not so much on nature directly but on technologies that lift the cup of nature to the lip of consumption.

Preservationists traditionally have avoided the economic approach to valuing ecosystems. They have tended to see and describe nature as a refuge from economic activity rather than as a resource for it, and they have characteristically appealed to the intrinsic, not the instrumental, value of nature, such as a remote wilderness or rare species, to justify the economic sacrifices often needed to protect it.

Today, many environmental activists, including many scientists, stand the traditional development-versus-preservation debate on its head by arguing that ecosystems should be preserved in their natural condition *for* rather than *in spite of* economic values and concerns. They argue that unspoiled nature provides long-term economic benefits that offset the short-term disadvantages involved in forgoing development. Environmental scientists now argue that wild and natural ecosystems provide directly for our needs and, therefore, that we have sound instrumental reasons to leave nature alone.

A group of ecologists has written, "Humanity obtains from natural ecosystems an array of ecosystem goods – organisms and their parts and products that grow in the wild and that are used directly for human benefit."[6] Unfortunately, a "lack of awareness" of the economic value of undisturbed ecosystems "helps drive the conversion of natural ecosystems to human-dominated systems (e.g., wheatlands or oil palm fields)."[7] These scientists may agree with Muir in valuing nature for aesthetic, ethical, and spiritual reasons, but like Pinchot they favor economic arguments, possibly because they regard them as more effective. In the words of one, "The ethical arguments for saving biodiversity and the environment are not winning the war."[8]

The Catskills Parable

Environmental scientists understand the power of examples. They know it is easy to find examples of human-dominated ecosystems – farms, campuses, roads, homes, resorts – that may appear more serviceable than, say, the wild savannas, wetlands, or forests they have replaced. Is there any ecosystem that serves humanity better if it is left alone rather than if saddled and bridled by technology? What is wanted is an example that illustrates the instrumental value of ecosystems left in a relatively natural, wild, or undisturbed state.

During the past few years, scientists have presented a telling example to illustrate the economic rationale for preserving wild or natural ecosystems. In the literature of environmental policy and science, this example more than any other presents evidence of the economic benefits that land if left in its natural state can provide.

In 1998, in "fundamentally important work," two scholars "powerfully demonstrated through economic arguments" the value of undeveloped nature.[9] In a now routinely cited commentary in *Nature*, Graciela Chichilnisky and Geoffrey Heal,[10] economists at Columbia University, wrote, "In 1996, New York City invested between $1 billion and $1.5 billion in natural capital, in the expectation of producing cost savings of $6–$8 billion over 10 years." These authors explained, "New York City has floated an 'environmental bond issue' and will use the proceeds to restore the functioning of the watershed ecosystems responsible for water purification." Commentators have argued that this decision "demonstrated how New York City realized billions of dollars in economic benefits by sustaining the Catskills watershed as a water filtration system, rather than . . . building a new filtration plant."[11]

The belief that New York City, to restore the purity of its water supply, has paid around $1 billion to purchase and preserve land in the Catskills has led many scientists to accept an intuitively appealing hypothesis: we benefit more when we preserve nature than when we develop or cultivate it. Many scientists, including those on prestigious boards and panels, have elaborated this idea. An eminent biologist recently has explained that, for generations, New York City received plenty of clean water from Catskills communities. "As their population grew, however, they converted more and more of the watershed forest into farms, homes, and resorts." As a result, "the sewage and agricultural runoff adulterated the water, until it fell below Environmental Protection Agency [EPA] standards. Officials in New York City now faced a choice. They could build a filtration plant to replace the Catskill watershed, at a $6 billion to $8 billion capital cost, followed by $300 million annual running costs, or they could restore the watershed to somewhere near its original purification capacity for $1 billion."[12]

The National Science Board of the National Science Foundation, in calling for research into the services ecosystems provide, now notes at its website that historically the watershed of the Catskill Mountains filtered and purified water for New York City:

Over time, this watershed ecosystem became overwhelmed by sewage, industrial and agricultural runoff to the point that the water quality in the city fell below EPA drinking water standards. An economic analysis provided costs of two alternatives for restoring water quality. The cost of purchasing and restoring the watershed so that it could continue to provide the service of purification and filtration was calculated to be $1 billion. The cost of building and maintaining a water purification and filtration plant was $6–8 billion in capital costs, plus annual operating expenses of $300 million. The City has opted to buy and restore the watershed, i.e., to let nature work for people.[13]

In a paper published at the Ecological Society of America (ESA) website, a panel of scientists repeats the argument, reflecting the view of ecologists that the City could best secure the purification services of natural ecosystems by withholding land from development. The panel argues that "preserving habitat in the watershed and letting the ecosystem do the work of cleansing the water" is "as effective as a new filtration plant. Habitat preservation and restoration costs one-fifth the price of a new filtration plant, avoids hundreds of millions of dollars in annual maintenance costs, and provides many other ecological and social benefits to the region."[14]

Several scientific panels and groups use the Catskills example to show that ecosystems benefit human beings more when they are left to their natural course than when they are "improved" or "developed." According to a paper published by the RAND Corporation, for example, "ecosystem services are the processes through which natural ecosystems, and the plants, animals and microbes that live in those environments, sustain human life." This definition excludes agriculture, silviculture, and aquaculture, sewage treatment, and any service that depends on the manipulation of nature's course.[15] As its principal example of the value of natural ecosystems, the RAND study points to the "natural filtration services" the Catskills watershed provides New York City.

Chichilnisky and Heal, who wrote the original paper that provided the source of this information, noted there that in the Catskills, natural processes in the past "were sufficient to cleanse the water to standards required" by the EPA. "But sewage, fertilizer and pesticides in the soil reduced the efficiency of this process to the point where New York City's water no long met EPA standards." As Chichilnisky and Heal continued, "The city was faced with the choice of restoring the integrity of the Catskill ecosystems or of building a filtration plant. . . . In other words, New York had to invest in natural capital or in physical capital. Which was more attractive?"[16]

A century ago, perhaps, one might have agreed with Pinchot that society had to invest in physical capital, such as technological infrastructure, to transform nature for human purposes, turning wetlands into farms or savannas into cities, constructing dams, tunnels, pipes, and treatment plants. The Catskills parable, as heretofore related, has taught the contrary lesson.

Problems with the Parable

The story that New York City paid about $1 billion to restore or preserve the Catskills watershed is now often cited to show that ecological services can justify the preservation of nature even against well-designed development. Yet, the original paper cites no source as evidence for this story. An exhaustive study the National Research Council (NRC) published in 2000 found that the quality of New York City water had not declined in recent years. "Source water and drinking water in New York City are in compliance" with standards set by the Safe Drinking Water Act, the study reported, and "[t]he Catskill/Delaware water supply currently meets all necessary criteria."[17]

Nor is it evident that natural purification processes until recently "were sufficient to cleanse the water to standards required" by the EPA, as the original paper stated. Since 1910, the City has relied on chlorine to disinfect its water supply.[18] The chlorine residues are so infinitesimal that the City easily complies with the residual standard for free chlorine and "little difficulty is expected meeting this requirement in the future as long as the City maintains its current disinfection practice."[19]

The Catskills watershed acts like a huge cistern that collects rainwater, which is then captured in the reservoirs made by dams. It is not clear that rainwater needs to be purified or filtered by the Catskills ecosystem. Actually, rainwater approximates distilled water, albeit acidified distilled water in the northeastern United States, so impurities and surely pathogenic microorganisms are more likely to come *from*, rather than to be removed *by*, the landscape onto which rain water falls.

Through a complex of dams, reservoirs, aqueducts, pipes, and tunnels, New York City draws most of its water supply from 1,600 square miles in the Catskills and Delaware watersheds.[20] Working farms now occupy less than 5 percent of the watershed, and older farms, unable to compete with dairy and other operations farther west, are now largely reforested. Industrial and dense residential activity each account for less than 1 percent of the land use; most of the area is forest (68 percent) or otherwise vacant (10 percent).[21] According to the NRC study, the population of the Catskills watershed has hardly changed from what it was at the time of the Civil War. "In fact, the 1990 watershed population exceeded the estimated 1860 population by just 235 persons."[22]

The NRC study does note that microbes pathogenic to humans have increased enough from one source in the watershed in recent years to pose a serious problem. That source is wildlife. "Once extirpated from the region by marked hunting and trapping, white-tailed deer and beaver have rebounded during the last century." In regions where there is no livestock, "the background contamination from wildlife populations is apparent,"[23] and increases in fecal coliform bacteria, when observed in the principal reservoir, "coincided both spatially and temporally" with increases in waterfowl populations.[24] If water quality was to be assured, "Beaver populations may require active management in some parts of the watershed."[25]

If the quality of the water supplied to New York City had fallen below EPA standards, then people would have been in jeopardy. Fortunately, both source water and drinking water have remained in compliance with all necessary standards, according to the NRC. The statement that the "watershed ecosystem became overwhelmed by sewage, industrial and agricultural runoff to the point that the water quality in the city fell below EPA drinking water standards" has no identified foundation with respect to the Catskills watershed. In the Croton area, which provides about one-tenth of the water supply, quality did decline, but New York City immediately opted to build a filtration plant at a cost of nearly $700 million rather than to buy up or preserve watershed ecosystems.

Nor is there an evident basis for the statement that "New York City has floated an 'environmental bond issue' and will use the proceeds to restore the functioning of the watershed ecosystems responsible for water purification." A study of the archives of the New York City Municipal Water Finance Authority[26] indicates no such bond issue, and a telephone interview with the Authority's Director of Investment Relations confirmed that there was none.[27] In 1997, New York State authorized the Clean Water, Clean Air Bond Act, which committed $1.75 billion to a variety of environmental projects statewide but earmarked no funds for land acquisition in the Catskills, though some of the money could have been or still might be used in that way.[28]

If its water had not fallen from compliance with EPA standards, why did the City face a choice between (1) investing "between $1 billion and $1.5 billion in natural capital," supposedly the cost of purchasing and restoring the watershed, and (2) "building a filtration plant at a capital cost of $6 billion–$8 billion, plus running costs of the order of $300 million annually"? Nothing had changed with respect to the safety or the quality of the City's water supply. The significant change took place not in the City or in its watershed but in Washington, D.C. What changed were specific regulations and the regulatory approach EPA adopted toward water treatment and watershed management.

On June 29, 1989, EPA promulgated the Surface Water Treatment Rule (SWTR),[29] which, indeed, presented New York City with a choice. The SWTR required that every surface-water system serving more than 10,000 people, no matter how clean or safe its water, either filter that water or successfully petition EPA for a "filtration avoidance determination" (FAD). This requirement had nothing to do with New York City in particular; its water remained excellent. The SWTR applied nationwide and was intended largely to deal with *Cryptosporidium parvum*, a microbe that survives chlorination and that, despite the SWTR, in 1993 posed a serious problem in Milwaukee.[30]

To comply with the SWTR, the City could build a water filtration plant at a cost of $6 billion, with maintenance costs of $300 million annually. Since its water already met high standards for safety and quality, the City had little to gain from this course. *C. parvum* could have become a problem, however, with about 350 vertebrate species, many able to act as carriers, thriving in the watershed. The City, however, had already begun to experiment with ultraviolet irradiation, a recognized alternative to the filtration of water containing *C. parvum* and other chlorine-resistant pathogens.[31]

Second, the City could – and did – petition for an FAD. On January 21, 1997, the City and EPA signed a Memorandum of Agreement that outlined steps the City would have to take to obtain a five-year filtration-avoidance determination, which it did receive.[32] EPA, in keeping with the watershed management approach it had by then adopted, had to be assured that the City would respect and protect the value of nature's services.[33] The City therefore committed itself to partner with landowners and communities to build infrastructure – particularly to improve sewage treatment – to make sure economic development would not impair water quality.

In applauding these aspects of the Agreement, the NRC committee thought that "moderate population growth and a wide range of new economic activities can be accommodated in the watershed without deleterious impacts on water quality as long as . . . infrastructure investments now being planned are put in place."[34] These investments included subsidies for better sewage and septic systems and for improved farm waste management. Waste treatment is necessary precisely because nature does not adequately provide this service. These investments make long-term precautionary sense, though there are, in the NRC's words, "few signs that rapid increases in economic activity are likely in the region."[35]

Had the City invested only in "technological capital" or infrastructure such as septic systems and refused to acquire habitat for preservation, it might have affronted ecologists inside EPA and out who recommended, to quote the ESA panel, "preserving habitat in the watershed and letting the ecosystem do the work of cleansing the water." Since there was no scientific consensus about the amount of wildlife habitat that was needed to disinfect the water supply, however, the City and EPA had to make a political judgment about the number of acres the City would have to buy to satisfy those in authority who believed that biodiversity provides purification services. In the Memorandum of Agreement, the City committed to buy no set amount of land but to solicit the purchase of 355,000 acres.[36] The amount of habitat the City would have to preserve was left vague.

Since 1997, the City has made significant investments in dam and pipe renovations, waste-treatment and septic-system improvement, and farm-operations enhancements. The City has attempted to begin work on a controversial $680 million water filtration plant it seeks to site in Van Cortlandt Park in the Bronx,[37] and it has begun a multi-billion-dollar water tunnel project. In spite of the expectations of many environmentalists, it has not been as lavish, however, in the investments it has made in preserving wildlife habitat as a method for purifying its water supply.

In fact, the extent of the City's habitat acquisition has disappointed environmentalists. In April 2001, an environmental group said the City "only secured a measly 36 acres of land surrounding the strategic reservoir – the Westchester County source for 90 percent of the city's drinking water."[38] In a May 2000 report, EPA castigated the City for having bought only seventeen undeveloped acres of the one thousand available around a crucial reservoir in the Catskills system.[39] As of October 29, 2001, New York City had completed the purchase of only 17,250 acres across the entire watershed, most not by acquisition but through conservation easements.[40] A phone interview with City officials determined that as of the following February, only 19,200 acres had been purchased, at a cost of $63.8 million. According to a press release dated December 19, 2003, the City by then had committed about $135 million to acquiring land in both the Croton and the Catskills watersheds.[41] After September 11, 2001, the need to secure land around reservoirs as a protection against terrorism became evident, and land acquisitions could serve this purpose, yet the City has capped at $260 million the amount it may eventually spend.[42]

The City is unlikely to pick up the desultory pace of its investments in land reserves except as a buffer to bioterrorism. By 1997, the City had bought enough land – virtually none – to reveal its own working estimate of the economic value of the surface-water purification services undeveloped terrestrial ecosystems provide. Environmental scientists and others gave their version of this estimate. A document on the ESA website announced, "In 1996, New York City invested more than a billion dollars to buy land and restore habitat in the Catskill Mountains, the source of the city's fresh water supply." This was one of many publications that repeated and amplified the account published in *Nature* in 1998 without relevant references, citations, or sources.

The "Nature" in Nature's Services

To understand the economic value of nature's services, one must define to what the term "nature" refers. The term "nature," as John Stuart Mill wrote, can refer to either of two things. First, the term may denote "the aggregate of the powers and properties of all things. Nature means the sum of all phenomena, together with the causes which produce them; including not only all that happens, but all that is capable of happening."[43] In this sense, the opposite of the "natural" is the "supernatural." Plainly, humanity could not exist without nature in the sense of everything under the sun and the sun itself.

Nature in the sense of all phenomena is the subject of every natural science, including the physical, chemical, and biological sciences. These empirical sciences comprise humanity and all its activities under exactly the same rules, laws, principles, and processes as apply to any other object and its activities. For example, genetic selection is genetic selection, as Charles Darwin understood, whether it is "natural" or "artificial." The kind of genetic recombination and engineering that occurs in the laboratories of Monsanto complies with exactly the same natural laws, rules, and processes as characterize the evolution of wild varieties. Any law, rule, mechanism, or process that pristine nature follows is one that human beings can apply to transform the environment to serve human purposes. The mechanisms of genetic selection, for example, do not change when humans utilize them to improve crops for agriculture.

As John Stuart Mill notes:

[T]o ask people to conform their actions to the laws of nature when they have no power but what the laws of nature give them – when it is a physical impossibility for them to do the smallest thing otherwise than through some law of nature, is an absurdity. The thing they need to be told is what particular law of nature they should make use of in a particular case.[44]

Nature in the second sense, according to Mill, means "not everything which happens, but only what takes place without the agency, or without the voluntary and intentional agency, of man." The opposite of the "natural" in this sense is the "artificial." This distinction acknowledges a moral or a spiritual division between human beings and other creatures. Even though all objects conform to the same rules and principles from the perspective of the empirical sciences, human beings differ from other creatures because, as far as we know, only we possess free will and are thus morally responsible for what we do. The distinction between the natural and the artificial marks the difference between those things that God has ordained and those things for which human beings are accountable. This difference, even if it means nothing to empirical science, is foundational to our ethical, social, cultural, and spiritual lives.

In our secular society, we have come to depend on scientists, particularly ecologists and ecological economists, to remind us of the fundamental truths that clergy taught to earlier generations. Our dependence on God's spontaneity and beneficence cannot be overstated. Human beings, weighed down by sin and corrupted by the profit motive, are far less likely to improve upon than to spoil what God has made. This lesson, which once required only religious judgment and conviction, now carries the authority of scientific journals and prestigious panels. When we look to science to explain or justify our moral and spiritual obligations to respect and protect Creation, we encourage scientists to embrace stories such as the Catskills Parable to show that nature will care for us as it does for the lilies of the field. These stories, examples, and assessments teach the right lesson, and, therefore, like any homily, they do not have to stand up on the facts.

Can We Put a Price on Nature's Services?

One may not need the Catskills parable, of course, to show that nature provides many goods and services that we enjoy for free. For example, the atmospheric oxygen on which we depend was generated by cyanobacteria two or three billion years ago. One could argue that we do not appropriately value the work of these bacteria – they received no payment – unless we measure their labor in economic terms. Is there a way that economists might put a price on oxygen production during the Archean era, for example, by establishing how much the cyanobacteria might have charged for their services? One might ask how much oxygen sells for today or would cost to produce, say, from water. This exercise might teach us better to appreciate nature's free services and thus to protect nature from further alteration or development.

One might carry the same research program forward to attach a price to all of nature's services – everything we obtain from the uncompensated efforts of plants, animals, insects, microbes, and every other living thing. If this price were great enough, it should counsel us to protect and preserve nature, not just for aesthetic and ethical reasons but also for instrumental and economic ones. If we must in general preserve wild nature – rather than transform, manipulate, or develop it – to ensure the free services it provides, then the greater the value of these services, the stronger the economic rationale for preserving pristine environments. If nature undisturbed is economically worth more than nature domesticated, one might justify dismantling cities, abandoning farms, closing universities, and otherwise returning the earth to its unfettered course. By trusting to nature we could be far richer than we are today, if nature's services are worth more than those of industry.

A group of ecological economists led by Robert Costanza, then of the University of Maryland, reached something like this conclusion. In the prestigious scientific journal *Nature* (which also published the Chichilnisky and Heal article discussed earlier), Costanza and colleagues argued that if the importance of nature's free benefits could be adequately quantified in economic terms, policy decisions could "better reflect the value of ecosystem services and natural capital." Drawing upon earlier studies that have "aimed at estimating the value of a wide variety" of ecosystem goods and services – from waste assimilation and the renewal of soil fertility to climate stabilization and the tempering of floods and droughts – the research team has estimated the "current economic value" of the entire biosphere at between $16 trillion and $54 trillion per year. Its "average" value, according to these authors, is about $33 trillion per year.[45] Since this is almost twice the annual economic value of the product of the world's economy, one may surmise that every time we convert nature, we may diminish the total economic value (TEV) of the relevant resource, such as a wetland or forest, by as much as half. Each time we restore wild nature, for example, by turning suburbs to savannas, we increase our wealth.

Some of these authors, writing with others in a later article, make this point. They conclude from case studies that when ecosystems are developed for commercial purposes, "mean losses of TEV due to conversion run at roughly one-half of the TEV of relatively intact ecosystems." This implies that the conversion of wild ecosystems – wetlands, say, into residences – represents on average a major economic loss.

Might this suggest, for example, that society would be better off if it dismantled Boston's historic Back Bay in order to restore the fens and swamps that once functioned as trysting grounds for malarial mosquitoes? Perhaps. These authors do not necessarily claim that efforts to restore nature – for example, by tearing down universities and allowing campuses to revert to forest – would necessarily increase total economic output. They conclude, however, that any further conversion of nature to industrial or commercial purposes "does not make sense from the perspective of global sustainability."[46]

The estimate that nature's services are worth $33 trillion – especially because it was presented in a lead article in *Nature* – was bound to attract public attention. In stories with titles like, "How Much Is Nature

Worth? For You, $33 Trillion," and "What Has Mother Nature Done for You Lately?" dozens of newspapers and magazines, including the *New York Times, Newsweek,* and *U.S. News and World Report,* covered the Costanza study.[47] "What is the natural environment worth in cold cash?" asked the *San Francisco Chronicle.* "No one knows for sure, but a team of economists and scientists figures $33 trillion, more or less, for such 'free' goods and services as water, air, crop pollination, fish, pollution control and splendid scenery.... For comparison, the gross national product of all the world's countries put together is around $18 trillion."[48]

Costanza et al. acknowledge that their estimates are fraught with uncertainties; the study, they say, provides only "a first approximation of the relative magnitude of global ecosystem services." Their caution is understandable. No one can doubt that "ecological systems... contribute to human welfare, both directly and indirectly," or that the world's economies depend on the "ecological life-support systems" that nature provides for free. "Once explained the importance of ecosystem services is typically quickly appreciated," writes Gretchen Daily, an ecologist at Stanford University. And yet, as she goes on to say, "the actual assigning of value to ecosystem services may arouse great suspicion." This is because "valuation involves resolving fundamental philosophical issues" – about the role of economic values in the policy process, the relation between economic value and human welfare, and various methodological problems.[49]

Even so, Daily concludes that "nothing could matter more" than attaching economic values to ecological services. "The way our decisions are made today is based almost entirely on economic values," she told the *San Francisco Chronicle.* "We have to completely rethink how we deal with the environment, and we should put a price on it."[50] Since ethical, aesthetic, and religious arguments are not winning the battle, science must ride to the rescue.

Calculating Values

Environmentalists have long noted that many of nature's gifts, such as the availability of oxygen in the atmosphere, are not traded in commercial markets. "Because ecosystem services are not fully 'captured' in commercial markets or adequately quantified in terms comparable with economic services and manufactured capital, they are often given too little weight in policy decisions," Costanza and colleagues argue. Public goods notoriously lack market prices. If prices could be imputed to ecosystem services, wouldn't these numbers help us to better appreciate their worth?

The many studies that Costanza and colleagues have assembled use a great variety of methods by which to impute economic value to ecosystem services. Some employ experimental techniques, including contingent valuation, to estimate the aesthetic or "nonuse" value of natural settings. The large majority of studies, however, estimate either the value of ecosystem *outputs*, such as fish, fiber, and food, or the costs of *replicating* ecosystem services. Costanza and colleagues use estimates of these two kinds – output values and replacement costs – to account for most of the $33 trillion price tag they impute to ecosystem services. As we will see, however, neither kind of estimate can serve as a basis for measuring the economic value of ecosystem services, even though those services are essential to human well-being.

Costanza and colleagues gathered data about the market value of the world's fisheries, forests, and farms. They correctly observe that nature's free services – for example, the work of the cyanobacteria mentioned earlier – are essential to this output. They then take a crucial step; they suppose that if x is a necessary condition for y, the value of x is at least that of y. Having thus determined the total value of the resource x (i.e., by setting it equal to the economic output for which it is essential), the research team then took another innovative step. To determine the "marginal" value or the value of the "next" unit, they divided the total value by the number of units of the resource.

To calculate the contribution of ecosystem services to marine fisheries, for example, the Costanza team first multiplied the world's fish catch in kilograms by an average market price per kilogram. They used "price times quantity as a proxy for the economic value of the service." The value of the service, that is to say, was set equal to the value of the output. The researchers apparently reasoned that because ecosystem services are essential to harvests of fish, the economic value of these services should include the value of those harvests. They then used data about the value of the total harvest to calculate what they identify as "the 'incremental' or 'marginal' value of ecosystem services." To arrive at a "marginal" or "unit" price in fisheries, they divided the overall value of fish harvests by the number of hectares of ocean to reach an estimated annual ecosystems service contribution of $15 per hectare.

The researchers used a slightly different approach to measure the value of ecosystems services in forestry and agriculture. Timber values "were estimated from global value of production, adjusted for average harvest cost... assumed to be 20% of revenues." In this instance, the researchers used "the net rent (or producer surplus)" – that is, proceeds to producers minus their costs – to estimate the overall value of ecosystem services. The study used rents to farmers – that is, the value of crops less production costs – to compute the value of ecosystem services to agriculture. To obtain a "per unit" value for forestry and agriculture, the researchers divided the resulting timber values and crop values by the number of hectares of forests and farmland. The method derives the value of the ecological service from some part of the value of the economic product. It divides the value of the economic product (e.g., crop) by the number of hectares or other units of area to derive a "per unit" or "marginal" value for nature's services.

Problems with This Calculus

It is understandable that Costanza and colleagues would want the economic value of ecosystem services to reflect the value of the industries to which they are essential. The very high estimate that results provides scientific evidence of the importance of protecting creation. To cavil with this estimate is to raise the suspicion either that one is callously indifferent to the fate of the environment (perhaps because one is allied with rapacious industry) or that one betrays reason and science. It is with trepidation, therefore, that I question this research.

It is a mistake to assume, however, that if x is essential to the production of y, the price of x can be inferred from that of y. One can see one flaw in this assumption when one acknowledges that several different ecosystem services, such as climate control and the nutrient cycling, are each essential to production in fisheries, forests, and farms. If a necessary input has the value of the output, each of these services should have a value equal to the economic product, since they are individually – not just collectively – necessary to the output of fishing, forestry, and agriculture.

This same difficulty arises with respect to inputs other than ecosystem services that may also be essential to production. Ships are indispensable for fisheries, saws for forestry, and seeds for farming. If we were to use the Costanza team's approach to estimate the value of these inputs, we would infer a price for each of them by dividing the number used into the net value of the industry. On this principle, in the aggregate, ships would be worth just as much as ecosystem services to fishing, because they are likewise essential. Let us suppose that there are ten necessary inputs to fishing, including boats, nets, refrigeration, trucks, labor, and so on. Since each is necessary to the output, it would have the same economic value, according to the reasoning published in *Nature*. The TEV of the inputs added together would be ten times that of the output. The more factors are essential, the greater would be their aggregate worth.

It is also a mistake to calculate the "marginal" value of each hectare of ocean in fishing, as do Costanza and colleagues, by dividing the value of the fish by the number of hectares of the seas. This method could be compared with determining the marginal value (or market price) of each saw by dividing the value of all felled trees by the number of saws that were used – perhaps adjusting up the shadow price of the saws that were used most often. Similarly, the method proposed by Costanza et al. would estimate the marginal value of a ship by dividing the total value of fish captured by the number of fishing boats.

Actually, there is a glut of fishing boats on the market today partly because of dwindling wild stocks, a turn toward aquaculture, and policy decisions that encouraged their overproduction. The marginal economic value of a ship equals the amount it fetches in a market in which shipwrights compete for buyers on the basis of quality and price. The market price of a fishing boat, in other words, is to be determined by the relation of the supply of boats to the demand for them, not by the price of fish divided by the number of boats used to hunt them.

Arguably, one could set up an auction in which firms that engage in fishing would bid for the rights to given areas; this would indicate the market value of particular hectares of ocean for fishing. Given the very small margins that characterize the fishing industry, competition from aquaculture, and the volatility of other expenses, such as fuel, insurance, and interest rates, it is baffling even to conjecture what, if anything, firms would bid for fishing rights to a random or average hectare of ocean.

In any case, the marginal or market values of many terrestrial environments are observable in prices paid for land. Thus, if a developer pays a farmer to turn a dell into a deli, an arcadia into an arcade, a meadow into a mall, or a paradise into a parking lot, then the market hath spoken. It makes no difference how many favors Mother Nature bestows on any of these places; the marginal value of each acre, favors included, is observed in its market price. Prime farm land is lost to development because there is a glut of grain but a shortage of tract mansions, relative to effective demand. Thus, prices for grain continue to fall while housing prices soar. Thus speaketh the market in setting marginal values.

Perhaps the most puzzling aspect of the Constanza et al. study and of the effort to "price" nature's services generally lies in its assumption that by attributing prices to goods, we somehow measure the benefits they bestow. This assumption derives directly from the "price-equals-marginal-benefit" rule I questioned in Chapter 4. This rule is untenable. Price does not equal benefit or provide information, in that sense, about economic value. Goods that trade at higher prices may simply cost more to produce; in other words, the higher production cost of a diamond explains why it is more expensive than water. The "next" or "incremental" drink of water, even if it is free, may be a life-saving necessity, as it is for those who have just run a marathon, while the diamond, albeit expensive, is only a luxury, perhaps a bauble.

If the costs of supplying ecosystem services are zero – if Mother Nature offers them free – then the prices (and, in that sense, the economic value) of these services may approach zero as well. This is true because competition among suppliers for buyers tends to drive prices down to costs. This does not suggest that nature's services have no instrumental value; it suggests only that in a competitive market, they will trade at very low prices. Many of nature's services are not scarce; like the best things in life, indeed, they are free. Their marginal or exchange value is negligible. The correct price approaches zero. This says nothing, however, about their value in use or the benefit they provide. That is immense, but it is not what prices represent.

To get to a higher price for nature's services – a price that reflects their importance – ecological economists may switch their attention from market prices to benefit or utility, which may be associated with the maximum or total amount people are willing to pay for a commodity or service. This takes supply – or the costs of production – out of the equation that settles price. If nature, rather than producing and giving away its goods for free, sought to operate as a discriminating monopolist, gouging consumers at demand values (total WTP), it could run up prices. This is essentially the situation that ecological economics envisions as a basis for valuation. In that event, however, the government would rightfully either set the price of an ecosystem service at a small percentage above costs (as it does with utilities) or break up Ma Nature into competing units (as it did Ma Bell).

Substitution and Replication

Costanza and colleagues also use the costs of creating technological substitutes for ecosystem services as a basis for inferring their incremental or marginal value. In an accompanying article in *Nature*, Stuart Pimm illustrates this process by explaining how the researchers determined that the nutrient-cycling services of the world's oceans are worth $17 trillion:

> If the oceans were not there, re-creating their nutrient cycling would require removing the nutrients from the land's runoff and returning them. The estimate of this service's $17 trillion value is arrived at by multiplying the cost of removing phosphorus and nitrogen from a liter of waste water by the 40,000 cubic kilometers of water that flow from the land each year.[51]

Similarly, Costanza and colleagues estimate what it would cost to re-create, with levees and other structures, natural flood control and storm protection ($1.8 trillion); to replicate artificially the pollination of plants ($1.8 trillion); to provide substitutes for natural waste treatment and breakdown of toxins ($2.7 trillion); and to replace the outdoor recreation and "esthetic, artistic, educational, spiritual, and/or scientific" benefits people find in natural places ($3.83 trillion).

The use of substitution costs as a way to measure the value of nature, however, raises two concerns. First, to be fair, one should balance the benefits that nature provides, for example, by mitigating floods, with the costs or damage it imposes, for example, by causing them in the first place. In general, one should subtract from the benefits of nature's services the costs of nature's disservices. These disservices include plagues, cancer, heart disease, pests, storms, days that are too hot or too cold, drought, mountains and rivers that are in one's way, hills to climb up or to fall down, the thousand natural shocks that flesh is heir to, universal death, and all the infirmities and miseries we encounter because we are not gods.

Second, when mainstream economists speak about substitution, they do not generally refer to alternative and more costly methods of providing some good or service. Rather, they refer to consumer indifference between alternatives at given prices. For example, the economic value of a beefsteak will be determined in part by the price at which consumers will switch to some other item on the menu. In the absence of cattle it would be very expensive to produce beef. This fact suggests nothing, however, about the goods people would substitute for beef if prices go higher.

To impute economic value, one would have to determine the price at which people would cease to demand a given service and spend their money on some other source of satisfaction instead. A $17 trillion price tag on the oceans' work of "pure ablution round earth's human shores" (as the poet John Keats described it) would price these services out of the market. Pimm notes that people would not think these services are worth that kind of money: "In the short term, many would not notice (and perhaps not care) what happens to the elements as they flow into the ocean." The force of the Costanza et al. argument may lie in the truism that we cannot live without nature. This tells us nothing, however, about marginal value or market price.

Sauce for the Gander

As might be expected, mainstream environmental economists did not sit still for the Costanza et al. study. Among many articles that criticize it, one by Nancy Bockstael and co-authors is representative.[52] Bockstael et al. write, "In economics, valuation concepts relate to human welfare. So the *economic* value of an ecosystem function or service relates only to the contribution it makes to human welfare, where human welfare is measured in terms of each individual's own assessment of his or her well-being."[53] These authors suggest that the Costanza study failed to understand this point.

Yet Costanza and his colleagues are not to be faulted for this reason. They try to measure the contribution the "incremental" or "marginal" unit of an environmental good makes to human welfare. As they point out, this measure of economic value includes "the 'consumer surplus' or the benefit the individual receives over and above the price paid in the market." In an earlier chapter, I used the example of medicine to illustrate this idea. The individual who buys a life-saving generic antibiotic would have paid or have been willing to pay a much higher price for the medicine – the price that it might have fetched before its patent expired. The higher price the individual is willing to pay – not the negligible one he does pay – relates to the benefit he or she receives from the prescription. Costanza and co-authors try to measure this contribution to well-being, in other words, the maximum WTP for the next unit consumed.

Bockstael and co-authors offer a second conception of economic value to criticize the Costanza study. "When they say they are valuing a change, economists are really defining a tradeoff between two situations," these authors write.[54] This second approach to valuation does not measure the contribution the next unit of a good makes to well-being. Rather, it measures the additional amount a person would pay for the next best substitute – or would demand to accept the next worst alternative. This approach to economic value, for example, concerns the difference in welfare or WTP between alternative brands of basically the same antibiotic; it does not reflect the contribution the antibiotic makes to that person's welfare, for example, by saving his or her life.

Bockstael and co-authors illustrate this approach with the example of a power plant that "is being considered for a location that would eliminate a swimming beach."[55] The economic value of the beach, on this second conception of economic value, does not refer to the contribution it makes to the well-being of any individual. Rather, it measures the *difference* between that contribution and the benefit the individual would obtain from the next-best alternative or substitute. "Economic value measures the amount a person would pay or be paid (in compensation) to be as well off with the power plant as without it."[56]

The tradeoffs economists seek to measure, Bockstael and co-authors write, "are sensitive to the circumstances of the choices. Is there a similar beach a short distance away that is not affected?"[57] The compensating or equivalent variation – the amount the individual would require or would give to be as well off with the power plant as without it – depends on the availability of and price of substitutes for the beach in question. If good beaches are a dime a dozen, the lost economic value of the given beach would be negligible, because the individual would demand little to go to the next beach instead.

The example of manna that falls from Heaven illustrates the relation of these two conceptions of economic value to ecosystem services. Let us suppose that a family, having just completed a long religious fast, collects enough manna to make a delicious and satisfying dinner. Plainly, the economic value of that amount of manna can be quite large if by "economic value" one means "the contribution it makes to human welfare." The value of the manna is negligible if by "economic value" one means "the amount a person would pay or be paid (in compensation) to be as well off" with that unit of manna as without it. As much and as good manna is readily available at no cost.

For more than a decade, I have tried to understand whether the economic value of the incremental unit of manna is immense because of the benefit the family obtains from it or inconsiderable because substitutes are so readily available for it. By "economic value," in other words, do economists refer to (1) the contribution of the marginal unit of a good to welfare (which includes consumer surplus) or (2) its market price, in other words, supply in relation to demand? If (1) is the case, then economic value is related to benefit but has no relation to price. If (2) is the case, economic value is related to price but not to the benefit the good provides. At most, economic value in the second sense relates to the often small amount more one would pay to buy a different brand or version of a product or demand to accept or switch to a slightly inferior one.

Economists may reply with the stricture that marginal benefit – the economic value of the "next" or "incremental" unit of a good – always equals the price the individual pays. According to this rule, which I criticized in Chapter 4, the benefit you receive from the antibiotic that saves your life, for example, just equals the amount the pharmacy happens to charge for it. Similarly, when you get a flat tire, the amount that is advertised in the newspaper exactly equals the benefit you obtain from the replacement. To paraphrase Tertullian, the only reason to believe the "price-equals-marginal-benefit" rule is that it is absurd.

The eighteenth-century philosopher G. W. Leibniz argued that a pre-established harmony exists between what goes on in our minds and what happens in the world. He invoked the power and beneficence of God to account for the perfect parallelism between our ideas and the facts they represent. Similarly, many economists apparently believe that a pre-established harmony or equality exists between the contribution a given incremental unit of a good makes to the welfare of an individual (the "marginal benefit") and the market price the individual pays for it. They base this remarkable pre-established harmony on the principle of declining marginal utility, the unobjectionable idea that the benefit of a resource declines the more of it one already has. To get from this principle to the price-equals-marginal-benefit rule, however, is to assume that everyone has stocked up on everything from toothpaste to tires to medicine exactly to the point that the benefit of the "next" unit purchased equals its price. Nobody has time, patience, or shelf space for any such thing. I believe that if economists thought critically about the "marginal-benefit-equals-market-price" rule, they would agree with me that it lacks empirical support and confounds common sense.

If I were an economist, I would define "economic value" as a measure of the scarcity of a good (or the next unit of same) relative to effective demand. Thus, the economic value of the incremental unit of manna would be negligible since manna is very plentiful. The "total" value of manna, construed as the economic value of the incremental unit (nothing) times the number of units consumed, would also be negligible. The economic value of an ecosystem service would generally be negligible as long as nature provides plenty of it for free. On this account, to show that nature's services are economically valuable one need not show that they make a big contribution to welfare – of course they do – but that they are scarce relative to effective demand. Economic value represents a function of supply and demand, in other words, value in exchange, and it is not a function of the contribution a good makes to welfare or well-being. In stating the well-known diamonds-and-water paradox, Adam Smith tried but apparently failed to make this point.

In Chapter 7, I shall argue that scarcities of natural resources are not in the cards. The "limiting" factor in production is now knowledge – and the skill to apply it. For example, I shall suggest that the production of fish such as salmon is not limited by wild stocks or by the ecosystem services that sustain them. Rather, current limits in the ability of technologists to engineer high-protein fish feed from vegetable matter may for now prevent fish production from being as efficient as the production of poultry. I shall argue in the next chapter that ecological economists have not made the case that ecosystem commodities or services are scarce relative to demand; therefore, they have not shown that these goods possess a lot of economic value.

Economists should decide whether "economic value" refers to (1) a measure of scarcity relative to demand, as Adam Smith believed, or (2) a measure of benefit or utility. If (1), economists would consider market prices, observed or hypothetical, as signals for the efficient allocation of resources. Cost-benefit analysis would make some sort of sense. If (2), economists start down a long road of "benefits estimation" and "valuation" at the end of which Costanza et al. are waiting for them. As an attempt at economic valuation, that is, as an attempt to measure maximum WTP and thus the benefits of marginal units of ecosystem services, the Costanza study is as good as it gets. It may have its problems, as I have argued earlier in this chapter, but at least it is not as awash in conceptual confusion as are the criticisms mainstream economists lodge against it.

The Basis of Decision-Making

The need to determine economic values for ecological services, Costanza and colleagues write, is inseparable from the choices and decisions we have to make about ecological systems. These authors continue:

Some argue that valuation of ecosystems is either impossible or unwise, that we cannot place a value on such "intangibles" as human life, environmental aesthetics, or long-term ecological benefits. But, in fact, we do so every day. When we set construction standards for highways, bridges and the like, we value human life (acknowledged or not) because spending more money on construction would save lives.

Many people share the suspicion that public policy is often based on implicit valuations that have never been articulated or defended. Part of the appeal of the Costanza study lies in its insistence that these matters of valuation be confronted directly.

Contrary to what Costanza and colleagues suggest, however, risk regulation does not necessarily provide an implicit economic valuation of "intangibles" such as human life. Decisions in this area more typically respond to public attitudes, statutory guidance, and relevant legal history. This is why our society protects human life and the environment much more stringently in some moral contexts than in others. We do not seek to save lives up to some predetermined economic value. Rather, we control risk more or less strictly on a number of moral grounds – for example, insofar as risks are involuntary or coerced, connected to dreaded ills such as cancer, associated with industry and the workplace, unfamiliar, unnatural, and so on.

To be sure, one can infer an imputed or implicit economic value for human life from any of thousands of governmental regulations. Mandatory seat belt laws cost $69 per year of life saved, while laws requiring uranium fuel-cycle facilities to purchase radionuclide emission-control technology cost an estimated $34 billion for every year of life saved. Safety controls involving chloroform at paper mills weigh in at $99 billion cost/life-year. For any number you pick between $20 (motorcycle helmet requirements) and $20 billion (benzene emission control at rubber tire manufacturing plants), there is a governmental program from which that number can be inferred as the value of a statistical year of life.

Every situation – every regulatory decision – responds to different ethical, economic, political, historical, and other conditions. A national speed limit of 55 miles per hour on highways and interstates would save a statistical year of life at a cost of only $6,600, but it is politically unpopular. Strict enforcement of such a speed limit, even more unpopular, would save an additional life/year at a cost of $16,000. Still more unpopular are random motor vehicle inspections – but these could save lives at even less expense. Can we infer that people value their lives at only a few thousand dollars? No; it is simply that people fear and resent some risks less than others, and least of all those risks they control themselves. These moral factors affect private and public decisions about risk. To impute a value-per-life/year to any regulation or policy, such as highway construction, is to create an epiphenomenon, a statistical abstraction, or descriptive convention, but not to identify a value judgment that necessarily affected that program.

Cigarettes illustrate the difficulty inherent in setting prices to reflect benefit. The price of cigarettes (before taxes) has no relation to human well-being as society judges it. As a society, we have reached a judgment that cigarettes have a negative welfare value – a deleterious effect on actual human well-being. The more consumers are willing to pay to smoke, the worse off they are, according to doctors and other respected social authorities. Cigarettes, therefore, have a positive exchange value but a negative value in use.

Suppose a well-meaning team of economists, seeing that cigarettes are bad for health, wished to correct the price of tobacco to make it better reflect its negative welfare effect. These economists would try to show that the economic value of cigarettes is very low, indeed, negative, because they are so harmful to health. If these economists thought – as the Costanza team apparently does – that prices should reflect the contribution a product makes to welfare, they would recommend lowering the price of tobacco. Indeed, one might argue that people should be paid to smoke, so that the negative market price reflects the negative welfare outcome.

It is much more sensible, however, to start from the fact that no relation holds between value in exchange and value in use, in other words, between market price (settled by competition among suppliers for customers) and benefit (however determined). We might then as a society make tobacco products more expensive to discourage their use. This policy decision, however, could not be justified as "correcting" a market failure. Rather, we set prices contrary to those of a competitive market to provide incentives that help society achieve some legitimate political result.

Growth versus Development

In important and insightful earlier essays, Robert Costanza and other ecological economists have criticized GNP as a measure of human welfare and economic growth as a goal of public policy. Improvements in the quality of human life, as these analysts have argued, are not to be confused with increases in the size of the economy. "As far as anyone knows," ecologist E. P. Odum observed, "there are no limits to quality development but there are certainly limits to economic growth that is based on increasing consumption in a finite world."[58] Costanza wrote elsewhere that economic growth "cannot be sustainable indefinitely on a finite planet." Development, in contrast, "which is an improvement in the quality of life . . . may be sustainable."[59]

In these writings, Costanza and others have made a distinction similar to the one that Adam Smith draws between "value in exchange" and "value in use." Economic growth concerns value in exchange; it is the rate of increase of GNP, which is to say, the total market value of all goods and services produced or consumed as measured in current prices. Development has to do with value in use – true human flourishing, including happiness and contentment, and is measured in the context of moral theories of the good life. There is no doubt that ecosystem services contribute immensely to human development; their contribution to human well-being in this substantive sense cannot be overestimated. The exchange value of ecosystem services, however, can be overestimated. This is true because exchange value has no clear relation to value in use, that is, to the substantive contribution a good or service makes to human flourishing and development. By seeking to "get the prices right," Costanza and others impute a high exchange value to ecosystem services. This confuses a measure of economic growth with a measure of human development.

Our dependence on ecosystem services cannot be overstated, and our efforts to sustain them can never be too great. To try to "get the prices right" as a way to protect nature, however, is to lend support to economic measures of welfare, such as economic growth and GNP, ecological economists rightfully reject. The effort Costanza and colleagues undertake to estimate what they call "the 'incremental' or 'marginal' value of ecosystem services" might be seen as undermining the more important program of understanding and promoting human development. Efforts such as this to "get the prices right" succeed only in lowering the credibility of ecological economics while increasing the legitimacy of the standard cost-benefit policy framework most likely to weaken attempts to protect the natural environment.

By relying on economic or instrumental arguments, moreover, environmentalists appear to join those who, according to Muir, "instead of lifting their eyes to the God of the mountains, lift them to the Almighty dollar." Environmentalists may eventually lose in credibility what they initially may gain in persuasiveness. They appeal to an instrumental ethic antithetical to their legitimate, indeed, laudable moral and religious beliefs. Environmentalists embrace an instrumental logic likely to defeat the intrinsic values that actually ground their convictions and make their goals praiseworthy and legitimate.

7

Carrying Capacity and Ecological Economics

When the tempest arose, "the mariners were afraid . . . and cast forth
the wares that were in the ship into the sea, to lighten it of them." This
passage from the Book of Jonah anticipates a strategy many environmentalists recommend today. Nature surrounds us with life-sustaining
systems, much as the sea supports a ship, which will sink if it carries
too much cargo. Environmentalists therefore urge us to "keep the
weight, the absolute scale, of the economy from sinking our biospheric
ark."[1]

This concern about the carrying capacity of earth, while it may remind us of the fearful sailors on Jonah's ship, marks a departure from
traditional arguments in favor of environmental protection. These arguments did not rest on prudential considerations. Early environmentalists such as Henry David Thoreau cited the intrinsic properties of
nature, rather than economic benefits, as reasons to preserve it. They
believed that economic activity had outstripped not its resource base,
but its spiritual purpose. As we saw in the last chapter, John Muir did
not call for improved cost-benefit analysis. He condemned the "temple destroyers, devotees of ravaging commercialism" who "instead of
lifting their eyes to the God of the mountains, lift them to the Almighty
dollar."[2] Nineteenth-century environmentalists, seeing that nature is
full of divinity, regarded its protection less as an economic imperative
than as a moral test.

By opposing a strictly utilitarian conception of value, writers such
as Muir saved what little of nature they could from the "gospel of

efficiency." Today, however, environmentalists themselves often preach this gospel. They construct integrated multiscale ecological-economic models and assessments online, utilizing the results of adaptive, bio-complex, computational, cross-cutting, holistic, integrated, interactive, interdisciplinary, multifactorial, multifunctional, multiscale, networked, nonequilibrial, nonlinear, simulational, synthetic, externally funded research, addressing uncertainties, vulnerabilities, complexities, criticalities, and surprise scenario forecasts. Thus they adopt in a contemporary form the very economic and utilitarian approach their predecessors deplored.

In this chapter, I want to continue to question attempts by today's environmentalists, particularly some of those who identify themselves as ecological economists, to vindicate environmental protection on instrumental grounds. I shall cast doubt on the hope that the utilitarian logic of ecological economics can succeed better than the utilitarian logic of mainstream economics to provide a foundation for the cause of environmentalism. I shall argue here, once again, that a reliance on economic reasoning merely abandons at the start the very grounds that most validly justify efforts to protect nature from commercial and industrial exploitation.

The Debate Between Mainstream and Ecological Economics

Mainstream economists, such as James Tobin, Robert Solow, and William Nordhaus, typically believe that nature sets no limits to economic growth. Trusting to our intelligence and ingenuity as we seek to satisfy our preferences and achieve well-being, these economists argue that we can "choose among an indefinitely large number of alternatives." They believe that the earth's "carrying capacity" cannot be measured scientifically because it is a function or artifact of the state of knowledge and technology.[3] For these economists, the limits to knowledge are the only limits to growth.

In Chapter 2, I described an essay by John V. Krutilla, "Conservation Reconsidered," which accurately presented the view mainstream economists had reached by the late 1960s.[4] I mentioned that Krutilla cited studies to show that advancing technology has "compensated quite adequately for the depletion of the higher quality natural resource stocks."[5] He observed that "the traditional concerns of conservation economics – the husbanding of natural resource stocks for the use of future generations – may now be outmoded by advances in technology."[6] Krutilla, along with other environmental economists in the 1970s, rejected the Malthusian idea that natural resources place intractable limits on economic expansion. Ecological economics arose in the 1970s as an academic discipline largely to challenge the assumption by mainstream economists that technology can always find cheap substitutes for resources that become scarce.[7]

Ecological economists believe that sources of raw materials and sinks for wastes ("natural capital") are fixed and therefore limit the potential growth of the global economy. They reject the idea that "technology and resource substitution (ingenuity) . . . can continuously outrun depletion and pollution."[8] Herman Daly, an ecological economist at the University of Maryland, has written that to "delude ourselves into thinking that growth is still possible if only we label it 'sustainable' or color it 'green,' will just delay the inevitable transition and make it more painful."[9]

The concept of a "limiting factor" helps identify the difference between mainstream economists and ecological economists. According to Daly, we have "entered a new era" in which "the limiting factor in development is no longer manmade capital but remaining natural capital."[10] Mainstream economists argue, in contrast, that as long as knowledge advances, the economy can expand. Where there is effective management, Peter Drucker has written, "that is, the application of knowledge to knowledge, we can always obtain the other resources."[11] He adds: "The basic resource – 'the means of production,' to use the economist's term – is no longer capital, nor natural resources (the economist's 'land'), nor 'labor.' *It is and will be knowledge.*"[12]

The idea that knowledge is the key resource reflects theoretical and empirical results Robert Solow presented in 1956 and 1957 and summarized in 1970. Solow found that economic growth depends "simply on the rate of (labor-augmenting) technological change," and that "most of the growth of the economy over the last century had been due to technological progress."[13] Economists following Solow adopted a standard model of growth that contains two factors: knowledge and the labor to apply it. (Drucker's favorite example is the surgeon in whom these factors of production are combined.) This differs from the classical model of Ricardo and Malthus because "[natural] resources, the third member of the classical triad, have generally been dropped."[14]

Mainstream economists offer at least three arguments to show that knowledge and ingenuity will always alleviate resource shortages. First, reserves of natural resources "themselves are actually functions of technology. The more advanced the technology, the more reserves become known and recoverable."[15] Recent examples of reserve-increasing technologies include the use of bacteria to leach metals from low-grade ore and the application of computer analysis to seismic vibrations to locate deposits of oil.[16] As a result of such advances, reserves of many nonrenewable resources have increased in recent decades, despite rising global consumption. Between 1987 and 1990, estimates of proven recoverable reserves of petroleum, for example, rose 11.4 percent, and those of natural gas rose by 17.9 percent.[17]

Second, advances in technology allow us not only to increase available reserves but also to substitute away from resources that may become scarce. When mainstream economists speak of *substitutability* in this context, they generally refer to the substitution of one resource for another or "the ability to substitute away from resources that are becoming scarce."[18] As Robert Solow explains, "Higher and rising prices of exhaustible resources lead competing producers to substitute other materials that are more plentiful and therefore cheaper."[19] Daly correctly ascribes to economists William Nordhaus and James Tobin the view "that in the aggregate resources are infinite, that when one flow dries up, there will always be another, and that technology will always find ways to exploit the next resource."[20]

The third argument offered by mainstream economists is that the power of knowledge continually reduces the amounts of resources needed to produce a constant or increasing flow of consumer goods and services. "If the future is anything like the past," Solow writes, "there will be prolonged and substantial reductions in natural resource requirements per unit of real output."[21] Knowledge increases the productivity of natural resources just as it increases the productivity of labor. Glass fibers, for example, not only substitute for but vastly improve upon copper cables in transmitting messages. The transmission capacity of an optical fiber cable increased by an order of magnitude every four years between 1975 and 1992. Today, a thin cable using optical amplifiers and erbium-doped fibers powered by laser diode chips can carry one-half million phone calls at any moment. Computers become stronger as they grow smaller; the world's entire annual production of computer chips can fit into a single cargo plane. Moreover, energy requirements continually decrease per unit of economic output; for example, the amount of energy needed to produce a unit of household lighting has decreased many fold since the time of candles and oil lamps. For reasons such as these, "virtually all minerals have experienced long-term declines in real prices during the last two generations."[22]

Reflecting on these trends, the World Resources Institute questions the idea that shortages of nonrenewable resources must limit the global economy. It states in a *Report*: "Even without more resource-sparing policies, . . . the cumulative effect of increasing reserves, more competition among suppliers, and technology trends that create substitutes suggests that global shortages of most nonrenewable resources are unlikely to check development in the early decades" of this century."[23] The *Report* also dismisses "the frequently expressed concern that high levels of consumption will lead to resource depletion and to physical shortages that might limit growth or development opportunity." The evidence suggests "that the world is not yet running out of most nonrenewable resources and is not likely to, at least in the next few decades."[24]

Some mainstream economists, it should be said, are less than convinced that there are no natural resource limits whatever to economic growth. Some mainstream analysts have proposed careful models for measuring price trends;[25] others have explained how difficult it is to obtain measures of scarcity;[26] and many others have explored problems created by externalities and common property regimes.[27] Some ecological economists have tried to find common ground with mainstream economists with respect to residuals management and intertemporal equity,[28] and others have emphasized adaptive management approaches to particular environmental and resource problems.[29] Not every ecological economist may agree with Paul Ehrlich[30] and Herman Daly,[31] moreover, that we confront an age of scarcity in the near or, at best, the medium term.

While both mainstream and ecological economics comprise a variety of positions, sometimes intersecting, I want to single out for criticism in this chapter a series of arguments ecological economists, such as Paul Ehrlich, Herman Daly, Robert Costanza, and the late Donnella Meadows, have mounted against the "growth" model of neo-classical economics, as defended by Barnett and Morse, Nordhaus, Tobin, Solow, Stiglitz, and others. To show that these arguments fail, as I shall try to do, is to prove neither that the standard model is correct nor that there are no ecological or resource limits to growth. In fact, the thesis that there are significant natural limits to growth remains intuitively appealing. Accordingly, I believe that my attempt to subject arguments for that thesis to criticism is a friendly and constructive one, if by this means they can be strengthened and improved. The preservation of nature is an important and legitimate goal. I argue only that it is too important to leave to economists – including ecological economists.

Energy and Entropy

In their dissent from the prevailing mainstream view, many ecological economists cite a theory stated by Nicholas Georgescu-Roegen, which depends on two premises to refute the standard model of economic growth. The first cites the Second Law of Thermodynamics, which requires that in "entropy terms, the cost of any biological or economic enterprise is always greater than the product."[32] There is always an energy deficit. Second, the free or usable energy ("low entropy") that is used up to replace this deficit represents a fixed and dwindling stock. Since we are running down low-entropy terrestrial resources, ecological economists contend, "nature really does impose an inescapable general scarcity" and it is a "serious delusion to believe otherwise."[33]

The first premise is unexceptional: the global economy must consume energy. After running through its reserves of fossil fuel, it must get power from some other source. The second premise, however, is controversial. Are energy resources limited to a fixed and dwindling stock?

If we ignore pollution problems, fossil fuels could subsidize the global economy for quite a while. According to physicist John Holdren, "one sees no immediate danger of 'running out' of energy in a global sense.... At 1990 rates of use, resources of oil and natural gas would last 70 to 100 years," counting conventional sources only, and there is "a 1500-year supply of coal."[34] The World Bank estimated fossil fuel reserves at more than 600 times the present rate of extraction. The Bank said, "fears that the world may be running out of fossil fuels are unfounded."[35]

The well-known problems associated with "greenhouse" gases, however, argue for a conversion to nonpolluting energy sources, such as solar power and geothermal energy. These sources – which dwarf fossil fuels in the amount of energy they make available – seem so abundant that they may be regarded as infinite. Kenneth Townsend observes, for example, that "the spontaneous flow of energy on earth from low- to high-entropy states may be offset by solar flow."[36] Georgescu-Roegen recognizes that it may be possible "to make greater use of solar radiation, the more abundant source of free energy."[37]

The sunlight continually reaching the surface of the Earth – not including vast amounts diffused in the atmosphere – is unimaginably immense. At the equivalent of 1.73×10^{14} kilowatts (kW) of power, it represents an annual energy "income" or "subsidy" of 1.5×10^{18} kW hours, about ten thousand times the amount of energy the global economy now consumes.[38] Even with today's technology, conversion efficiencies of sunlight to electricity are good – 23 percent on sunny days and 14.5 percent on average annually for Luz solar trough systems, and about 11 percent (with performance improving rapidly) for current advanced amorphous silicon, copper indium diselenide, and cadmium thin-film photovoltaic systems.[39] Analysts who study the falling prices and increasing efficiency of solar energy agree with Lester Brown that "technologies are ready to begin building a world energy system largely powered by solar resources."[40]

While photovoltaics currently enjoy the greatest interest, water, wind, and biomass also provide promising methods of harnessing superabundant solar energy. Hydropower now supplies 24 percent of total world electrical generating capacity.[41] Rapid gains in capturing wind power have made it competitive with other energy sources; in California, for example, wind machines now produce enough electricity to meet the residential needs of a city the size of San Francisco. Energy plantations, using fast-growing plants to remove carbon from the atmosphere, may build on the Brazilian fuel-alcohol program.

One survey found that by "the middle of the 21st century, renewable energy technologies can meet much of the growing demand at prices lower than those usually forecast for conventional energy."[42] This survey brings together well-respected authorities who review enthusiastically the potential of hydropower, crystalline-and-polycrystalline-silicon solar cells, amorphous silicon photovoltaic systems, photovoltaic concentrator technology, ethanol and methanol production from cellulosic biomass, advanced gasification-based biomass power generation, wind energy, and various other environment-friendly power sources. The book also describes the exceptional prospects of nonsolar alternatives, such as tidal power, which captures gravitational energy, and geothermal power, which employs heat coming from the earth's core. The energy accessible to modern drilling technology from geothermal sources in the United States, for example, is thousands of times greater than that contained in domestic coal reserves.[43]

Amory Lovins, like others who study energy technology from the "bottom up," has argued that advanced technologies are commercially available that can "support present or greatly expanded worldwide economic activity while stabilizing global climate – and saving money."[44] Lovins writes that "even very large expansions in population and industrial activity need not be energy-constrained."[45] If available geothermal, solar, and other sources of nonpolluting energy exceed global demand by many orders of magnitude, and if efficiency alone can greatly increase economic output with no additional energy inputs, it is not obvious how the Second Law of Thermodynamics limits economic growth. The world's economy has grown immensely over the centuries, without disturbing any natural law. The question is whether the global economy can use energy more efficiently and provide cleaner and more abundant sources of energy. This question is best addressed by engineers, not economists.

Rather than refute Amory Lovins and other experts in their own terms – that is, with arguments showing the limited potential of solar and other technologies – ecological economists tend to rebuke them *ad hominem*. Those who look for technological solutions are denounced as either hirelings of industry or dupes of their own optimism. "This blind faith in technology," four ecological economists have written, "may be similar to the situation of the man who fell from a ten-story building, and when passing the second story on the way down, concluded 'so far so good, so why not continue?'"[46] Another writes that those unalertable to intractable scarcities "believe in perpetual motion machines" and "act as if the laws of nature did not exist."[47]

The Complementarity of Human-made and Natural Capital

Ecological economists attempt to refute the mainstream position not only by citing the Second Law of Thermodynamics but also by arguing that "the basic relation of man-made and natural capital is one of complementarity, not substitutability."[48] Extra sawmills, for example, cannot substitute for diminishing forests, more refineries for depleted oil wells, or larger nets for declining fish populations. Daly concludes that "material transformed and tools of transformation are complements, not substitutes."[49]

The problem with this argument, however, is that it fails to respond to the underlying contention of the mainstream model "that increasing resource scarcity would always generate price signals which would engender compensating economic and technological developments, such as resource substitution, recycling, exploration, and increased efficiency in resource utilization."[50] The examples Daly offers seem to support the mainstream position. The use of solar energy increases when prices for petroleum rise. As prices for lumber or seafood increase, silviculture and aquaculture rapidly supplement and even underprice "capture" or extractive forestry and fishing. Food prices in general stand at historical lows because of continuous and continuing improvements in the science and practice of agriculture.[51]

The standard model of economic growth, as we have seen, assumes that human knowledge and ingenuity can always alleviate resource shortages so that "natural capital" sets no limit on economic growth. One may say that the standard model holds that knowledge can "substitute" for resources, then, in the sense that ingenuity can always find a way to get around scarcity – for example, by extending reserves, by substituting between resource flows, and by improving efficiency. This does not imply, of course, that nets can replace fish, saws replace trees, or that the economy can do without resources altogether. As Robert Solow summarizes: "It is of the essence that production cannot take place without the use of natural resources. But I shall assume that it is always possible to substitute greater inputs of labor, reproducible capital [e.g., technology], and renewable resources for smaller direct inputs of the fixed resource."[52]

Daly concedes, in effect, that silviculture and aquaculture do alleviate scarcities just as mainstream economists would predict. When he considers what he calls "cultivated natural capital," including "agriculture, aquaculture, and plantation forestry," he writes that "[c]ultivated capital does substitute for natural capital proper in certain functions – those for which it is cultivated."[53] The facts bear out this optimism. Tree plantations worldwide "spread rapidly during the 1980s, rising from 18 million hectares in 1980 to more than 40 million hectares by 1990."[54] The 1990s might be called the decade of silviculture, since millions of hectares of land went into new industrial tree plantations each year, producing trees genetically engineered for various properties including rapid growth. During the 1990s, China planted almost 60 million hectares of tree farms, and India now plants four trees for every one it commercially harvests.[55]

The progress of aquaculture may be gauged from the fact that most freshwater fish that are sold are farmed. Only 8.2 million metric tons of freshwater ("inland") fish were harvested from the wild, whereas almost 20 million metric tons were produced by aquaculture, according to a 2000 United Nations Food and Agriculture Organization (FAO) report.[56] Today, more than two-thirds of all freshwater fish are farmed rather than taken from nature, and this proportion is bound to continue to increase. One can imagine a time when nearly all commercial freshwater fish are aquacultural products and wild fisheries are reserved for recreational use or conservation. The problem will lie in keeping enough "wild" systems intact so that they can be valued aesthetically. Our concern must lie not simply with the yields or productivity of wild fisheries (aquaculture can and will replace them) but with converting too many wild places to commercial aquacultural plantations and thus losing their aesthetic, recreational, and spiritual value. The goal of environmentalism may be to protect nature *from* rather than *for* instrumental or economic purposes – a goal that an instrumental calculus defeats.

The FAO predicts that by 2030, at least half of all food fish by weight will be farm raised and more than half by value or price. A problem that must be solved involves converting the diets of a few carnivorous species, such as salmon, to soy and other vegetable-based proteins. At this time, salmon eat in the wild about ten times their weight in other fish; in captivity, salmon eat only three times their weight in fish meal. To fully relieve wild ecosystems of the burdens of commercial fishing, research needs to be done to engineer bacteria – or to find some other method – to convert plentiful vegetable matter to high-protein fish and chicken meal.

As aquaculture becomes more efficient and feed prices fall, supplies of many species, such as salmon, have increased and prices have tumbled worldwide.[57] Eventually, salmon may become as inexpensive to produce as chickens, since the feed-to-flesh ratios of these species are broadly similar. Technologies that improve salmon feed will also help address concerns about safety. "We must realize that what is happening to the salmon industry in Europe now is similar to what happened in the chicken industry decades ago," a trade journal reports. "Salmon is becoming a low-cost food, and we shall just have to find ways to live with this."[58]

The Four Causes

The argument ecological economists propose concerning the complementarity of technological and natural capital can be most clearly understood in the context of the four "causes" Aristotle (*Metaphysics*, I. 3–6) identified: material, efficient, formal, and final. The material cause in the example Aristotle uses, a statue of a horse, consists in the bronze of which it is made. The tools the sculptor applies are the statue's efficient cause. The formal cause consists in the idea, plan, image, or design – in short, the knowledge – that guides the artist. And the final cause is the reason or purpose – to celebrate a victory or pay off a debt – that led the sculptor to make the statue.

Daly has asserted his basic premise of ecological economics in clear and precise Aristotelian terms: "[T]he agent of transformation (efficient cause) and the substance being transformed by it (material cause) must be complements."[59] All of Daly's examples – nets and fish, sawmills and trees, oil drills and oil reserves, trowels and bricks – illustrate the complementarity between efficient and material causes, or, as he says, "the main relation between what is being transformed and the agent of transformation."[60]

Daly thus asserts with great force and insistence what mainstream economists would never have thought of denying, namely, that one "cannot substitute efficient cause for material cause."[61] At the same time, he offers no argument to refute the principle that mainstream economists assert and defend, namely, that the formal cause of production, that is, design, knowledge, innovation, and ingenuity, can always overcome shortages in resources or materials. Thus, mainstream economists know, for example, that harpoons and whales are complementary; one cannot produce more whales after a point by casting more harpoons. Mainstream economists point out, however, that advances in knowledge and invention have compensated for shortages of resources such as whale oil for uses such as lubrication and lighting. Similarly, advances in biotechnology applied to silviculture and aquaculture can and do produce a lot more trees and fish – but not as a consequence of producing more saws and nets. Similarly, while refineries cannot substitute for petroleum reserves, mainstream economists assert that human knowledge and ingenuity can find substitutes for petroleum – for example, by harnessing the inexhaustible resources of the sun. Nature need not limit economic growth, they propose, as long as knowledge increases and the sun shines.

The Question of Scale

When ecological economists speak of the limits of growth or warn that growth is unsustainable, they use the term "growth" in an idiosyncratic sense. "*Growth* refers to the quantitative increase in the scale of the physical dimension of the economy, the rate of flow of matter and energy through the economy, and the stock of human bodies and artifacts."[62] Daly adds: "*Scale* refers to the physical volume of the flow of matter-energy from the environment as low-entropy raw materials and back to the environment as high-entropy wastes."[63]

What ecological economists mean by "growth" – an increase in physical scale, quantity, or volume – has no analog in mainstream economic thought. While "growth" is not a scientific term in mainstream economics, it is used generally to refer to the rate of increase of Gross Domestic Product (GDP), defined as the value of everything the economy produces in a year at then-current prices. Quantitative increase in the physical dimension of the economy is neither necessary nor sufficient for economic growth in the conventional sense, which has to do with the *value* of production rather than the physical *size* of whatever is produced or consumed. If ecological economics possesses a central thesis, it is that the "term 'sustainable growth' when applied to the economy is a bad oxymoron."[64] Whatever ecological economics says about "sustainability," however, has no apparent implications for what mainstream economists mean by "growth."

If energy consumption or carbon emissions may serve as indicators of economic "scale" or "quantity," as ecological economists use these terms, we can see that the scale of an economy may not vary with GDP. Between 1973 and 1986, energy consumption in the United States, for example, remained virtually flat while economic production expanded by almost 40 percent.[65] In Japan, GDP per capita has doubled – from about $8,000 to $16,000 – since 1973 with no increase in per capita emissions of carbon dioxide. Primary energy demand in the United Kingdom in 1990 was less than it was sixteen years earlier, although the GDP grew.[66] Since 1973, France and Germany (West Germany before 1990) have decreased per capita emissions from fossil fuels as their economies have expanded. In France between 1973 and 1991, the economy grew by about 30 percent while per capita emissions declined by about 40 percent.[67] Although emissions sometimes increase with GDP, no general relation holds between "growth" in the conventional sense and the "scale" ecological economists believe is unsustainable.

Ecological economists assert that economic growth, as they define it, is unsustainable because it stresses the carrying capacity of the earth. Economic growth in the conventional sense, however, bears no general relation to environmental stress. Societies with big GDPs, such as Sweden, protect nature, while nations in the former Soviet bloc with much smaller GDPs, such as Poland, have devastated their environments. The Scandinavian countries use their affluence to help countries with smaller economies, like Poland, clean up the environmental mess they have made. Richer countries may use cleaner technologies than poorer ones; they may also turn more pristine areas to golf courses. The relation between wealth or affluence and environmental quality turns on political decisions, not the tautologies of ecological economics.

In impoverished nations, as Norman Myers observes, people may "have no option but to over-exploit environmental resource stocks in order to survive," for example, "by increasingly encroaching onto tropical forests among other low-potential lands."[68] The poorest of the poor, Myers writes, are often the principal cause of deforestation, desertification, and soil erosion as well as of the extinction of species.[69] It is the *absence* of economic growth rather than its *presence*, then, that causes forest destruction, desertification, erosion, and loss of biodiversity.

No one believes that economic growth will lead automatically to environmental protection. I can find no reason to agree with the contention of ecological economics, however, that economic growth in the sense of greater GDP or affluence leads automatically to resource depletion and ecological demise. If the "scale" or "size" of an economic activity, moreover, is measured in terms of the volume or quantity of the flow of matter-energy that runs through it ("throughput"), it bears no clear relation to environmental quality. The physical quantity of detergents used to do laundry, for example, may be the same whether or not those detergents contain phosphates; the ecological consequences, however, will be vastly different. Similarly, a twelve-ounce can of hair spray that uses chlorofluorocarbons (CFCs) will damage the environment much more than a twelve-ounce can that substitutes a harmless propellant. Since quantities of water exceed those of any other material in our industrial metabolism, the most efficient way to limit scale might be to cut back on that fluid, but no one believes we would thereby greatly protect the environment. One would cry over a gallon of spilled mercury but not over a gallon of spilled milk.

Presumably, ecological economists know that some forms of "throughput" are worse than others even in the same amounts. If ecological economists were to discriminate, however, on some basis other than quantity among kinds of "throughput" that harm the environment, they would find themselves embarking on a path at the end of which mainstream economists (such as those at the World Bank) are waiting for them. Rather than decry "throughput" in general, measured in terms of "quantity," mainstream economists believe some pollutants and practices are worse than others, and so they address well-defined problems, such as CFC loadings, rather than the "size" or "scale" of "throughput" as a whole. Mainstream economists reject the idea that the dose alone makes the poison; accordingly, they adopt a case-by-case approach that looks for solutions to specific market and policy failures.

If ecological economists were to relativize the concept of "scale" to *kinds* of throughput, they would also confront the problem of identifying and dealing with the pollutants, practices, and policies that are particularly harmful to the environment. They would have to decide which economic activities create risks greater than benefits, which "externalities" markets fail to price, and so on. If ecological economists conceded that water vapor even if greater in scale is not as destructive as CFCs, in other words, they would have to move on as economists to risk-benefit analysis, the "pricing" of externalities, and the "correction" of market failures. Many ecological economists have done just that. Thus the ecological-economics paradigm has begun to collapse into that of mainstream economics.

Ecological economists distinguish between "growth" and "development." Growth, "which is an increase in quantity, cannot be sustainable indefinitely on a finite planet." Economic development, in contrast, "which is an improvement in the quality of life...may be sustainable."[70] One must ask how ecological economists propose to measure "improvement in the quality of life." If they adopt an economic measure, such as utility or macroeconomic indicators of prosperity, what they mean by "development" collapses into what mainstream economists mean by "growth." If they propose some other measure, they strike their tents as economists and set out on the high seas of moral philosophy to discuss the good life and the values that enter that life.

"Co-opting" Nature

To give empirical content to theoretical arguments about why the global economy can no longer grow, ecological economists often refer to what one describes as the "best evidence" that economic expansion has reached its natural limits.[71] This is the estimate Peter Vitousek, Paul and Anne Ehrlich, and Pamela Matson published in 1986, stating "that organic material equivalent to about 40% of the present net primary production [NPP] in terrestrial ecosystems is being co-opted by human beings each year." The article by Vitousek and colleagues uses the verb to "appropriate" interchangeably with to "co-opt," concluding that "humans now appropriate nearly 40% ... of potential terrestrial productivity."[72] Two commentators conclude: "If we take this percentage as an index of the human carrying capacity of the earth and assume that a growing economy could come to appropriate 80% of photosynthetic production before destroying the functional integrity of the ecosphere, the earth will effectively go from half to completely full during the next ... 35 years."[73]

Many ecological economists believe the photosynthetic capacity of the world limits economic growth, indeed, that the growing affluence of human populations already tests those limits. Paul Ehrlich, for example, cites the scarcity of NPP to refute the "hope that development can greatly increase the size of the economic pie and pull many more people out of poverty."[74] He calls this humane hope "insane" because of "the constraints nature places on human activities." Such an expansion of economic activity, Ehrlich contends, "implies an assault on global NPP far beyond that already observed."[75]

By referring to an "assault" on NPP, Ehrlich and others invoke the traditional Malthusian belief that only a limited amount of food can be produced and that a growing population creates demands that exceed or will exceed that limit. In the current restatement of the Malthusian argument, the earth can produce only so much phytomass (NPP) each year, of which humans already consume directly and indirectly more than 40 percent. According to this argument, the assault on NPP implied by the rising numbers and living standards of the world's poor would surely tax NPP even more and thus destroy the integrity of the world's ecosystems.

I know of no ecologist who has questioned the argument Vitousek and colleagues presented in their immensely influential and constantly cited essay, "Human Appropriation of the Products of Photosynthesis." In its wake, some biologists have dropped the concept of "co-opt" and state flatly, "humans consume 40 percent of net primary productivity (NPP) on land."[76] In a recent manifesto, *The World According to Pimm*, ecologist Stuart Pimm updates and recalculates the figures and reiterates the conclusion. Pimm asks, "What percentage of the land's annual plant growth do we consume, directly or indirectly?" Referring throughout his book to the Vitousek et al. calculation, he writes, "The answer is 42 percent."[77] He adds, "Forty-two percent and counting, since our numbers increase every year."[78]

Vitousek et al. calculated the human assault on global NPP first by estimating the amount of vegetable material human beings eat annually – about 1 billion metric tons, according to Pimm's recalculation.[79] This is less than 1 percent of the total terrestrial NPP, an amount Vitousek and colleagues estimate at 132 billion metric tons.[80] To the 1 billion tons of direct consumption, they add roughly 2 billion tons of grass and feed domesticated animals consume and another 2 billion tons of plant growth people use for fuel and wood.[81] Vitousek et al. aggregate these and other uses to peg direct human consumption at "about three percent of the biosphere's total annual NPP."

To put this finding into context, we may compare the percentages of NPP other species consume. Insects rival large herbivores as consumers of vegetative matter; for example, "many ant species harvest annually as much phytomass per unit area as do elephants."[82] Consider termites. According to Vaclav Smil, the biosphere's "nearly 250 quadrillion termites ... process between one-third and two-fifths of all phytomass in their tropical and subtropical habitats, that is, perhaps as much as one-quarter of all terrestrial NPP." Thus, termites represent a direct assault on global NPP – that is, they eat it – almost ten times greater than that of human beings. Other creatures, such as beetles and ants, may be as prodigious. If human consumption is a problem, then consumption by termites (and then beetles, earthworms, ants, etc.) must be a far, far greater problem. They eat much more than we do, and thus – if eating is a problem for ecology – they must pose a greater threat to the integrity of the world's ecosystems.

In fact, eating, in other words, decomposition, does not necessarily upset ecosystems. Vegetable matter as it passes through the gut of a termite or through the digestive tract of a human being ends up the same way. Some of it provides energy, and some goes off as waste. People return to the earth when their lives are done – dust to dust – and thus everything is recycled. Besides, human beings greatly increase the amount of biomass areas produce. As British writer Colin Tudge has remarked, "cultivated systems, whether of intensive grain or for fish, are always more productive than wild systems"; indeed, they "often out-produce wild systems by 100-fold or more."[83]

What is the problem, then? Food has never been less expensive; famine plainly represents a shortage of effective demand (people are prevented by war, oppression, and destitution from buying it) rather than a shortage of supply.[84] Those who use the occurrence of famine as an argument to show that resources are inadequate divert attention from the true causes of starvation, such as civil war and oppression. There is more than enough food – and capacity to produce food – to feed current and future populations. Human consumption of the earth's NPP is no more an assault on ecosystems – it is certainly more modest – than that of many other species. Why is human digestion of farm-raised food a threat to ecosystems on which humans depend?

Getting to 40 Percent

In any event, Vitousek and colleagues calculate at only 3 percent the direct use humans make of NPP. To get to the 40 percent estimate, Vitousek and co-authors consider the amount of phytomass human beings "co-opt." By "co-opted" NPP, the authors "mean material that human beings use directly or that is used in human-dominated ecosystems by communities of organisms different from those in corresponding natural communities."[85] No meaning is given – or probably could be given – to the phrase "corresponding natural communities." The implication that human-dominated environments (farms, suburbs, etc.) are not "natural," however, provides a clue to a suppressed premise of the argument. Since what humans do – including all they consume – is tainted by original sin or something, it is "unnatural." By definition, human beings, corrupted as we are by sin, must threaten and contaminate ecosystems simply by changing them. Thus, the human assault on nature is basically not a biological assault but a moral or spiritual one. If human beings affect an ecosystem, they "co-opt" and threaten it. If termites affect an ecosystem in exactly the same way, they merely assist in its natural functioning – even if the results are the same.

According to Vitousek and co-authors, the amount of NPP that "flows to different consumers and decomposers than it otherwise would" amounts to about 19 percent of terrestrial NPP. I imagine this means that when human beings change the character of a place, its natural history changes, for example, the way the ecology of New England changed under the tutelage of the Amerindian tribes, then the Puritan settlers, the farmers, industrialists, and so on.[86] As farming moved west, New England forests grew back. They are different; nature is no longer what it would have been. This is the criterion of co-option, that is, ecological changes caused by human beings, which are always and by definition bad, unlike those caused by "natural" organisms.

As a theological statement, the assertion that human beings co-opt or appropriate nature by changing it makes sense because humanity differs spiritually from other creatures. As a biological thesis, however, human beings are completely natural – meaning, we are not super-natural – and everything we do in and with nature is 100 percent natural, consistent with nature, and true to nature's course. Human beings are bound by and follow exactly the same laws of nature as any other animal and cannot take nature away from the course those laws require.

The 40 percent figure mentioned earlier – the one constantly cited – refers to the percentage of NPP that "human beings have 'co-opted' and potential NPP lost as a consequence of human activities."[87] Thus, all the NPP humans produce on farms – even if it is many times more than would have been produced by wild areas – is "lost" because it is not "natural" in an apparently spiritual sense. To calculate this amount, Vitousek et al. consider as "lost" whatever landscape human beings farm or affect in any other way. For example, farmers in the Imperial Valley of California have created largely by irrigation and fertiliza-tion an immense garden out of what was a desert. Vitousek calculates this tremendous increase in NPP as a loss because whatever natural vegetation might have grown in that area is forgone. To be sure, agri-culture may completely dwarf nature – the way amber waves of grain plainly represent more biomass than whatever grasses formerly sur-vived on the plains. The more humanity produces, however, the more is "lost" in the sense that Vitousek and other ecologists somehow understand.

Consider, for example, that American farmers now average about 7 tons of corn per hectare (t/ha), but when challenged, as in Na-tional Corngrowers Association competitions, they easily triple those yields.[88] Varieties of rice developed recently are expected to boost yields dramatically above the present 3.5 t/ha, with a conjectural bi-ological maximum of about 15 metric tons per acre.[89] According to the weird logic of the Vitousek et al. argument, the more farmers pro-duce, the more is lost – because this production results from human activity.

Vitousek and colleagues recognize that the NPP output of cultivated land may exceed that of natural ecosystems – but when it does, "the amount of potential NPP co-opted by human beings increases."[90] This is logically true, insofar as "to co-opt" means "to affect or influence." Suppose the Imperial Valley produced ten pounds of NPP per acre before the European settlement and ten tons per acre today as a result of irrigation, fertilization, and biotechnology. According to the Vitousek et al. calculus, human beings would have co-opted both the ten pounds and the additional ten tons – both the amount that they replaced and the amount they produced. Production for which human beings are responsible, directly or indirectly, is appropriated or co-opted. If humans affect the whole world, then it is all co-opted, and there is nothing left to appropriate.

The idea that nature becomes something else – photosynthesis no longer counts as "natural" but only as "co-opted" – when influenced by human agency may make sense in the context of theology. Seventeenth-century theologians believed that human activity by its very essence must disturb the Great Chain of Being that God created.[91] Ecologists today interpret this lesson to mean that only nature uncorrupted by human influence is capable of producing *real* NPP; human beings must logically assault, contaminate, and corrupt the NPP God has made. This may be a plausible lesson of religious faith, but it makes no sense in the context of biology.

As early as 1854, George Perkins Marsh observed that humanity had long since completely altered and interfered with the spontaneous arrangements of the organic and inorganic world.[92] Other authorities agree that the landmass of the globe has been thoroughly "co-opted," as Vitousek et al. define that term, for more than a century.[93] Bill McKibben in *The End of Nature* argues eloquently that not a nook or cranny on earth is free of human influence.[94] A persuasive article by Charles Mann in *The Atlantic* argues that the pristine rain forests of the Amazon are largely human contrivances.[95] The earth and its NPP have been totally co-opted and appropriated in the sense of Vitousek, the Ehrlichs, and Matson, and this has been so for 500 years.

What can we conclude from the fact that NPP has been virtually 100 percent "co-opted" or "appropriated," as Vitousek et al. use these terms, for centuries? Nothing. Plainly, while Vitousek et al. believe that the economy expands only at the expense of NPP – only by further appropriating and co-opting it – the evidence suggests otherwise. The global economy has grown immensely over the past five centuries, even though the global environment – and therefore NPP – had long ago been completely co-opted. Accordingly, NPP does not limit economic growth.

Conclusion

This chapter has criticized arguments many ecological economists assert concerning the "carrying capacity" of the earth. The first concerns whether entropy limits economic growth. "The question that confronts us today," Georgescu-Roegen has written, "is whether we are going to discover new sources of energy that can be safely used."[96] This question is better answered by engineers than by economists. The engineering literature, especially with respect to solar power, suggests that safe, abundant, and inexpensive new sources of energy have already been found.

Second, mainstream economists believe and history confirms that knowledge, ingenuity, or invention – the formal causes of production – find ways around shortages in raw materials, either by increasing reserves, substituting between resource flows, or making resources go farther. In reply, ecological economists answer that tools of transformation – the efficient causes of production – are complementary to and therefore cannot substitute for the material causes. While true, this reply is irrelevant. Technological optimists argue that formal causes (knowledge and ingenuity) not efficient causes (tools) can substitute between resource flows and therefore away from scarcity. The complementarity of efficient and material causes has no significance.

Third, ecological economists define economic "growth" in terms of the physical dimensions of "throughput," which, as they point out, cannot expand indefinitely. This tells us nothing, however, about "growth" as mainstream economists understand that term, which has to do with the value rather than the physical dimensions of production. The concept of "throughput," moreover, is too amorphous to be measured; its relation to environmental deterioration therefore cannot be determined.

Fourth, ecological economists employ as an "index of how full the world is of humans and their possessions" a calculation that 40 percent of NPP "passes through the human economy, or is in some way subject to human purposes."[97] This argument rests on two premises: first, that total NPP is fixed or limited by nature and, second, that economies, in order to grow, must "co-opt" correspondingly more organic matter. Both premises are false.

The central principle of ecological economics, the concept of carrying capacity, fails to show that economic growth is unsustainable. Ecological economists are unable to point to a single scarcity of "natural capital" that knowledge and ingenuity are unlikely to alleviate. Moreover, no one "really knows scientifically how large the carrying capacity of the earth is now or could be in the twenty-first century," as Stephen Schneider has written. Carrying capacity is an elastic notion depending on "social, economic, industrial, and agricultural practices."[98]

Environmentalists a century ago pointed to the intrinsic rather than to the instrumental value of the natural world. Like Thoreau, they found Heaven not only above their heads, but under their feet. They thought of nature as a divine mystery; the term "natural capital" would have been lost on them. If a leaf of grass, as Walt Whitman wrote, is no less than the journeywork of the stars, there is no need to conjecture about its economic benefits. E. O. Wilson has correctly said that the destruction of biodiversity is the crime for which future generations are the least likely to forgive us.[99] The crime would be as great if a computer could design or store all the genetic data we might ever use or need. A device may someday produce genomes to order; the ability to design and redesign species – to produce biodiversity at will – does not lie far off. The reasons to protect nature are moral and spiritual far more often than they are economic.

To this, ecological economists may reply that morality and prudence teach the same lesson, so that one will reinforce the other. Morality and prudence, however, teach very different lessons. Morality teaches us that we are rich in relation to the number of things we can afford to let alone; that we are happier in proportion to the desires we can control, not those we can satisfy; and that a simpler life is more worth living. Economic growth may be morally undesirable even if it is ecologically sustainable.

Prudence, in contrast, teaches – in the immortal words of Miss Piggy – that "More is More," as long as you can get away with it. Advances in technology may expunge, one by one, the instrumental reasons for protecting nature, leaving us only with our cultural commitments and moral intuitions. To argue for environmental protection on utilitarian grounds – because of "carrying capacity" or "sources of raw materials" and "sinks for wastes" – is therefore to erect only a fragile and temporary defense for the spontaneous wonder and glory of the natural world.

We might, then, take a lesson from the mariners who introduced this chapter. When lightening the ship of its cargo failed to overcome the danger – the tempest only worsened – they looked for a moral rather than a physical explanation of their plight. They found it: Jonah confessed his crime in fleeing from God's commandment. When the sailors transferred Jonah from the ship to the whale, the seas became calm. Today, we are all aware that the seas may rise up against us. Like the mariners, however, we might consider not just the weight of the cargo but also the ethical compass of our biospheric ark.

8

Cows Are Better Than Condos *or* How Economists Help Solve Environmental Problems

The French singer Maurice Chevalier (1888–1972) is credited with coining the adage, "Old age isn't so bad when you consider the alternative." Does cost-benefit analysis, like growing old, seem acceptable in view of the alternative? Throughout this book, I have criticized the attempt to assess environmental policies "by evaluating their consequences in terms of prior preferences."[1] What is the alternative? "Without cost-benefit analysis," Herman Leonard and Richard Zeckhauser have written, "we would be forced to rely on an unpredictable political process. That process frequently leads to stalemate and reliance on the status quo; at other times it careens in response to popular perceptions and whims of the moment."[2] Environmental economist Barry Field has made the same point. He has written, "It is the politician's job to compromise or seek advantage," while economists "produce studies that are . . . as objective as possible."[3]

The Commanding Heights in Environmental Economics

In step with the Progressive movement prominent more than a century ago, welfare economists contrast policy science with politics. Edith Stokey and Richard Zeckhauser, for example, argue that cost-benefit analysis provides a scientific, objective basis for policy making, while the alternative, a political process, is uncontrollable. "The benefits and costs accruing to all . . . will be counted on a dollar-for-dollar basis. Benefit-cost analysis is a methodology with which we pursue efficiency and which has the effect of limiting the vagaries of the political process."[4] Centralized planning based on scientific evaluation, according to this approach, brings to policy making an objective, neutral basis that political institutions and processes lack.

In the same Progressive spirit, Nobel laureate Kenneth Arrow, writing together with a group of economists, states, "Benefit-cost analysis should be required for all regulatory decisions."[5] People are too often swayed by ethical views, moral beliefs, and aesthetic judgments that can lead to environmental policies that are inconsistent with the welfare criterion. Accordingly, Arrow and co-authors argue that society should look to science – to an expert community of economists, such as themselves – to judge and justify policy. The goal of environmental policy – net benefits maximization – is revealed by social science and may be thwarted by politics. No political process – however transparent, fair, or democratic – can guarantee outcomes that will pass the cost-benefit test.

According to Arrow and co-authors, "economic efficiency, measured as the difference between benefits and costs, ought to be one of the fundamental criteria for evaluating proposed environmental, health, and safety regulations." The other criterion would be fairness or distributive equity, since "policies inevitably involve winners and losers, even when aggregate benefits exceed aggregate costs."[6] Policy analysis will "identify important distributional consequences," but it must "focus primarily on the overall relation of benefits and costs."[7] Redistributive goals are better pursued by separate policies, for example, direct transfers to the poor.

While Arrow and co-authors acknowledge that redistributive concerns can inform policy, they deny that any other ideological, moral, or political view should count. They write, "Benefit-cost analysis is premised on the notion that the values to be assigned to program effects – favorable or unfavorable – should be those of the affected individuals, not the values held by economists, moral philosophers, environmentalists, or others."[8] Of course, when Arrow and co-authors recommend efficiency or net benefit maximization as the goal of social policy, they believe that they express not a *value* but an objective scientific *fact*. Those who advocate any opposing view about social policy, no matter how well they might argue for it, express not an objective fact but a subjective preference, and this value or preference is only as good as their willingness to pay for it.

To judge a policy on cost-benefit grounds, experts have to perform a complex maximization exercise. Since they must gather and analyze the relevant data anyway, they might as well formulate the policy in the first place. Science must enter at the beginning if it is to be found at the end. To allocate resources efficiently, economists must apply scientific principles to correct the notorious failures of both market and political institutions. Why should cost-benefit analysis succeed, however, when other attempts at scientific management, such as socialism, failed?

To say that the "values to be assigned to program effects . . . should be those of the affected individuals" is roughly to repeat the tenet of Marx and Engels that goods be allocated "to each according to his needs." To be sure, Marx and Engels thought centralized planning could satisfy only the needs of individuals, while Arrow and company would satisfy all preferences, insofar as possible, on a willingness-to-pay (WTP) basis. Scientific management of the economy would seem to invite the same abuses whether the commissars are found in the Kremlin or in the Office of Management and Budget.

Joseph Stiglitz has written that "the failure of market socialism serves as much as a refutation of the standard neoclassical model as it does of the market socialist ideal." Stiglitz sees little difference between neoclassical and socialist economics. He has explained "that if the neoclassical model . . . had provided a correct description of the economy, then market socialism would indeed have had a running chance of success."[9]

The Policy Forum written by Arrow and a team of economists may represent the high-water mark of the Progressive Era faith in scientific expertise as the basis for correcting the notorious and ubiquitous failure of both markets and political institutions to allocate resources correctly. Marxist and neoclassical economists differ in details but not in their fundamental belief that social science gives them the authority to occupy the commanding heights from which to direct social policy. Those who possess a science are too soon possessed by it. They may dismiss opposing views as displays of ignorance or of a corrupt unwillingness to see the truth. Worse still, opposing beliefs may be included, on a WTP basis, in the calculus on which social decisions are to be based.

The Institutional Alternative

On the other hand, many contemporary economists may agree with Stiglitz that "what is at issue in the analysis of how the economy allocates its resources is more than just the solution to a complicated maximization problem; economics is far more complicated, and more interesting, than the engineering approach," such as that embodied in the Policy Forum.[10] A current trend toward an institutional perspective suggests that economists need not be in the business of valuation. Instead, economic theory may assess, criticize, and seek to improve not a given allocation of goods but an institutional arrangement or social process for allocating them. Many environmental economists have begun to deemphasize the attempt to measure benefits. Instead, they would help to design social processes, practices, and institutions through which people can more effectively make exchanges, collaborate, resolve conflicts, and achieve common aspirations.

Many economists do not believe they should occupy the commanding heights to evaluate policy. They regard the alternative to cost-benefit analysis, namely, democratic deliberation, not as irredeemable but as capable of reform and improvement. Members of this group are likely to have been persuaded by Ronald Coase, Peter Drucker, and others that cooperation rather than competition – organization rather than optimization – defines a modern economy.[11] The role for economists is not to declare every outcome to which anyone objects a "market failure" that requires a cost-benefit remedy, but to strengthen the institutions – the processes of organization, cooperation, and exchange – that enable individuals or their representatives to participate in and become accountable for the decisions that affect them.[12] Economists assist in these cooperative efforts by designing and informing arrangements – from "cap and trade" markets for pollution allowances to collaborative agreements among stakeholder groups – to allow those affected by a policy to engage more effectively in the process of shaping it.

Many of the most helpful, cost-effective, and sensible reforms in environmental policy have resulted from the suggestions of economists about how society, by altering incentive structures, can better reach its goals. By "its goals," I plainly do not refer to economic efficiency or net benefits maximization. Not a single statute proposes economic efficiency as a criterion and many major environmental statutes preclude it. Rather, the goals of society, for example, clean air and water, the protection of species, and the maintenance of wild and scenic areas, are intelligible to those without (but perhaps not to those with) advanced degrees in policy analysis. The question society must answer is how and where it can pursue these goals most effectively, that is, at the lowest political and economic cost. Economists often provide ideas and analyses society needs particularly to pursue its goals in cost-effective ways. Economists can show how traditionally opposed groups can gain more through compromise than by perpetual conflict.

The structures economists propose to improve social processes of decision-making include well-known and by now well-proven innovations, including pollution offsets and banking, risk "bubbles," transferable development rights, tradable pollution allowances ("cap-and-trade" strategies), environmental audits of industry, labeling requirements (e.g., California's Proposition 65), Toxic Release Inventories and other "benchmarking" information strategies,[13] liability schemes, subsidies for technological research, and other decentralized strategies to serve social goals. These innovations have been well studied in the literature, and I can add nothing to their analysis here.[14]

In the remaining pages of this chapter, I offer three brief case studies to show how economists have successfully tried not to supplant but to strengthen and inform social and political processes of environmental decision-making. The final chapter of this book will present an extended case history of an instructive example of environmental negotiation in which opposing groups turned conflict into collaboration to resolve a major dispute.

The War on the Range

For over a century, ranchers have grazed sheep and cattle on public lands in the West. As a result of the Taylor Grazing Act of 1934 and subsequent legislation, ranchers have operated under a complex set of regulations and fees that nobody believes makes sense. The Taylor Act assigned to qualifying ranches ("base properties") a number of AUMs ("animal unit months," i.e., forage for a cow and a calf for a month), based on a conception of the carrying capacity of a given parcel of public range. The Bureau of Land Management (BLM) administers about 10 million AUMs, the Forest Service another (roughly) 8 million. In Montana, an AUM averages about 20 acres; the national average is somewhat less. Grazing occurs on roughly 260 million acres of public rangeland and forest.[15] The rancher pays the government rent on his allotment of about $1.35 per AUM.[16] The BLM and the Forest Service in 1998 took in about $20 million in grazing fees. These agencies spend an estimated $75 million to over $200 million annually to administer the program, for example, to set allotments.[17] In managing this system of grazing permits, the government spends perhaps about $10 for every $1 it takes in. Even if the BLM charged the full market value of AUMs, proceeds would cover only one-third of the costs of administering the program.[18]

For fifty years, environmental groups argued that the AUM system did little to restore and much to damage the ecology of the western range. According to *Sierra Magazine*, cattle "trample whatever hasn't been eaten, crumble riverbanks, foul water, and otherwise make life miserable and sometimes impossible for the plants, birds, fish, and amphibians dependent on these rivers of life."[19] Organizations such as the National Wildlife Federation and the Natural Resource Defense Council contend that taxpayers subsidize this devastation because the government charges for AUMs only a fraction of what they are worth. The market prices of AUMs, as they transfer with the sale of ranches, range from $36 per AUM in Wyoming to $89 in New Mexico.[20] While these prices appear much greater than the dollar or two the rancher returns to the government, the rancher arguably pays for them in the purchase price of the associated ranch.

As early as 1963, Delworth Gardner, a leading agricultural economist, proposed that the government create "perpetual permits covering redesignated allotments . . . and issue them to ranchers . . . in exchange for those now in use." Gardner explains: "These permits would be similar to any other piece of property that can be bought and sold in a free market."[21] Those who valued the permits most – whether ranchers, sheepherders, hunters, or environmentalists – could then purchase them, thus redirecting the use of the public lands through voluntary, noncoercive exchange. Many economists supported this analysis, adding evidence to show that environmentalists would probably retire the ecologically most fragile parts of the range by purchasing the rights from cattlemen.[22]

Leading environmentalists, including many of those most fiercely opposed to ranching interests, accepted this economic analysis. Dave Forman, founder of the radical Earth First! movement, likewise called for a program to "buy out grazing permittees." He observed, "The butting-heads battles with ranchers over grazing in Wilderness is bad for all involved. The most practical and fairest way...is to buy 'em out."[23] Johanna Wald, a senior attorney with the National Resources Defense Council (NRDC), who won a landmark case against the BLM (*NRDC v. Morton*, 1976), approved an approach based on "incentives and markets." If grazing rights were privatized, environmentalists "will have market options, like buying out all or a portion of a rancher's permit."[24]

Two Views from the Same Window

Conflicts over the use of the public range have grown more intense in the last decade as the demography of the West has changed dramatically. Ranchers, loggers, and others who exploit natural resources see themselves as an embattled minority representing a small and dwindling part of the economy. As one writer, Sharman Russell, describes the rural valley in southwestern New Mexico where she lives:

In these last ten years, we have grown from a small community of farmers and ranchers to a larger community of farmers, ranchers, retirees, school teachers, entrepreneurs, small gardeners, and others. We are increasingly polarized. "Cowboys" on one side. "Environmentalists" on the other.[25]

According to Russell, ranchers and environmentalists see two different landscapes when they look out the same window. Ranchers see land that is healthy – in far better condition than fifty years ago – the productivity of which has improved over their lifetimes. They have been good stewards of the public domain. Environmentalists

read from a history book that vividly paints the West that was *before* the cattle came: grass up to a horse's belly, perennial rivers alive with beaver and trout, a wolf's resonant howl in the distance.... We backpack in the Gila Wilderness and find our camping sites littered with cow pies. We worry about things like the growing desertification of the West and the destruction of wildlife habitat. We see degradation.[26]

These contrasting aesthetic and ethical perceptions – each of which can be backed up by scientific studies – produced an impasse. In a 1994 opinion piece, Andy Kerr, a prominent environmental activist, argued, "In the long run, environmentalists have more people, more power, and more money than do the Elite Welfare Ranchers." He added, "Their battle is 'better' grazing. Our battle must be no grazing."[27] Ranchers feel threatened by environmental regulations, such as the Endangered Species Act, and by the environmental movement. Many or most ranchers believe that they can hardly survive economically in any case, largely because of foreign competition and low meat prices, though they hang on to protect what they regard as their heritage and way of life.

While the economic transformation of the West, as Andy Kerr observed, brings environmentalists people, money, and power, it also brings tremendous residential and commercial development. The choice is often not between ranching and wild land – the two landscapes seen out the window – but between ranching and retirement villages, golf courses, resorts, manufacturing campuses, research parks, and so on. As one rancher pointed out, "The subdivisions stop when they reach our property, and then there's this big swath of open space."[28] The values of ranchers and environmentalists may not seem all that different – better grazing might be an acceptable compromise – if the realistic alternative to grazing is a wave of residential development and commercial sprawl.

Economists and other analysts, alarmed by a polarization between ranchers and environmentalists that had begun to find expression in violence, wondered if a different sort of social structure could achieve agreements rather than aggravate antagonisms. The underlying problem, according to resource economist Robert Nelson, who teaches at the University of Maryland, lay in the amorphous nature of grazing rights. By practice and expectation over many decades, rights to AUMs had become vested in the associated ranches and transferred with them; indeed, they added so significantly to the value of the ranch that they could be used as collateral for mortgages. On the other hand, the rancher could not transfer the right other than by selling the ranch, and the right to the range could be used only for grazing. An environmental group who wished to purchase AUMs, even from a willing seller, to retire them in order to preserve ecological values could not do so. According to the 1978 Public Rangelands Improvement Act, a rancher could lose his permit if he failed to graze 90 percent of his allotted animals.

Nelson, who served for many years in the policy office of the Department of Interior, reiterated that a regime of well-defined transferable property rights would allow environmentalists to retire grazing permits in those places where they believe grazing is ecologically the most destructive. Nelson wrote:

For decades ranchers have pressed for a more formal establishment of their tenure status on federal rangelands. Today some prominent members of the environmental movement are reaching similar conclusions. The delineation of formal rights to use would promote a more responsible environmental management and federal rangeland resource use. The lack of any clear rights on the federal rangelands has resulted in blurred lines of responsibility which have been as harmful to the environment as they have been to the conduct of the livestock business.[29]

Leaders and activists from both environmental and cattlemen groups welcomed in principle the idea that ranchers could own grazing rights in fee simple and treat them as transferable like any other property right. The winner-take-all or zero-sum confrontation between ranchers and environmentalists could give way to voluntary exchanges that encourage cooperation and accommodation. The rancher and the environmentalist who look out the window, then, might come to see the same landscape.

Reform on the Range

By the middle 1990s, environmentalists such as Andy Kerr and Dave Foreman, who had been hostile critics of cattlemen, began to advocate a free-market or voluntary approach to conservation. In a lengthy analysis published in *Wild Earth* magazine in 1998, Kerr praised the buyout option even though it recognized that ranchers have a property right in their permits to graze cattle and sheep on public land. Kerr argued that the government loses so much on administering the grazing program, it would save hundreds of millions of dollars if it bought back the AUMs at fair market value, that is, at whatever competitive price a rancher demanded. Kerr reasoned that under the current graze-it-or-lose-it approach, stockmen have no choice but to run cattle on public land, and environmentalists have "no option but to exercise traditional environmental protection strategies in the areas of administrative reform, judicial enforcement, and legislative change." These methods "can cause social and political stress and are not always successful. To take advantage of the voluntary retirement option, some conservationists – and some ranchers – would need to rethink their traditional strategies."[30]

During the Clinton administration, then Secretary of Interior Bruce Babbitt introduced administrative amendments that opened the way to grazing permit trading by deleting the term "engaged in the livestock business" from the regulation governing who could own a grazing permit.[31] This opening to voluntary buyouts of AUMs has been pursued on a restrained, case-by-case basis. Every example is its own story. In one instance, the Grand Canyon Trust, a conservancy group, purchased a base property, the Last Chance Allotment, in part to retire associated grazing rights on the Grand-Staircase-Escalante National Monument. As property owner, the Trust would be held accountable for the condition of the associated range.

Environmental activists were quick to see that with ownership comes accountability. Once someone owns the AUMs, a buyer may become responsible for the subsequent condition of the land. This may lead to cooperative arrangements with stockmen. For example, if a rancher sells his AUMs on the public range to a conservancy group or back to the government, what will he do with his ranch? That private property will be sold, most likely, to developers, since they are willing to pay the most for it. Environmentalists who wish to preserve the open landscape, then, may have an incentive not to get rid of cattle but to subsidize or otherwise keep the rancher on the land, if they cannot outbid the developer.

The Nature Conservancy, when it announced its purchase of the Dug Out Ranch near Canyonlands National Park, said the ranch would continue in the livestock business. The organization sought to "move beyond the rangeland conflict and into collaborative efforts with livestock operators." A Conservancy spokesperson noted that "cows are better than condos, and increasingly in the West, this is the only choice we face."[32]

Visibility at the Grand Canyon

Environmentalism in the American West is often directed at preserving a magnificent landscape against the encroachment of commercial, industrial, and residential development. Perhaps the greatest symbol of the landscape of the West can be seen at the Grand Canyon – if, indeed, one can see it. During many summer days, prevailing winds dramatically impair visibility in the Grand Canyon by transporting emissions from the Los Angeles basin and other urban and industrial areas to the west. During the winter, when visibility in the Canyon is at its best, it is far from perfect, many environmentalists have charged, because occasional surface winds moving east to west bring sulfur emissions – the precursor of smog – from the Navajo Generating Station (NGS) located only 12 miles east of the edge of the Grand Canyon National Park.[33]

In 1977, Congress had amended the Clean Air Act (CAA) to require that the Environmental Protection Agency (EPA) promulgate regulations to assure "reasonable progress" toward preventing "any future, and the remedying of any existing, impairment of visibility" in the national parks. This amendment responded to complaints about pollution in areas such as the Grand Canyon, where, according to press accounts at the time, "the spectacular scenery is dulled by a murky, polluted haze.... Occasionally, the air is so foul that the daily quota of 12,000 visitors can hardly see to the bottom of the mile-deep gorge."[34] In 1982, the Environmental Defense Fund sued EPA to force it to regulate NGS emissions under the 1977 CAA amendments to improve visibility, especially during the winter at the Canyon.

NGS, which burns a maximum of 24,000 tons of coal a day, was constructed near Page, Arizona between 1971 and 1976. It had installed no pollution-control equipment because the air in the area is so clean that the marginal increase in sulfur dioxide did not threaten human health.[35] When NGS received its construction permit, however, it understood it would have to retrofit later with some kind of scrubber technology. A study the National Park Service (NPS) released in 1987 found that on some winter days NGS contributed up to 70 percent of the sulfates detected in the air over the Canyon. Although the National Research Council and other groups challenged this finding on scientific grounds – air transport models are notoriously inexact – it galvanized public opinion.[36] Public opinion, the 1977 CAA Amendments, and legal pressure by environmental groups made it inevitable that EPA would require NGS to do something. Leadership within EPA, particularly in the program office for Air and Radiation, moreover, saw in the controversy over NGS an excellent opportunity to bring industry and environmental groups together to work out a collaborative agreement.

The Economic Analysis of Visibility

Economic analysis affected the regulatory history of NGS in two ways. First, since visibility need not affect human health, regulations to protect it may consider and perhaps even balance costs and benefits. Accordingly, EPA could try to measure the benefits of increased visibility at the Grand Canyon in economic terms. Second, EPA needed to determine how much incremental control of NGS emissions actually cost. This would establish a supply-side price for marginal improvements.

EPA was obliged to estimate the benefits of regulation because an executive order promulgated during the Reagan administration required major environmental regulations to pass a cost-benefit test. EPA in addition had to respond to rules issued by the Office of Management and Budget (OMB) and later by the Competitiveness Council that required the quantification of benefits associated with major environmental rulemakings. The attempt to quantify the benefits associated with greater visibility in national parks began in the early 1980s and comprised much of the early research in contingent valuation (CV) methodology.[37] Economists understood that many citizens believed that pollution in places like the Grand Canyon is wrong. Therefore, these citizens could be said to benefit from environmental protection, even if they never visited the places in question. CV methods seek to measure as WTP the moral beliefs, aesthetic judgments, and spiritual concerns economists identify as "existence" or "nonuse" values.

By 1990, CV research had shown that people cared about environmental quality even in those places they did not ever plan to visit. Motivated by religious, aesthetic, and ethical judgments and convictions, many respondents to CV questionnaires reported significant WTP for the protection of visibility from industrial pollution; the totals could be staggering when aggregated across all households in the nation.

By revealing stupendous hypothetical WTP for "bequest," "option," and "existence" values, the CV approach offered EPA the numbers it needed to get a regulation by the Competitiveness Council. A CV analysis gave "juice" to regulations headed to OMB for cost-benefit review.[38]

To meet the OMB cost-benefit requirement, EPA relied on an extensive and expensive CV study it commissioned (with NPS) in 1988 to quantify the benefits associated with visibility improvement (or protection) in national parks in the Southwest and elsewhere. In this study, respondents were shown photographs that represented a range of summertime visibility in different national parks. Answers to the survey instrument indicated that respondents who did not plan to visit the park – whose values were wholly disinterested – were on average willing to pay about \$24 for a given improvement in visibility (155 km to 259 km) and \$21 to prevent that much degradation. The analysts excluded outlying bids that, if included, would have raised the average bid by a third.[39]

EPA somehow extrapolated these numbers to the Grand Canyon wintertime scenario; it then "applied the option, bequest, and preservation values to the entire population of the United States."[40] Not surprisingly, the annualized WTP for improved visibility at the Grand Canyon – as much as \$190 million for a 70 percent and \$250 million for a 90 percent reduction in emissions – was found to be well in excess of the costs. CV surveys such as this one provide the numbers environmentalists need to counter industry claims. These methods perform this feat by redescribing ethical beliefs as economic benefits for which people are willing to pay, thus turning moral and aesthetic judgments into data for economic analysis. To be sure, CV surveys are costly, but EPA officials saw past that problem. "You get the numbers you are willing to pay for," one said.[41]

Dueling Cost-Benefit Analyses

When the operators of NGS learned from EPA that it was preparing to quantify the benefits associated with regulating emissions, they saw the political need to commission their own analysis, which they tailored specifically to the Grand Canyon case.[42] As in the EPA study, respondents were shown photographs of different visibility conditions – although on the basis of a daily variation rather than seasonal variation. Like the EPA study, the NGS assessment produced a great many outlier bids, so the manner of handling these made a huge difference in both instances. The NGS consultants found that when they trimmed outliers according to the method they used, WTP for visibility improvements (or to prevent degradation) differed by an order of magnitude from that of the EPA-funded study. According to one summary, "the NGS benefits analysis estimated that first-year (1995) benefits would be $1.4 million for the 70% control option and $2.3 million for the 90% control option."[43] This was less than a tenth of the EPA estimates.

Leland Deck, who as an EPA economist served as the lead technical analyst for the NGS negotiation, has written a detailed and thoughtful review of the usefulness of benefits estimation in determining the regulatory outcome at the Grand Canyon. He observed that the differences between the two dueling benefit analyses were never resolved. "Ultimately the parties agreed to disagree about the benefits estimates," and they worked together instead on discovering how they could make the most reductions in emissions at the lowest cost. In other words, both sides abandoned cost-benefit analysis for cost-effectiveness analysis or, more precisely, knee-of-the-curve analysis. They consulted engineers to find ways to reduce emissions inexpensively and thus to make the greatest improvements possible within a bearable expense.

Deck asked why the two attempts to measure the benefits of visibility came to such dramatically different conclusions. He noted that the two studies represented the state of the art; contingent valuation had been very well developed in this area. Deck wrote that by the early 1990s there was already "a long history of available visibility valuation studies."[44] The disagreement might have arisen, Deck conjectured, because the nonuse benefits associated with environmental goods are hard to measure, because of structural differences in the way the studies were designed and implemented, or even because "of the influence of the sponsor."[45] It would be interesting to see if two groups of economists tasked with the same benefits estimation but working independently of each other and for sponsors with opposing interests would ever arrive at anything like the same estimates. In this instance, "the competing estimates effectively became a standoff."[46] The bad news was that benefits analyses were attempted. The good news was that they canceled each other out.

The Contribution of Costs

Although economists working for EPA and those working for NGS differed dramatically in their estimates of the benefits of regulation, they easily worked out whatever disagreements they had about the costs. They found, among other things, that owing to the "lumpiness" of available scrubber technologies, the marginal cost of reducing emissions from 70 percent to 90 percent was actually less than the average cost per unit of the reductions to 70 percent. While one usually assumes that emission reductions become more expensive as they increase, in this instance the more effective technology costs little more than a less effective one, so that the marginal cost curve declined. This economic information suggested that NGS could accede to a 90 percent reduction, thus accommodating environmentalists, without a significant additional expense.

Scrubbers that remove sulfur often have to be shut down for servicing; during these periods, emissions will increase. If NGS had to maintain a 90 percent reduction at all times – or as an average per hour, day, or even month – it would have to purchase at a cost of billions of dollars backup scrubbers that could take over when its main scrubbers were serviced. On the other hand, if the emissions were averaged over a year, there would be no need to purchase backups, because the plant could make up the difference by getting better than 90 percent reductions at some times to compensate for less at others. If servicing took place mostly during the summer – or at other times when winds blew from the west – this would not impact visibility at the Grand Canyon.

This interesting cost profile suggested the basis for a win-win compromise. If environmentalists agreed to yearly averaging, NGS might agree to purchase scrubbers to reduce emissions by 90 percent while avoiding the need to pay billions to install backup scrubbers. The problem, however, was that each side distrusted the other and insisted on its own benefits analysis. How could EPA broker a political compromise to keep industry and environmental groups from endlessly tying each other up in lobbying and litigation? How could EPA get the opposing sides to collaborate rather than fight each other in Congress, OMB, and the courts?

EPA found a brilliant strategy to move antagonism to collaboration. It threatened to impose a regulation that would be disastrous for both sides if the stakeholders did not come up with their own compromise. In 1991, the agency proposed a 70 percent level of control, which antagonized environmentalists, who insisted on 90 percent. It also proposed thirty-day averaging, which would require NGS to purchase backup scrubbers for each of three units, which the electric utility regarded as an impossible expense. The Assistant Administrator for Air then brought representatives of concerned environmental and industry groups together under the threat – equally terrifying to both – that if they did not come up with a win-win alternative, EPA would impose this lose-lose regulation.

Since the default regulation EPA threatened to impose was equally anathema to both sides, the stakeholders had the proper incentive to collaborate. As they investigated the costs of pollution control, they found that because of the way scrubber units are built, it would cost very little more to achieve a 90 percent reduction than a 70 percent reduction, although backup scrubbers would cost billions of dollars in order to meet short-term averaging requirements. By controlling pollutants down to 90 percent, moreover, NGS would produce sulfur emissions credits it could sell in the emerging market that had been created for them. After two months of intense negotiations in which information about costs – not benefits – proved decisive, the parties agreed on a regulation that would achieve a 90 percent reduction calculated on an annual average basis. On October 3, 1991, EPA formally adopted the compromise plan as its final rule.

President George Bush, in a well-publicized ceremony at the Grand Canyon, signed the rule into law. A front-page article in the *New York Times* hailed EPA's use of negotiations as an alternative to "the lawsuit system."[47] In fact, some disgruntled power consumers did sue, but the Ninth Circuit Court dismissed their petition, noting that "the Final Rule is the result of a site-specific informal rulemaking process that included virtually unprecedented cooperation between the governmental agency and the affected parties."[48] The way to include the interests of the affected parties is to bring them or their representatives together in stakeholder negotiations and give them an incentive to work something out. Collaboration provided a better alternative to cost-benefit analysis.

Project XL

The Clean Air Act was written with industries like coal-burning power plants such as the NGS in mind. These industries rely on large-scale mature technologies, for example, boilers, coke ovens, refineries, smelters, and so on, which are the principal point sources of pollution. A major goal of the statute is to force the operators of these plants to install the best available pollution-control technology and continually to develop better and cheaper means and methods of reducing emissions. An improved method or mechanism for controlling pollution on one smokestack, smelter, coke oven, or refinery might be required of others. The trick was to give industry incentives – such as marketable pollution permits – to develop new technology rather than to suppress it.

During the decades since 1970, however, American industry has become more and more integrated into a global manufacturing and marketing system in which competitive advantage results primarily from introducing new processes and products. A company such as 3M, for example, which manufactures high-tech goods from adhesives, batteries, and ceramics to fuel cells, imaging equipment, and optical fibers, survives by innovating. This company, like many others, tries to live by the rule that a third of its products by sales should not be any more than four years old.[49] Accordingly, it must constantly change its manufacturing processes, often in the course of developing a product, and this is not consistent with filing scores of permit requests for different kinds of emissions, preparing cost-benefit analyses, and waiting years for approvals.

In response to the challenge of regulating companies such as 3M that require timely permitting if they are to operate in this country, the Clinton administration developed Project XL to give industries "the flexibility to develop alternative strategies that will replace current regulatory requirements, while producing even greater environmental benefits."[50] Project XL requires a stakeholder committee – including local, state, and federal officials, industry representatives, and representatives of citizen and nongovernmental organizations – to develop and then oversee the implementation of Final Project Agreements. These Agreements set forth the steps an industrial facility will take to mitigate its effect on the environment and assure its standing with the community.

The Agreement requires that a company or facility demonstrate a superior environmental performance – including less pollution – than it would have achieved under current regulation. In return, the facility as a whole would be considered as a single source – all of its emissions would be placed, as it were, under a "bubble" – and the operators can decide how to keep the total output well under allowable levels. This would free the industry from the necessity of filing for a permit for every new process and from having to install control technologies that might otherwise have been mandated. Indeed, a facility can be approved in advance for changes in flows of emissions as long as the totals in general kinds for the plant as a whole remain within the agreed-upon limit.

At least three difficulties have limited the number of Project XL success stories. First, the negotiation process among federal, state, and local agencies, the stakeholder committee, and the company can easily become more involved, time consuming, and demanding than conventional permitting. Indeed, lengthy negotiations involving an XL application by 3M for one of its major plants proved intractable, adversarial, and fruitless. According to one careful account, both EPA and 3M took calculated positions and engaged in strategic bargaining, not collaborative problem solving. "In the end, this was not conducive to a deal."[51]

Second, Project XL presupposes environmental performance superior to that required by conventional regulation. This baseline – the emissions conventional regulation might permit – is hard to establish in industries that have to innovate, to change processes, and to switch among flows of materials and emissions in response to market conditions. The difficulty of determining a baseline – the default level of emissions the industry had to improve upon – proved intractable in the 3M case.

Third, while environmental groups, such as the National Resource Defense Fund (NRDC), are often asked to participate in the stakeholder process, they have little incentive to do so, at least insofar as they regard all pollution as wrong and oppose any level of industrial

emissions. Strategically speaking, they may do better not to participate in but to challenge any collaborative agreement as dangerous to
human health and the environment. Environmental groups had an
incentive to collaborate in the NGS permitting process because EPA
established a "default" option so disastrous to both sides that industry representatives and environmentalists had to agree on something
better. Perhaps EPA should have threatened to permit an independent company to operate a horrendous incinerator near the 3M site –
anathema to both sides – if negotiations failed.

Absent such a threat, the NRDC, which did not join the 3M stakeholder process, prepared a detailed and bitter challenge to the proposed agreement that emerged from it. Why allow industry to poison
the air for profit? Can one trust a stakeholder process that industry
alone has the resources to dominate? Since Project XL has no clear
legislative basis, EPA and 3M had to worry about an NRDC legal challenge. Concerned with the possibility of litigation, which would undo
whatever advantages in speed the XL process offered, EPA and 3M
gave up what was in any case a contentious and frustrating effort.[52]

Intel – A Success Story

In spite of its difficulties, Project XL can claim several successes. In the
late 1990s, Intel proposed to build at its Ocotillo Campus in a suburb
of Phoenix, Arizona, two major fabrication facilities for its Pentium
microprocessor chip. Microprocessor design and manufacture can be
understood in effect as an on-going experiment in which engineers
constantly change manufacturing methods in view of the results. A microchip manufacturer finds troubling the idea that routine changes
in manufacturing processes might be subject to months of review by
county, state, and federal authorities. Intel, which also operates fabrication plants in Ireland and Israel, publicly stated that lengthy permitting
requirements for every process change led the company to "seriously
question whether it could remain committed to the construction and
expansion of our U.S. sites."[53]

Intel applied to EPA for an XL permit that would "bubble" its entire
720-acre Ocotillo site as a single source and allow the company to do as
it liked as long as its total emissions remained under the caps in broad
categories – such as volatile organic compounds, particulate matter,

hazardous air pollutants, nitrogen oxide, and carbon monoxide. According to one technical publication, the manufacture of a six-inch wafer of microprocessors can require 20 pounds of various chemicals and more than 3,000 cubic feet of gases, all subject to scores of changes each year.[54] Intel wanted a single agreement to be administered by a lead regulatory authority rather than a variety of pacts with ten county, state, and federal agencies. A fifteen-member stakeholder counsel of industry representatives, officials from local, state, and federal regulatory agencies, and local citizens met over a hundred times starting in January 1996, educating each other about the technical aspects of microchip production and emissions reduction and control.

The Final Project Agreement that emerged from the lengthy and stressful stakeholder negotiation held Intel to strict requirements. The negotiators determined that in the absence of historical data – the planned facilities were new – they would consider the baseline against which to measure superior performance the theoretical maximums allowed a "minor source" by the Clean Air Act. Intel agreed to cap emissions at less than half the allowable levels – 100 tons per year – of carbon monoxide, nitrogen oxide, and volatile organic compounds. The company committed itself to emit only five tons of sulfur dioxide and particulate matter and ten tons of organic and inorganic hazardous air pollutants, as compared with far greater allowances under conventional regulation, for example, 250 tons of sulfur dioxide. Intel undertook to build and maintain a $25 million water treatment facility for the town and, of course, to furnish computers to the local schools. After the agreement was formalized, Intel constructed two large fabricating plants, one completed in 1998, the second in 2001. They produce Pentium microchips.

Cars, trucks, and other nonpoint sources of pollution, such as lawn mowers and barbecues, are overwhelmingly responsible for air pollution problems in the Phoenix air shed as in many other urban areas. According to the Intel website, its Arizona facilities produced in 2001 about the same amount of volatile organic compounds as 680 cars and the same amount of carbon monoxide as 80 cars. As one study states, "The company agreed to an air permit with, on balance, much more stringent emissions limits than what the alternative, a regular Maricopa County permit, would have required."[55] The NRDC issued a press release complaining that the agreement did not go far enough to protect health and the environment, but the group did not threaten to sue. It would have exhausted a good deal of political capital to force all microchip manufacturing overseas.

The Wampler Factor

The principal problem confronting the stakeholder group involved determining a baseline in comparison to which Intel would be required to do better. Intel suggested that the baseline be set at current regulatory requirements for a new minor pollution source in Maricopa County. Indeed Intel had designed the size of its facilities, with the "minor source" designation in mind, which allowed the industry to be subject strictly to state and county rather than federal requirements. Critics pointed out, however, that microchip manufacture is generally a cleaner activity than refining, smelting, electric generation, and other industries and so should be held to a much higher standard. A more relevant baseline might be taken from the environmental performance of Intel and other microchip manufacturers. Intel might be required not only to come well under minor source standards but to improve on its own past performance and that of the industry generally.

Accordingly, the Final Project Agreement allowed Intel to increase its emissions up to the overall cap only if it increased production proportionately. The stakeholder group wanted to preclude the possibility that Intel might produce fewer, "dirtier" chips under the overall cap, while encouraging them to produce more, cleaner ones by improving the chip-to-emission ratio. This production-based standard has been called the "Wampler Factor" and credited to David Wampler, an economist in the EPA regional office.[56] The stakeholder group encountered a conceptual difficulty in determining how to measure the quantity of microprocessors produced, for example, whether to use the number of chips or wafers, the computing power (which doubled every 18 months), the revenue, or some other yardstick. The Final Project Agreement in this matter as in most others states a complex technical formula; it is characterized in the endnote.[57]

Economists who have studied the Intel XL project point out that the crucial economic analysis did not attempt to measure the benefits of microchip production generally or of the existence of a domestic microprocessor industry. Instead, economic analysis proved most helpful in establishing a baseline – such as the production-to-emission ratio – and in suggesting ways to limit abatement, compliance, and transaction costs. Intel appeared most concerned about the transaction costs that would make it prohibitive to file for permits for every change in chemical processing, since microprocessor manufacture might require thirty or forty such changes per year. It also worried about having to install enormously expensive control devices on temporary and relatively insignificant sources. Thus, the appeal of the campuswide "bubble" – a concept originally suggested by economists – lay in the flexibility it allowed to offset emissions under a general cap rather than have to deal with each source separately. The company was willing to make significant concessions concerning the total allowable emission level to preserve flexibility in its treatment of individual sources that contributed to that total.

In a perceptive study, three economists conclude that the main benefit to be considered lay in the overall cost reduction – primarily a reduction in transaction costs – to Intel. These economists summarize, "In Intel's case, where production processes are constantly changing during a one-year chip development process, the firm faces the prospect of costly delays every time it has to modify its production process."[58] Intel did well to invest in the initially higher transaction cost of a stakeholder negotiation rather than bear the ongoing expense and uncertain prospects of conventional regulation. It certainly had to avoid the expense involved in preparing cost-benefit analyses to justify each change it might make in its emissions, product line, and chemical processes.

Conclusion

The chapter began by asking whether cost-benefit analysis, like old age, appears more acceptable in view of the alternative. What is the alternative to cost-benefit analysis? In many instances, the alternative may involve economic concepts and analyses of other kinds. In the case studies this chapter has briefly described, economists played crucial roles in the successful resolution of environmental disputes. Economists contribute to environmental policy making primarily in three ways. First, they help set up institutional arrangements, such as markets in tradable grazing permits, that enable traditional antagonists to gain the benefits of exchange. With exchange comes trust and collaboration. We cannot be too grateful for the contribution of institutional and other social economists who suggest frameworks that allow individuals to participate in determining the outcomes that affect them, for example, by buying and selling grazing, emission, and other rights. This is a very different approach from that of microeconomists who favor scientific management and centralized planning based on their own expertise.

Second, economists may suggest useful concepts that help society measure environmental progress. One such concept, which deserves more attention than it receives, defines the "knee of the curve" in a graph that represents pollution reduction on one axis and cost of abatement on the other. The "knee" occurs in the region at which the costs of controlling additional units of pollution begin exponentially to increase. In the NGS case, economists were able to point out that no "knee" occurred between 70 and 90 percent emission reduction. The operators of the plant, therefore, became more willing to bargain in terms of the 90 percent target.

Another concept, the product-to-emission ratio, became crucial to the Intel agreement. Economists who study the problem of global climate change have shown how this concept may also be relevant to reducing atmospheric loadings of carbon dioxide and other greenhouse gases. They have suggested that treaties adopt a target ratio between a country's per capita GDP and its emissions – for example, dollar GDP per pound CO_2 – and that wealthier nations help poorer ones obtain the needed cleaner technology.[59]

Third, economists have shown that they can helpfully measure the costs of pollution control and environmental protection and suggest ways to minimize those costs. The negotiations that led to the NGS and Intel agreements succeeded because the stakeholders could agree on the compliance costs associated with different regulatory options. The stakeholders could search, then, to get the most environmental protection at the lowest cost. In other words, all could agree that regulations should be cost-effective even if there is no way or need to determine whether they are cost-beneficial.

Perhaps the most important concept economists have contributed to policy analysis is that of the transaction cost. Plainly, the Intel agreement was motivated by the company's eagerness to avoid the massive transaction costs involved in standard command-and-control regulation. Industries like Intel may be willing to comply with tougher requirements if they were streamlined, say, if companies dealt with a single agency under clear mandates that allow the industry the greatest flexibility in complying with them.

The alternative to cost-benefit analysis may be economic analyses of other kinds – institutional analysis, transaction cost analysis, cost-effective analysis, and so on. Cost-benefit analysis does not look better when compared to these other ways economists helpfully inform environmental policy. Indeed, in comparison to the many important ways economists contribute to environmental policy, cost-benefit analysis only looks worse.

9

The View from Quincy Library *or* Civic
Engagement in Environmental Problem Solving

On their own initiative, about twenty residents of the northern Sierra Nevada, including environmentalists, timber industry representatives, and local officials, held a series of meetings beginning in 1993 at a library in the logging town of Quincy, California, and after months of deliberation and negotiation they agreed on a plan to manage the surrounding Plumas, Lassen, and Tahoe National Forests. They had chosen the library, it was said, so that they could not scream at one another – and by all accounts, the strategy worked. "After fifteen years of fighting . . . the idea that we would sit in one room and recognize each other's right to exist was a new one," said Michael Jackson, an environmentalist in the Quincy Library Group (QLG). A newspaper serving the area explained, "Local combatants were forced to deal directly with each other or to remain in perpetual struggle and gridlock."[1] Laura Ames, who directs an alliance of grassroots environmental groups, noted that deliberation succeeded where litigation failed. "We are in a new era," she said.[2]

Across the United States, and especially in the West, hundreds of citizen associations like the QLG bring together environmentalists and their adversaries in face-to-face collaboration to manage shared resources. The more inclusive these associations become – for example, by engaging public officials and representatives from national business and environmental groups – the more democratic are their deliberations and the more legitimate their results. This chapter examines the "new era" – or at least the new hope – that the rise of civic environmentalism creates. The current "winner-take-all" system of confrontation and litigation may be yielding to more deliberative and representative and therefore more democratic decision-making.

Science as a Surrogate

The QLG might be seen as a long-delayed response to the expectation with which the U.S. Congress in the nineteenth century encouraged settlers to migrate to the West. By giving settlers land in modest plots – usually about 160 acres – the Homestead Act of 1862 and the land acts that followed sought to build a Jeffersonian democracy of small freeholders throughout the arid West. These landowners were supposed to form associations patterned on town meetings to settle controversies that might arise among them. In refusing to allow public rangeland to be fenced, Congress in 1885 perpetuated the hope that settlers could collaborate to manage the pastoral commons. "It was a noble idea," writes Karl Hess, a scholar of the social history of the West. "It was the expectation that every citizen would be a stakeholder in an experiment of direct, hands-on democracy."[3]

Over most of the West, however, the climate conspired with everything else to doom this hopeful experiment. Herds of cattle require enormous tracts of land – sometimes 100 square miles – where forage grows slowly. Farms of modest size cannot succeed with only 16 inches of rain a year. By the end of the nineteenth century, timber, cattle, railroad, and mining "barons," after concentrating their economic and political hold on western land, plundered places and ravaged resources Congress hoped associations of farmers, tradesmen, and other small landowners would protect. Theodore Roosevelt spoke for the conservation movement by demanding that corporations "be so supervised and regulated that they shall act for the interest of the community as a whole."[4] The sparse citizenry and the inchoate local government of the West, however, could hardly challenge mining, timber, and grazing barons who created jobs and brought in money.

By the 1870s, Congress had become aware that "cut and run" timbering practices had created horrendous problems of disease, fire, and erosion in many areas of the northern and western forests. The "tragedy of the commons" played out even more dramatically on the range, where enormous herds of cattle quickly grazed off the prime forage.⁵ At the turn of the century, one federal official observed flocks of sheep and cattle

passing each other on trails, one rushing in to secure what the other had just abandoned as worthless. Feed was deliberately wasted to prevent its utilization by others. . . . Transient sheepmen roamed the country robbing the resident stockmen of forage that was justly theirs. . . . Class was arrayed against class – the cowboy against the sheepman, the big owner against the little one – and might ruled more often than right.⁶

Faced with the failure of hands-on democracy on the western range, Karl Hess writes, "a new vision of the West arose from the ashes of the old – a vision of a federal range governed by scientifically objective and politically neutral government agencies." The growing power of the timber barons – Weyerhaeuser practically owned Washington State – lent urgency to the formation of the U.S. National Forest Service, which, along with the General Land Office and, somewhat later, the Grazing Service, was to manage western public land in the public interest. Conservationists believed that professionals in agencies, not politicians in Congress, could be trusted to determine on neutral, rational grounds what the public interest requires. "Reflecting the will of the people, these agencies would be manned by men and women steeped in the value of public service and thoroughly trained in the science and technology of land management, use, and conservation."⁷

Conservationists such as Gifford Pinchot, the founding chief of the Forest Service, argued that in the absence of centralized control, public or private, competition among thousands of "cut and run" operators, each trying to beat the others to market, would destroy the resource base. In harmony with the Progressive movement, these conservationists believed the government should retain control of public lands rather than cede them to corporate oligopolies. "If scientific management in fact required large organization," writes policy analyst Robert Nelson, "then the public sector was preferable to the private sector, or so it seemed to many Progressives. Rather than create one or more new Weyerhaeuser-type empires, Progressives preferred to create the Forest Service instead."⁸

Pinchot and his successors fought on two fronts – first, against large corporations, and second, against politicians who might make a pork barrel out of the West. To keep corporations at bay, Pinchot railed against the "vast power, pecuniary and political, [of the] ... railroads, the stock interests, mining interests, water power interests, and most of the big timber interests."[9] After Pinchot retired, the Forest Service continued to attack timber practices on private land. "Laissez-faire private effort has seriously deteriorated or destroyed the basic resources of timber, forage, and land almost universally," the Service reported in the 1930s. The private sector "has felt little or no responsibility for the renewal of the resources on which its own industries must depend."[10] This was not entirely fair. By the 1950s, millions of acres in tree farms, as one expert noted, received "more intensive forest management than ... most of the publicly owned lands."[11]

To keep public lands out of the pork barrel, conservationists including Presidents Theodore Roosevelt and Woodrow Wilson tried to free agencies from political control. According to historian Samuel Hays, conservationists preached a "gospel of efficiency" asserting that "social and economic problems should be solved, not through power politics, but by experts who would undertake scientific investigations and devise workable solutions."[12] Hays writes, "The crux of the gospel of efficiency lay in a rational and scientific method of making basic technological decisions through a single, central authority."[13] Experts using "technical and scientific methods should decide all matters of development and utilization of resources, all problems of allocation of funds. Federal land management agencies, rather than the parties themselves, should resolve conflicts among livestock, wildlife, irrigation, recreation, and settler groups."[14]

Why should land management agencies rather than the parties themselves resolve conflicts? The question had an obvious answer at the time. Few held out much hope that the processes of representative democracy would flourish amid the "pressure politics" of the Gilded Age. The shoot-out at O.K. Corral in 1881 illustrated the alternative dispute resolution (ADR) and "stakeholder" arbitration techniques then available. More to the point, conservationists believed that the truth and objectivity of science offered a sounder basis than majority (or mob) rule for determining the public interest. The objectivity of science was supposed to put political decisions above class and faction. The conservationist movement, an analyst writes, believed that a "sense of political community may be regenerated by the adoption of science as the common language of discourse, bringing about an end to irrationality, rivalry of power, and authoritarianism."[15]

Today, nobody utters the words "scientific management" and "centralized planning" except pejoratively, calling up images of Five-Year Plans. And indeed, scientific management in the form of forest fire prevention led directly to, among other things, the insect-infested dying forests that surround Quincy Library. Yet, in the early 1900s, Congress had to decide whether to transfer the great resources of the West to empire builders – the railroads, Weyerhaeuser, and a few other corporations – or to keep its options open by retaining control of public lands.[16] What population existed in the relevant landscapes had all it could do to keep rudimentary law and order. Congress created the Bureau of Reclamation (1902) and the Forest Service to manage natural resources scientifically in the public interest – call it communism if you like – as the alternative to establishing private empires and baronies in the Western states and territories.

If deliberation means discussion of the substance of proposals rather than jockeying for influence, if it means adducing considerations that others can understand as reasons rather than logrolling for results, one could as plausibly look for deliberation among scientists and professionals as among the representatives of the people. For these reasons, scientific management seemed to conservationists to be a good enough surrogate for democracy.[17] At the time, how but by some appeal to "objective" science could the government identify a legitimate public interest in managing western resources? Local communities of diverse "stakeholders" and libraries in which to meet hardly existed within national forests or public rangeland prior to the Second World War. Even if scientific expertise and professional judgment amounted to reading the entrails of chickens, no one offered a better way to determine the public good.[18]

The Illusion of the Ideal Administration

The twenty or so citizens who met at Quincy Library did not convene to protest a Forest Service decision. Rather, they came together as a result of Forest Service indecision. The Service, according to a local newspaper account in 1997, had become "a weakened, disoriented agency that used to run the national forests. Today, the forests are run by judges, by environmentalists working through the Clinton admin-istration, and by the timber industry working through Congress."[19] QLG organizer Michael Jackson explains that "because no one knows how to manage the forests, all sides in Congress hack away at the Forest Service. The Republicans attack science, recreation, and implementa-tion of wildlife protection. The Democrats go after roading and other natural-resource budget items. The result is a shrinking agency that spends much of its time wondering when the next blow will fall."[20]

In its heyday before the Second World War, the Forest Service had the benefit of savvy political leadership. Legislation enacted in 1897, moreover, gave the Forest Service a clear and politically feasible mandate, namely, to secure water flows and "to furnish a continuous supply of timber."[21] With this mandate, the Forest Service derided the views of preservationists such as John Muir. "The object of our forest policy," Pinchot wrote, "is not to preserve the forests because they are beautiful . . . or because they are refuges for the wild crea-tures of the wilderness . . . but the making of prosperous homes."[22] In Pinchot's time experts in agencies knew something; they spoke with moral certainty born of scientific objectivity, and it hardly mattered if what they knew wasn't so.[23] Given a clear mandate – to maximize sustained yields – scientists could in principle reach a working consen-sus. This is not as easy if the goal is to do the right thing, to maximize each of a hundred conflicting uses, or to appease violently opposed groups, each with its own scientists to attest to its view of the values to be protected in the environment.

After the Second World War, in the rapidly growing new West, hunters, fishers, skiers, and preservationists came into conflict with miners, loggers, grazers, farmers, and developers. Environmental or-ganizations, such as the Sierra Club, as well as industry, recreational interests, and other groups, built up their own staffs of scientists, economists, and other experts to challenge the Forest Service on its own professional grounds. The agency meanwhile had become inbred; its chiefs, always appointed from within the agency, lacked the political savvy of Pinchot. The Forest Service lost ground figuratively and liter-ally after the War: against its howls of protest, preservationists managed to carve several wilderness parks from the national forests.

To block further attempts to turn forests into parks, the Forest Service prodded Congress to enact the Multiple-Use Sustained-Yield

Act of 1960, a vague document instructing the Service to manage "the various renewable surface resources of the national forests so that they are utilized in the combination that will best meet the needs of the American people."[24] Although the agency hoped that this delegation of legislative authority would increase its power, it had the reverse effect. Such an indeterminate delegation, as law professor Louis Jaffe wrote, yields only controversy and litigation "when results do not comport with one or another individual's concept of what the 'public interest' requires. Thus, paradoxically, the more vague a delegation, the more likely the charge that the agency has failed to fulfill its congressional mandate."[25]

When Congress provides an agency, such as the Forest Service, with no instruction more precise than to regulate in the public interest, it creates not legislation but legislators. Congress similarly delegates its legislative powers to others when it sets an impossible goal – that the workplace shall be hazard-free, for example – and then modifies it with weasel words, such as "to the extent feasible."[26] Chief Justice William Rehnquist, reviewing the Occupational Safety and Health Act, described the phrase "to the extent feasible" as one of many examples of "Congress simply avoiding a choice which was both fundamental for purposes of the statute and yet politically so divisive that the necessary decision or compromise was difficult, if not impossible, to hammer out in the legislative forge."[27] He implored the Supreme Court to invalidate the vague and precatory laws that support today's regulatory state. These statutes, he said, "violate the doctrine against uncanalized delegations of legislative power."[28]

What is wrong with uncanalized delegations of legislative power? Critics of the administrative state sometimes offer the pseudosophisticated reply that agencies to which Congress fails to give a clear political mandate will be captured by the industries they are supposed to regulate. Other critics, including those associated with public choice theory, argue even more cynically that bureaucrats will feather their own nests, for example, by endorsing on "neutral" and "scientific" grounds whatever policies bring more money or more power to the agency. If putting out fires brings in money, then science requires the suppression of fires; if further studies attract big bucks, then more research is required. While there is something to be said for these familiar criticisms, agencies acting even with the best intentions lack authority to make the political tradeoffs Congress delegates to them. As a result, little more may be expected from these agencies than regulatory rigor mortis, paralysis by analysis, and an endless loop.

During the 1960s and 1970s – years in which it enacted the nation's basic environmental statutes – Congress acted consistently with the conservationist premise that policy should be professionalized rather than politicized. The National Environmental Policy Act of 1969 (NEPA), for example, hailed at the time as "an environmental bill of rights,"[29] in fact reiterated the conservationist faith that the agencies could spin scientific straw into political gold if they gathered enough of it.[30] The statute told the agencies to "[u]tilize a systematic, interdisciplinary approach which will ensure the integrated use of the natural and social sciences and the environmental design arts in decision-making which may have an impact on man's environment."[31] If a single scientific discipline failed to make an agency sufficiently diverse, democratic, or deliberative, perhaps a passel of different disciplines – including the social sciences – would do.

No matter how many scientific specialists an agency brought on board, the NEPA-mandated Environmental Impact Statements (EISs) it prepared quickly became the targets of litigation. In a representative case, *National Resources Defense Council (NRDC) v. Morton*, an environmental group forced the Bureau of Land Management (BLM) to produce not one (as it planned) but 212 major EISs for the areas for which it granted grazing rights.[32] Ranchers appealed, arguing that the NRDC, which hoped "to run them off the range," had colluded with the BLM, which saw that "its budget allotments would be greatly strengthened"[33] to pay for the EISs. The ranchers then turned to their senators, who held posts in key oversight committees, to protect their interests from any BLM action.

An "Iron Triangle" – the inevitable result of the overdelegation of legislative authority to the executive branch – now defines environmental policy making as a three-cornered tug-of-war. At one vertex of this triangle, the administrative agencies, such as the Forest Service or the BLM, try to promulgate policies. At the next vertex, the special interests, including industry and national environmental groups, challenge any policy they do not like, often taking the agency to court. At the third vertex, members of Congress intervene with the agency to obtain policies their constituents or contributors desire. Any decision taken at one of these vertices will be appealed and probably blocked at another – and eventually the dispute will wend its way through the judicial system, the fourth corner of this infamous triangle. The Iron Triangle as surely sinks public policy as the Bermuda Triangle sinks ships – and equally well serves the public interest.[34]

If Congress had either leased the Lassen and Plumas forests to Sierra Pacific Industries or designated them as wilderness, the people of Northern California would live with the results. In a democracy, citizens are supposed to accept and comply with a statute the legislature enacts even if they do not agree with it. As long as no one is accountable for the national forests, however, the citizenry must get along with no decision at all – just indecision, starts and fits of policy in one direction or another, contradictory statutes, and endless litigation. The Forest Service would fiddle with further studies, the locals thought, even while the Sierras burned.

Torn in opposite directions by well-heeled environmental and industry lobbies, each with its own credentialed scientists and special friends in Congress, the agencies have become Push-Me-Pull-You's utterly unable to make the hard political choices Congress delegates to them. The appearance of civic environmental associations, such as the QLG, has an ironic quality in this context. The very political choices civil society pays Congress to decide have come back full circle to civil society again.

The Solace of Science

Almost a century ago, the Forest Service enjoyed both a clear political mandate and a solid scientific consensus among experts about how to achieve it. Congress told the Service to protect water flows and to maximize the sustained yield of timber. Foresters and other professionals knew (or thought they knew) how to do these things. Today, when the Service has no instruction more determinate than to "best meet the needs of the American people," what role can science play in agency decision-making? It must play an even greater role, one might say, because the agency has to rely on science to determine its ends as well as the means it uses to achieve them. The alternative to scientific management would seem to be pressure politics; then there would be no role for science.

Speaking to American foresters in the 1970s, economist John Krutilla declared that the Forest Service must base policy on science or endure "indignities at the hands of one or another group insisting that the national forests satisfy their mutually incompatible demands."[35] Recommending his own discipline of resource economics, Krutilla announced that the agency's goal must be "to manage the national forests in order to maximize benefits," that is, "to pursue economic efficiency."[36] Robert Nelson comments, "Krutilla argued that the time had come to make good on the original promise of Gifford Pinchot, who preached only scientific management."[37]

Economists like Krutilla preached the "gospel of efficiency" throughout the 1970s, arguing as scientists that the public interest lay in maximizing social utility. Seizing upon this opportunity to add another level of bureaucratic review to stifle regulatory actions, Ronald Reagan, upon becoming president in 1981, issued an executive order requiring a cost-benefit justification of all major regulatory actions, except as prohibited by law.[38] Administrative agencies obediently hired economists to pour the old political wine into new bottles, labeled "costs" and "benefits," from which to decant their usual views of the public interest.

Seeing their own opportunity in this alchemical project, national environmental organizations hired economists able to demonstrate scientifically that the policies they favored corrected a "market failure" and thus were economically efficient. Krutilla himself authored a number of spectacularly innovative analyses to demonstrate that the costs of economically promising projects, such as the proposed Hell's Canyon dam, actually exceeded the benefits.[39] Traditional combatants carry on venerable political, moral, and ideological battles by arguing over externalities, existence values, discount rates, and the economic returns of ecosystem services.

Attempts by economists and other professionals to place public policy on a scientific and objective footing, however, have made agency decisions only the more vulnerable to "pressure politics." One reason for this is obvious: all sides to a political controversy can hire their own scientists and economists to refute the other fellow's experts. Nobel laureates tend to cost so much that only industry can hire them, but there is hardly an interest group, however modest, that cannot afford to enlist reputable expert witnesses to testify at administrative hearings and then in court. Scientists outside a regulatory agency second-guess everything it says or does, so that the agencies must employ blue-ribbon science advisory boards or commission National Research Council studies to vouch for their objectivity.[40] Cost-benefit analyses, ecological models, toxicological studies, and other analyses cancel each other out. As expert economic and other assessments fracture along traditional political fault lines, public confidence in science erodes.

By the 1970s, the public recognized that science simply could not answer many of the questions regulators asked of it.[41] Hume's edict about inferring an "ought" from an "is" became a commonplace caution to policy makers against mixing "facts" and "values." The tendency of newer "policy sciences" beginning in the 1960s to extend their reach to the "trans-scientific," that is, to normative and political questions, aroused public suspicion. Meanwhile, the business of science – the competition for grants, the constant claims to "paradigm shifts" that adorn proposals, and the millions of dollars wasted on "big science" fiascoes such as the International Biology Program – fed skepticism about the honesty, objectivity, and neutrality of expertise.

Chastened by the public's distrust, some scientists have become circumspect, qualifying their claims to the point of making them vacuous or abandoning "relevant" research topics altogether. Others find themselves preoccupied with policing the boundaries between "real" and "junk" science. As journalists have taken up the science beat, moreover, debates between experts have become routinized, presented like theater or restaurant reviews, as matters of taste, or reported like sports events, as competitions. The press tends to "balance" every assertion with an equal and opposing one, however implausible. While science has plainly added much to the store of human knowledge, it has also made us aware of how much we do not know. Accordingly, as science advances it creates the need for more science – and creates with it the opportunity to avoid hard political choices by funding further research.

As more people attend college and observe scientists in their university habitats, they are less likely to venerate science and more inclined to judge scientific claims for themselves. When the public does seek to judge for itself, however, it finds less and less in these claims that it can understand. Local knowledge, for example, of the dying, sticklike forests near Quincy, often bears no relation to scientific models, such as those concerning "forest succession," "climax communities," or "sustainable yields." Funds flow to "high priori" abstract and theoretical research, such as the mathematics of biocomplexity, although these arcane Neoplatonic studies cannot possibly bear on management decisions.

As the models become more mysterious, the assumptions more gnostic, the mathematics more hairy, expert opinion loses relevance to public concerns. Sheila Jasanoff, a leading commentator on science policy, has written, "The gap between what experts do and what makes sense to people accounts for a massive public rejection of technical rationality in modern societies."[42] Not science itself but the conservationist or Progressive faith that it can always be our guide has led to disillusionment – to the widespread belief, as Jasanoff reports, that "science, far from being part of the solution, may in fact be part of the problem."[43]

The Mischiefs of Faction

One does not have to look long at the history of the Forest Service to see what James Madison described as the "mischiefs of faction." The single-issue strategies of many lobbying groups routinely "gridlock" policy in the Iron Triangle.[44] For these groups, conflict provides the principal method to deal with issues and to mobilize support. Deliberating with others to resolve problems undermines the group's mission, which is to press its purpose or concerns as far as it can in what it regards as a zero-sum game with its political adversaries. Anything less than demonizing opponents – for example, negotiating with them – would disarm and demobilize one side in comparison with the others. When an interest group joins with its enemies to solve a problem, it loses the purity of its position; it ceases to be a cause and becomes a committee.

The strife of factions around the Iron Triangle has become professionalized. It benefits the lawyers, lobbyists, and expert witnesses who serve as mercenaries, but it produces no policy. If the crumbling Plumas and Lassen forests go up in flames, carrying away the habitat of species as well as that of human beings – as they surely will absent a management plan – environmental groups can celebrate their victory: they will have thwarted the timber industry. The timber industry can savor its victory in having kept the area from becoming a designated wilderness. Like the dead trees that hang upon each other in the forest, interest groups shore each other up, each sustained and supported by its holy war against the forces of evil on the other side.

Political theorists suggest two strategies for dealing with the mischiefs of faction. First, neoconservatives believe that public resources such as the national forests should be privatized. Second, some liberals suggest that representatives of opposing groups could form "stakeholder" committees to work out some compromise – as happened in the Arizona power plant example described in the last chapter. There are ways to combine these strategies. One model for doing this might be found in the Smithsonian Institution, which is governed by a group of trustees who represent different constituencies and are accountable for what the organization does. Why not incorporate each national forest, for example, under its own board of trustees and let them experiment with different approaches to management? That way, society would have management and management decisions rather than an endless loop that in the end gives nobody authority and thus leaves everyone out.[45]

By creating boards of trustees to govern the national forests, society could create authority rather than diffusing it. Opposing groups represented on these boards must reach consensus or lose their mandate. As things stand, these groups simply vie with one another for favors – "rents" in the technical lingo – from government. The public ownership of resources, as Friedrich Hayek has said, leads to the "domination of government by coalitions of organized interests" and the growth of "an enormous and wasteful apparatus of para-government" needed to placate, reward, and defend against interest groups.[46]

Incorporation under trustees is not the only strategy to avert the mischiefs of faction. Among liberal theorists, Joshua Cohen and Charles Sabel have described a system of federalism "with multiple centers of decision-making, including central and local decision-makers, and separate spheres of responsibility for different units."[47] Laws that prohibit nuisances or torts – for example, laws controlling pollution – may be administered centrally, since everyone has the common-law right to be free of trespass. Representative citizen groups and stakeholder councils, however, are best situated to respond to problems arising in their communities not related to civil, political, or personal rights. Cohen and Sabel also note that deliberative associations seeking to manage localized resources have much in common. Compromises environmentalists and industry groups reach in one place may provide a model or "benchmark" for results elsewhere. These problem-solving groups should be networked so that they can learn from each other's efforts.

A Step toward Democracy

Beginning in the early 1970s, the Forest Service encouraged this kind of federalism by bringing the views and interests of local user groups into its decision-making process. In 1972, the agency initiated its Inform and Involve program, which served as a model for other agencies eager to engage stakeholders in policy discussion. The National Forest Management Act of 1976 called for public participation in the preparation of the long-term forest plans it required.[48] Officials in the Department of Agriculture prodded the Forest Service to implement the participatory mandates of the law.[49] A cadre of foresters tried to tease out the public interest by talking with the public; indeed, the Forest Service became preoccupied with public outreach and engagement.

During this period, the Forest Service brought together stakeholder groups, thus preparing the way for the one that met a decade later at Quincy Library. Carmen Sirianni and Lewis Friedland, who work with the Civic Practices Network, point out that "some forests developed programs characterized by genuine dialogue and consensus-seeking among various user groups, and staff began to nurture deliberative regulatory cultures to complement and modify a professional ideology based on the scientific management of the land."[50] In response to NEPA, the Forest Service redoubled its efforts to solicit public "input."[51] In the decade-long process to prepare an EIS for areas to be given wilderness status, Sirianni and Friedland report, the Service "involved fifty thousand people in providing input into the scope of the EIS, seventeen thousand in workshops," and thousands more who sent in comments. Over two decades, the Forest Service has engaged stakeholders throughout the West in "deliberative, consensual and other face-to-face" discussions, including "intensive workshops to clarify and classify different user values" and "weekend retreats to build trust and empathy among traditional opponents."[52] These traditional opponents, when dealing face-to-face with each other, start considering reasons rather than stating positions and thus move from mobilizing support to solving problems.

Rather than simply seeking "input" for a decision agency experts are to make, the Forest Service can do more to let stakeholder councils make the decision themselves, once they have been offered expert information and advice. As long as individuals trust their representatives in negotiations with delegates of opposing groups, they are bound to accept the outcome as equitable or as the best that could be achieved. They are likely to challenge the same outcome if reached by an administrative process on the basis of technical or scientific considerations.

Science cannot determine the public interest. A bureaucracy may implement clear political goals, but it is hopeless when it tries to resolve what are essentially political disputes. The public itself, through a representative and deliberative process, must make out where its interest lies. Unlike the Iron Triangle, where pressure is the only principle, local stakeholder councils, properly constituted, can be places, as Cohen and Sabel write, "where practicality in the form of problem-solving meets political principle in the form of deliberation."[53]

The story of the QLG is typical of these deliberative problem-solving coalitions, which draw together diverse interests and ideological groups. When actors find they cannot defeat each other and that it is better to solve problems than to rally around positions, as Sirianni and Friedland write, face-to-face meetings and social networks give them the opportunity to find common ground "based on the development of trust and recognition of legitimate interests." With respect to the national forests, "more deliberative cultures, and the use of alternative dispute resolution, open decision-making and ecosystem management emerged only in the wake of an extended period of conflict" in which adversaries remained tied to inflexible positions.[54]

Management strategies worked out by deliberative and representative citizen groups, of course, become targets of criticism by those who seek to advance a priori positions – for example, to permit or to prohibit logging on all public lands – which they insist reflect the best available science. Thus, any consensus-based compromise reached by those trying to resolve an impasse will be "attacked by environmentalists, timber and mining groups, and other backcountry users as providing too much or too little wilderness protection."[55] In spite of their vulnerability to end-runs by interest groups, stakeholder councils have gained enough strength to prompt Robert Gottlieb and Helen Ingram to hail the emergence of a "new environmentalism." They describe a "grass-roots, community-based, democratic movement that differs radically from conventional, mainstream American environmentalism, which always had a strong nondemocratic strain."[56]

In an article titled "Land-Use Democracy," ecologist Aldo Leopold wrote in 1942, "One of the curious evidences the 'conservation programs' are losing their grip is that they seldom have resorted to self-government as a cure for land abuse. ... [We] have not tried democracy as a possible answer to our problem."[57] Instead of trying democracy, the nation has generally kept Pinchot's faith (to quote Julia Marie Wondolleck) "that scientifically trained land managers will be able to acquire the appropriate information with which to ... reach outcomes that advance the public's interest." Whether a forest should be mined, timbered, hunted, roaded, or designated as wilderness, however, is a political not a professional judgment, which an agency must hide under the cloak of technical analysis. Scientific expertise provides a smokescreen for political judgment. Wondolleck writes, "Like the emperor's new clothes, however, this technical cloak now hides little and ... the masses are not quiet about what they see."[58]

Community Survival in Place

The QLG was born of desperation. Decades of litigation had tied loggers, environmentalists, and officials in knots – a legal Laocoön from which no one could break loose. Through a series of administrative appeals and suits challenging nearly every timber sale during the 1980s, local wilderness advocates such as Michael Jackson and Linda Blum had forced logging companies, notably Sierra Pacific Industries, to cease most operations, depressing the economies of Quincy, Loyalton, and other towns. When a timber sale did go through, a local newspaper reports, the driver of the truck carrying the big logs was likely to make a detour to pass under Jackson's office window "taunting the environmental litigator with the sight of another fallen giant, before stopping for a celebratory beer on the town's main street."[59] In 1986, laid-off workers made threatening remarks at public meetings, and store owners displayed yellow ribbons in solidarity with the industry. Wilderness advocates gave as good as they got. "We blamed and ridiculed our neighbors," Jackson recalled. "There was sugar in the tanks of logging equipment. And they responded in the normal way, including gunshot wounds to windows."[60]

Ten years later, these adversaries found that face-to-face meetings in search of a compromise plan gave each side more than it could gain by struggling against the other. In spite of their earlier acrimony and mutual distrust, environmentalists, loggers, foresters, and public officials united in seeking what the leader of a prominent ecological restoration project in Northern California has called "community survival in place."[61]

How did these opponents manage to find common ground? First, they had to solve a problem rather than sustain a lobby. Second, they had arrived at an impasse detrimental to all. Unable to attract any attention from national environmental groups, local activists like Linda Blum had to act single-handedly to stop logging by filing administrative appeals of specific sales. "That meant driving deep into the forest to review every logging site and writing lengthy documents," said Blum, an environmental consultant in Quincy. "As a grassroots activist, I couldn't keep it up. It wasn't sustainable activism."[62] Logging companies found they could not pay their hundreds of employees in the area, thus sustaining the local economy, and still litigate against these diehard environmentalists. Neither side expected that the Forest Service would resolve the situation, for its interest plainly lay in budgeting for further scientific studies, not in making a decision. Everyone involved in the community around Quincy had come to his or her wit's end, and no one outside the community offered much hope or help.

Third, many of these people knew each other and deeply regretted the social animosity that had torn the community apart. "It is easy to take the moral high ground when you don't live in these communities," said Tom Nelson, a Sierra Pacific Industries forester, who joined the Quincy group. "It is tougher when you have to face these people every day."[63]

Fourth, the prospect of a horrendous forest fire functioned, like the proverbial hanging, to concentrate the minds of these traditional combatants. For thousands of years, Native Americans had used fire periodically to remove undergrowth and to thin dense stands of cedar and pine, allowing a few surviving trees per acre to become old and great. This regime of regular burning produced the park-like old growth that illustrates calendars issued by the Sierra Club and other wilderness organizations.[64] When the Lassen National Forest was first surveyed in 1908, trees over 30 inches in diameter dominated more than 70 percent of the land.[65] At about that time, however, the newly created Forest Service instituted fire prevention as part of its scientific management of the forests. (Fire suppression also brought enormous amounts of money into Forest Service coffers.) Gifford Pinchot wrote in 1917 that "the work of a Forest Ranger is, first of all, to protect the District committed to his charge against fire. That comes before all else."[66]

In an eighty-year effort that cost many billions of dollars, Smokey Bear nearly eliminated forest fires in many areas of the West. Partly as a result, in Idaho, California, and other western states, deadwood and brush blanket the floors of forests, and small trees in dense stands compete for water and light. "Such forests in the typical case have become economically less productive, subject to disease and insect infestation, aesthetically unattractive, and ironically now also prone to new and much greater fire hazards," writes Robert Nelson.[67] The conflagrations that ravaged Yellowstone National Park were no accident. "They were partly a result of a century of federal fire policy that has sought to eliminate fire from the western landscape but instead has merely changed its time and place."[68] According to Jackson, "In 1904, the number of stems [trees] was around 200 per acre," because fires regularly burned saplings, while larger trees survived. In 2000, as a result of fire suppression, "there was an average of 1,280 stems per acre" along wth immense stands of undergrowth in the forests surrounding Quincy, California.[69]

To relieve the tinderbox conditions in the surrounding forests, local environmentalists, including Jackson and Blum, along with industry foresters, revived a plan that national environmental groups, including the NRDC, the Sierra Club, and the Wilderness Society, had supported ten years earlier. It allowed timber companies to emulate the results of periodic fire by thinning small trees and clearing deadwood and undergrowth, while leaving larger trees untouched. "If I thought this forest could survive without being cleaned up, I would support zero cut," Jackson said. "After 150 years of pounding this is not a normal ecosystem. We've got 50 years' worth of work to get back to a natural cycle."[70]

The QLG Plan

On July 10, 1993, the QLG presented its management plan at a town-hall meeting attended by about 150 individuals representing every view, interest, and position in the surrounding communities. The attendees approved the plan nearly unanimously. In 1994, when a huge blaze in neighboring Loyalton destroyed spotted owl habitat, local activists including Blum saw no alternative to the Quincy plan. "It wasn't loggers versus owls that was the unresolved issue," she said. "It was owls versus fire."[71]

The Quincy Library Plan covered about 2.5 million acres that it hoped to return to the condition that existed in previous centuries, when periodic fires pruned away dead and small trees, leaving old growth to dominate the forest floor. Today, according to observers, fire suppression and other policies have turned the forest into "a thicket of 1,000 or more small trees per acre, with dead ones on the ground or leaning against the living trees." In this context, "the fear is that even small fires will quickly grow to catastrophic, landscape-scale conflagrations that will destroy all trees and habitat."

The plan put about a million acres of roadless forest into wilderness and other protected status – including 148,000 acres of roadless, old-growth forest now designated by law as timberland. In response to the threat of catastrophic fires, the Quincy Library Plan proposes that in the remaining 1.6-million-acre managed area, loggers each year would clear 40,000 to 60,000 acres of leaning dead trees, some young trees, and deadwood on the ground. All larger trees (those over 30 inches) would be protected. The plan also allows 10,000 acres within the managed area to be logged in selected small patches yearly, with a resulting rotation cycle in which each acre would be logged once every 175 years.[72] According to newspaper reports, the plan "limits the size of cuts to 2 acres at most, and takes 30 percent of the most sensitive of the 2.5 million acres off the timber base, including salmon habitat not yet protected by any recovery plan."[73] The group believes that the permitted harvest will allow enough work for loggers to sustain the local economy while at the same time helping to return the forest to its "pre-settlement" state.

Having reached a deliberative consensus on this strategy among traditional combatants in Northern California, the QLG had to convince the Forest Service to implement the plan. But this proved impossible. Wayne Thornton, the Forest Service supervisor of the Plumas National Forest when the Quincy group was formed, correctly surmised that national political groups that dominated the Iron Triangle – and to whom the Service was beholden – did not share the problem-solving spirit of the participants. "Every time I looked at them, I saw almost shadows looming behind them of larger constituencies," said Thornton. And it was not clear that "these individuals were doing what these larger constituencies wanted."[74]

Nor was it clear that the Forest Service was eager to find a solution. Critics suggest that increased funding for the Forest Service pays mostly for environmental impact and other scientific studies. Since studies can always be questioned, extended, confirmed, disconfirmed, and so on, getting the science right promises to become an eternal occupation. This is especially true when each side of a controversy earnestly believes its position reflects the best available science. Paralysis by analysis seemed the only prospect. "We'd been waiting for four years for the administrative solution," said QLG member Linda Blum, "and had gotten nothing but excuses and obfuscation and sabotage by various persons working for the U.S. Forest Service at various levels." Accordingly, Blum and her colleagues, perhaps following a lesson they had learned in high school civics, decided to go to their representatives in Congress.

The Politics of Environmental Policy

In 1996 – three years after they had first submitted their proposal to the Forest Service – members of the Quincy group approached their local representative to Congress, Republican Wally Herger, who joined with Senate Democrat Dianne Feinstein to convert the plan to legislation. On July 9, 1997, as the QLG members watched on C-SPAN, the House of Representatives debated and passed the bill by a 429-1 majority. "We were thrilled by the vote, of course, but the debate touched our hearts," Michael Jackson later testified. "To see Congressmen Herger and Fazio working together to include Congressman Miller's objectives in our bill reminded us of our own laborious negotiations in the early years. To see resolution, accomplishment, and good spirits reign for a morning on the floor of the House was soul-satisfying for us and many like us around the country."[75]

The passage of the Quincy bill in the House, while "soul-satisfying" for local collaborative groups, greatly angered national environmental organizations, such as the Audubon Society, the Sierra Club, and the Wilderness Society, which, along with the NRDC, had earlier supported the plan upon which the Quincy group was built.[76] The Sierra Club in the meantime had adopted a "zero logging" principle for the national forests and now opposed even the commercial cutting of deadwood to make firebreaks. The Audubon Society described the Quincy plan as "unfair and undemocratic" because it involved a "paradigm shift from national management of national forests to local management."[77] Louis Blumberg, a spokesperson for the Wilderness Society, shared the same concern. The Quincy bill "excludes 99 percent of the Americans who have an equal stake in national forests," he said.[78]

Except for the Sierra Club, which opposes all commercial logging in national forests, national groups objected to the Quincy plan less as a matter of substance than of precedent. "Just because a group of local people can come to agreement doesn't mean that it is good public policy," said Jay Watson, regional director of the Wilderness Society.[79] The National Audubon Society stated that Quincy-like bills "would allow a relatively small group of citizens to dictate public forest management, rather than agency officials receiving input from the public at large."[80] Michael McCloskey, chair of the Sierra Club, declared the bill was "designed to disempower our [national environmental] constituency, which is heavily urban."[81]

QLG members replied that national groups refused to send representatives to their councils. "We begged. We pleaded. They wouldn't come," said Michael Jackson. "What do you do when they won't come? Tell your neighbors we can't meet because they're too busy having cocktail parties down in San Francisco?"[82] Library group member Tom Nelson pointed out that Congress was responsible for making the decision. If Congress votes overwhelmingly for the bill and the president signs it, how is democracy slighted? "It is rewarding that a group of local citizens can take their ideas to a local representative and take it through the whole process," said Tom Nelson of Sierra Pacific.

"It is how democracy is supposed to work. That is what I learned in school."[83]

Speaking for the Wilderness Society, Blumberg urged the Quincy group – which he described as "only one special interest group" – to wait for the Forest Service to make its determination, however long it might take.[84] The League of Conservation Voters joined the Wilderness Society in defending the Forest Service process. In her letter to Congress, Deb Callahan, League President, wrote, "The Herger bill could have serious environmental consequences that can only be assessed through full public and scientific review."[85] Michael McCloskey of the Sierra Club joined the others in defending the Forest Service. Brushing aside the fifteen years local residents had awaited a decision from the agency, McCloskey said, "When they run to Congress to impose a negotiated agreement on a national forest, they certainly are displacing an agency's process."[86] Michael Yost, a Quincy environmental activist, replied, "After working eleven years with the national environmental organizations and four years with the QLG attempting to get an administrative solution, the best option is now to seek a legislative solution."[87]

The QLG Bill Becomes Law

After the House of Representatives passed the Quincy Library Bill nearly unanimously, the president announced his support, and the Senate put it on its agenda for quick passage. To stop the bill in the Senate, the National Audubon Society circulated a "Dear Senator" letter that defended the normal processes of the Forest Service. "Forest Service employees," the letter said, "are more likely on the whole to act in the public's best interest than local management coalitions, which don't have the national scientific backing of an agency."[88] The Society acknowledged that one of its "respected chapters, Plumas Audubon Society in Quincy, CA, is participating in and actively supporting the QLG's legislative strategy." The letter advised the Senate to ignore the position of the local chapter.

Local forest users can tell us a lot about their forest, like which areas are used by which species or which are most valuable for wood. They are not necessarily equipped to view the bigger picture of, for example, species declines, cumulative impacts, or policy trends. . . . Considering the big picture is the job of Congress, and of watchdog groups like the National Audubon Society.

The local Audubon chapter, stung and surprised by the "Dear Senator" letter from the National Society, wrote back that the national office was "unfamiliar with the individuals, expertise and diverse talents which have developed QLG strategies. Also, this rhetoric is, to put it politely, patronizing." The Plumas chapter, which had joined the Quincy Library negotiations from the start, asked, "How can a local chapter of Audubon remain viable when the National office abandons, sabotages or undermines local efforts to improve conservation on the local scene?" The chapter emphasized the specificity of place and the need for place-based solutions to environmental problems. "National folks could better understand the real meaning of 'place' if they would come to the 'places' in question."[89]

Sierra Club Chair McCloskey explained his group's opposition to stakeholder negotiations in a November 1995 memo issued to the Club's board. "Industry thinks its odds are better in these forums," McCloskey wrote. "It has ways to generate pressures on communities where it is strong, which it doesn't have at the national level."[90] Environmental leaders in Washington joined McCloskey in alleging that rural Westerners are easily snookered by slick-talking industry representatives. According to one newspaper report, literature from national groups often refers "to well-intentioned Bambi consorting with ravenous Godzilla, and naive chickens inviting sharp, high-powered foxes into the coop."[91]

In spite of opposition from national environmental groups, the local coalition prevailed; the Senate approved and the president signed the Harger-Feinstein Quincy Library Group Forest Recovery Act, which became law in October 1998. It required and directed the Forest Service to conduct a five-year pilot project, patterned on the QLG plan. The statute insisted that the pilot project be consistent with maintaining habitat for endangered species. This proved to provide a basis for scientific second-guessing of every contemplated action. At the time, though, hopes were high for some action. Representative Helen Chenoweth of Idaho, in oversight hearings, praised the QLG for its efforts in collaborative democracy. She congratulated the group for "bringing this community-based plan to a point where it can now be implemented as a pilot project. It offers hope to those of us who care deeply about balance in our national forests."

Killing the QLG

Congratulations were not in order. In spite of the clear directive of the legislation, the QLG plan was not implemented. Instead, the decision-making process has continued, and no end is in sight. Rather than implement the QLG legislation, the Forest Service conducted extensive and expensive scientific and environmental reviews, some of which became objects of litigation, throughout 1998 and 1999. Some of the further studies, such as were involved in several Environmental Impact Statements, also may have been required by law. In an effort to get the science right – to develop a management plan based in science not politics – the Forest Service brought or bought all sorts of academic and other experts into a debate over many alternative plans and assessments. The science fractured along political lines; more was required.

A $12 million study undertaken during the Clinton administration culminated in the Sierra Nevada Framework, a roughly 1,500-page document, hailed by environmental groups for limiting logging and thinning of national forests. Indeed, the Framework would cut logging levels by two-thirds on 11.5 million acres in eleven national forests and would prescribe burning as an alternative to thinning by lumber companies. However well the Framework conformed to the no-logging views of major environmental groups, it appeared to mock and reject the mandate of the QLG Act by blocking efforts to thin overgrown thickets. The QLG filed a lawsuit complaining the Framework violated the letter and spirit of the law. Frank Stewart, a forester in the QLG, stated that the Framework "does nothing to address fire, fuel loads and local economies. All it does is continue the process and ensure that fuel reduction will be accomplished" through catastrophic wild fires.[92] The QLG stated in a letter written to the Forest Service, "the Sierra framework decision effectively kills the Herger-Feinstein Quincy Library Group Project."[93]

This QLG statement is mistaken, even naïve, in one respect: it refers to a "decision." The only way to get a decision is to act as the QLG did, namely, to bring the stakeholders together and have them work something out. These stakeholders must then have the authority and responsibility to administer their agreement and be accountable for the results. As long as factions collide around the Iron Triangle – as long as interest groups can end-run agencies – there will be no decision. The Sierra Nevada Framework, though it received at first what seemed to be a blessing by the Bush administration, soon became one more dead tree in the overgrown thicket of studies, policies, and recommendations, all awaiting conflagration. On December 31, 2001, the supervisor for California's national forests announced that the Bush administration would review and revise the Framework. As of this writing, the Bush administration's Healthy Forest Initiative appears to swing the policy pendulum as far in the direction of logging as the abandoned Sierra Nevada Framework swung it in the direction of preservation. QLG members are worried. "If it goes too far, it's going to take well-thought-out plans like ours and make them seem like frauds," Michael Jackson said.[94]

There Will Never Be a Decision

It may be time to acknowledge that there will never be a decision, a plan, or a policy for the national forests. This is because no one but the local groups whose livelihood depends on the condition of the forests wants a decision. To be sure, local environmentalists and forest users can get together as they did in Quincy to hammer out their differences and get to win-win solutions. These people are united, for example, in the dread that the forest will explode in fire, surrounding their community with flames. They also need the assurance of a predictable policy for deciding what sorts of investments to make, careers to consider, houses to build, and so on.

Outside the local community, however, nobody wants a decision. In fact, all factions benefit from the endless process of indecision. This is plainly true of the Forest Service, whose budget depends on developing policies, undertaking analyses, and reviewing scientific findings. It is also true of the forest industry in general since it depends for timber production primarily on private forests. To open the national forests to logging – the situation has not changed since Pinchot's day – would be to depress lumber prices. Overproduction in the lumber industry, already a problem especially in view of competition from Canadian suppliers, would follow that of agriculture generally, so that the entire economy might depend on subsidies and bailouts. Plainly, some firms want to open the national forests, but others do not. Conflicts of interest within the industry make it easier to tolerate an absence of policy generally.

Environmental groups, such as the Sierra Club, have nothing to gain and much to lose by participating in stakeholder collaborations. It is better to fight for purity – and thus represent those who support the cause – than to settle for compromise. At one time, environmental groups could rightly worry that stakeholder collaborations would be captured by industry groups. Today, local communities include entrepreneurs of many sorts; for example, from the Sierra Nevadas to the Colorado Plateau, software developers greatly outnumber loggers. According to the *Atlas of the New West*, only a few counties remain in which 35 percent of the population is employed in mining, logging, farming, or ranching. The "West has moved beyond extracting natural resources to appreciating them in place: mountainsides not excavated for copper or molybdenum; rangeland homes for wolves instead of cattle; and old-growth forests rather than clear-cuts."[95]

National environmental groups remain suspicious of collaborative "stakeholder" processes for other and deeper reasons than the fear that industry flaks will co-opt local environmentalists. People who are willing to listen to each other and to find ways to solve the problems that divide them are likely to defect from the Manichean battles national groups wage around the Iron Triangle. "It is troubling that such processes tend to de-legitimate conflict as a way of dealing with issues and of mobilizing support," McCloskey wrote in his memo. "Instead of hammering out national rules to reflect majority rule in the nation, transferring power to a local venue implies decision-making by a very different majority in a much smaller population."

McCloskey added that there is a good reason national groups do not accept invitations to participate in councils seeking to govern localized resources. If representatives working at the local level sign on to a compromise to resolve a particular conflict in specific circumstances, the national group will be bound to accept it, even though it departs from national principles. "It is psychologically difficult to simultaneously negotiate and publicly attack bad proposals from the other side. This tends to be seen as acting in bad faith."

Since the Sierra Club has committed itself on both scientific and ethical grounds to a "zero commercial logging" national rule, it sees little to gain by negotiation or accommodation. "Too much time spent in stakeholder processes may result in demobilizing and disarming our side."[96]

Sociologist Robert Putnam has argued that battles environmental groups wage in Washington drain the strength of democracy to solve environmental problems in the nation at large. "We are shouting and pressuring and suing," he has written, "but we are not reasoning together, not even in the attenuated sense that we once did, with people we know well and will meet again tomorrow."[97] While recognizing the political clout of organizations like the Sierra Club, Putnam denies they build the social trust on which democracy depends. "For the vast majority of their members, the only act of membership consists in writing a check for dues or perhaps occasionally reading a newsletter. . . . Their ties, in short, are to common symbols, common leaders, and perhaps common ideals, but not to one another."[98]

Civic Environmentalism and Civic Renewal

Recently, Randal O'Toole, a respected authority on western resource issues, has warned that the environmental movement faces its greatest crisis. "One likely result is that the movement will fragment into two distinctly different movements, one that focuses on preservation and central control and one that focuses on management and decentralization." O'Toole presents this schism as a replay of the historical opposition between preservationists and conservationists. He may fail to see, however, that preservationists and conservationists now hold at least one view in common. Both appeal to science – whether environmental economics or forest ecology – to justify their position. They seek a scientific vindication not a political compromise.

Preservationists in the tradition of John Muir demand that the federal government protect as much of the nation's landscape as possible from human intrusion. "Research in ecology, fisheries, soils, and other areas," O'Toole comments, "seemed to support the preservationist claim that 'nature knows best.'" A "precautionary principle," moreover, suggests that it is perilous to alter nature if science cannot with certainty predict all the consequences that may result.

Conservationists believe that experts should manage nature intensively to maximize the long-run benefits it offers humanity. Like preservationists, however, conservationists favor scientific control of resources – for example, the management of the national forests by the Forest Service. Both preservationists and conservationists base their conceptions of land management – their "land ethic" – on what each takes to be the best available environmental science.[99] For preservationists, science involves succession and equilibrium models, feedback loops, stability-diversity associations, and notions of nature as a superorganism that has a "health" or an "integrity" upon which we all depend. For conservationists, science yields the principles of silviculture, genetic engineering, and so forth, on which sustainable forestry, agriculture, and the like are based. The best available science shows that humanity can prosper, even survive, only if it manages nature intensively (if you are a conservationist) or leaves it alone (if a preservationist). Each side, secure in the objectivity of its science, is certain of the rightness of its cause.

"As heirs to their conservationist forerunners' deference to expertise," Gottlieb and Ingram comment, "establishment environmentalists are embarrassed by the lack of scientific sophistication in the grassroots movements." Thus, a Sierra Club press release urges defeat of the Quincy bill in part because it "ignores the best available science."[100] Appealing, for example, to the theory of forest succession or to various equilibrium models of the order of nature, environmentalists may argue that the Lassen and Plumas forests will achieve the "climax" condition pictured on Sierra Club calendars if we just leave them alone. Science shows that nature knows best; all logging – indeed, all commercial activity in the wilderness – is therefore bad on scientific grounds.

Members of the Quincy Group, however, cannot see the old-growth forests pictured in Sierra Club calendars for the stick-like, dying trees that they perceive all around them. Their experience confirms what other ecologists believe, namely, that theories of forest succession, equilibrium, and so on serve essentially a political purpose, while nature itself (to quote environmental historian Donald Worster) "is *fundamentally* erratic, discontinuous, and unpredictable. It is full of seemingly random events that elude models of how things are supposed to work."[101] From this point of view, one could argue that selective logging, by thinning trees and clearing out brush, can replace fire regimes in the ecosystem. It may no longer be possible to leave the forest alone.

What is most striking about grass-roots movements, Gottlieb and Ingram have written, "is their democratic thrust. . . . Instead of embracing expertise, they have developed self-taught experts. . . . They have become organizations of active members rather than rosters of dues-payers on mailing lists."[102] Jordan and Snow add, "While the traditional groups have amassed memberships to underwrite staff experts in law, science, and policy, the grassroots groups are comprised of members who are personally involved in the issues." Jordan and Snow point out the difference. In "their base of support and the ways they select issues and strategies, the grass-roots groups are essentially political, while many of their establishment counterparts have become essentially technical."[103] This difference – rather than the historical divergence between conservationists and preservationists – accounts for the schism now dividing environmentalists.

Environmentalists today confront a fundamental choice whether to conceive their movement as political or as technical in its concerns, its program, and its justification. They cannot have it both ways. If environmentalists at the local level engage their opponents in a political deliberation ending in a compromise, this is bound to offend national leaders eager to vindicate the truth of their science-based position against wrong-headed, ill-intentioned, and unscientific beliefs. It is unsurprising that national groups like the Sierra Club and the Audubon Society reject the political efforts even of their own chapters in the affected regions. Environmental decisions cannot be trusted to amateurs whose objectivity and neutrality are compromised because they are invested emotionally and economically in the survival of their human communities in place. These locals do not have the requisite scientific expertise.

Lois Gibbs, who has criticized mainstream environmentalism ever since the Love Canal days, has argued that it is a mistake to think environmental goals can be framed or justified in technical – including economic and scientific – terms. They are political goals arising from competing beliefs, needs, interests, emotions, and ideologies. They are not matters of technical controversy to be settled by a more scientific, interdisciplinary approach. "Efforts to preserve and improve the environment are sure to be set back, if not fail outright, when advocates for the environment forget or ignore the fact that environmental causes are just as political as any other public policy issue."[104]

If environmental causes are political, advocates must seek to persuade or reach some accommodation with their adversaries who are regarded as equals in a joint effort of deliberation. This requires all the sides in a controversy to discuss possible ways to solve a problem, each offering considerations the others may regard as reasons to adopt one solution or another. Rather than denigrating one's opponents as motivated by private gain or as befuddled by bad science, one must engage them in a joint project of finding common ground. The alternative is to delegate political decisions to experts – to interdisciplinary teams of economists, environmental scientists, and lawyers who, as the Audubon letter said, are "equipped to view the bigger picture of, for example, species declines, cumulative impacts, or policy trends." This alternative lets a technical elite that has lost its democratic bearings govern. The Russian *nomenklatura*, as William Sullivan points out, offers a glaring example of "the fate of modern elites who lose their collective moral bearings, and slip from self-satisfaction into arrogance and finally deadening demoralization."[105]

Jean Cohen, a political scientist at Columbia University, argues that "participation as an equal in the exchange of opinions and in collective deliberations" gives individuals a sense of voice and democratic competence. Collaborative groups engender "internal publics" in which individuals have a voice. Cohen writes, "I suspect that only associations with internal publics structured by the relevant norms of discourse can develop the communicative competence and interactive abilities important to democracy." The efforts of deliberative associations to penetrate legislatures – as the Quincy Library Group has tried to do – far from being undemocratic, provide an important check on the state's administrative apparatus.[106]

If civic associations like the Quincy Library Group are unable to influence environmental policy, it is hard to see what political recourse they may have. National mass-mailing organizations, along with their special friends in Congress and the industry groups they oppose, own the Iron Triangle as a preserve for professionalism and expertise. Whatever its prospects for implementation, however, the Quincy Library

Plan has restored a sense of civility – even of common purpose – to the communities surrounding the Plumas and Lassen forests. Traditional adversaries are now on the same side. Democracy can and should accomplish just that result. Michael Jackson describes one sign of the civic renewal his group has achieved. "These days, when people wave at me, they use all five fingers," he said.[107]

Notes

Chapter 1

1. E. B. White, *Charlotte's Web* (New York: Harper & Row, 1952).
2. Ibid., p. 164.
3. Alan Randall has written that in the view of the economist, "What the individual wants is [in his estimation] good for the individual." G. Peterson and A. Randall, eds., *The Valuation of Wildland Resource Benefits* (Boulder, CO: Westview Press, 1984), p. 6.
4. Louis Kaplow and Steven Shavell, *Fairness versus Welfare* (Cambridge, MA: Harvard University Press, 2002) p. 23.
5. Ibid., p. 5.
6. Ibid., p. 409.
7. Jonathan A. Lesser, Daniel E. Dobbs, and Richard O. Zerbe, Jr., *Environmental Economics and Policy* (Reading, MA: Addison-Wesley, 1997), p. 42.
8. Kaplow and Shavell, *Fairness versus Welfare*, p. 16.
9. Ibid., pp. 21–22.
10. Willett Kempton, James S. Boster, and Jennifer A. Hartley, *Environmental Values in American Culture* (Cambridge, MA: MIT Press, 1997), p. 113.
11. For discussion, see David Takacs, *The Idea of Biodiversity* (Baltimore, MD: Johns Hopkins University Press), pp. 249–54.
12. Adam Smith, *An Enquiry into the Nature and Causes of the Wealth of Nations* (Oxford: Oxford University Press, 1776 and 1991), Book I, Chapter 4.
13. Ibid.
14. White, *Charlotte's Web*, p. 46.
15. Eban S. Goodstein, *Economics and the Environment* (Englewood Cliffs, NJ: Prentice Hall, 1995), p. 26.
16. Carlyle Murphy, "A Spiritual Lens on the Environment; Increasingly, Caring for Creation Is Viewed as a Religious Mandate," *Washington Post*, Feb. 3, 1998: A1.

17. Yi-Fu Tuan, *Topophilia: A Study of Environmental Perception, Attitudes, and Values* (New York: Columbia University Press, 1990); E. O. Wilson, *Biophilia* (Cambridge, MA: Harvard University Press, 1986).

18. White, *Charlotte's Web*, p. 183.

19. In defining the instrumental and aesthetic good, I follow the analysis of George Henrik von Wright, *The Varieties of Goodness* (London: Routledge & Kegan Paul, 1963), pp. 19–40. Von Wright, however, uses the term "technical good" where I use the term "aesthetic good."

20. "That which is related to general human inclination and needs has a *market price* ... But that which constitutes ... an end in itself does not have a mere relative worth, i.e., a price, but an intrinsic worth, i.e., a dignity." Immanuel Kant, *Foundations of the Metaphysics of Morals*, R. P. Wolff, ed. L. W. Beck, trans. (Indianapolis, IN: Bobbs-Merrill, 1959), p. 53 (emphasis in original).

21. "The same thing is good and true for all men, but the pleasant differs from one and another." Democritus (c. 460–370 B.C.). Democritus points out that the difference between good and evil, right and wrong, true and false involves objective judgment, so that where people disagree, the judgment should go to those with the better argument. Where subjective judgments of welfare are at stake, however, every man is his own authority. See Henry Spiegel, *The Growth of Economic Thought* (Durham, NC: Duke University Press, 1971).

22. Here, I follow the argument of Alan Holland in "Are Choices Tradeoffs," *Economics, Ethics, and Environmental Policy*, Daniel W. Bromley and Jouni Paavola, eds. (Oxford: Blackwell, 2002), pp. 17–34.

23. In Chapter 3, I note that Alan Kneese and Blair Bower at Resources for the Future found that market failures are so pervasive, at least with respect to environmental assets, that "the pure private property concept applies satisfactorily to a progressively narrowing range of natural resources and economic activities." They concluded, "Private property and market exchange have little applicability to their allocation, development, and conservation." A. V. Kneese and Blair T. Bower, *Environmental Quality Analysis: Theory and Method in the Social Sciences* (Baltimore, MD: Johns Hopkins University Press and Resources for the Future, 1972), pp. 3–4.

24. Barry C. Field, *Environmental Economics: An Introduction*, 2d ed. (New York: McGraw-Hill, 1997), p. 19.

25. For a similar view generalized to political decision-making, see Deborah A. Stone, *Policy Paradox: The Art of Political Decision Making*, rev. ed. (New York: W. W. Norton, 2001).

26. James G. March, *A Primer in Decision Making* (New York: Free Press, 1994), p. viii.

27. Ibid., p. 58.

28. See Gretchen C. Daily, ed., *Nature's Services: Societal Dependence on Natural Ecosystems* (Washington, DC: Island Press, 1997).

29. For discussion, see Elizabeth Anderson, "John Stuart Mill on Experiments in Living," *Ethics* 102 (4) (1991): 4–26.

30. Walter V. Reid et al., "A New Lease on Life" in *Biodiversity Prospecting: Using Genetic Resources for Sustainable Development*, Walter V. Reid et al., eds. (Washington, DC: World Resources Institute, 1993), p. 1.

31. Judy Foreman, "Drug Hunters Can't See the Rainforest for the Medicines," *Boston Globe*, March 27, 2001: C1.

32. David Galas, president of Darwin Molecular, quoted in Colin Macilwain, "When Rhetoric Hits Reality in Debate on Bioprospecting," *Nature* 392 (April 9, 1998): 535–40.

33. Macilwain, "Rhetoric Hits Reality." See also Thomas Eisner, "Hard Times for Chemical Prospecting," *Issues in Science and Technology* 19(4) (Summer 2003): 47–48.

34. Eugene Russo, "Ethics and War Challenge Biologists," *The Scientist,* March 25, 2003. For further reading on roadblocks to research that developing countries have erected to prevent the piracy of the presumed blockbuster drugs in their biota, see Randy Tinker, "Biopiracy Issue Stops Research," *Nature Medicine* 8(1)(January 2002): 9; Chikako Takeshita, "Bioprospecting and Indigenous Peoples' Resistances," *Peace Review* 12(4)(December 2000); Rex Dalton, "Political Uncertainty Halts Bioprospecting in Mexico," *Nature* 408(2000): 278; Rex Dalton, "The Curtain Falls," *Nature* 414(2001): 685. For a balanced postmortem of "The Eisner Model" – the basic theory of bioprospecting – see George M. Garrity and Jennie Hunter-Cevera, "Bioprospecting in the Developing World," *Current Opinion in Microbiology* 2(1999): 236–40.

35. Daniel Charles, "Seeds of Discontent," *Science* 294(5543)(Oct. 26, 2001): 772–75.

Chapter 2

1. Abraham Lincoln, "The Gettysburg Address" (1863), *Lincoln on Democracy*, Mario M. Cuomo and Harold Holzer, eds. (New York: HarperCollins, 1990).

2. George Will, "A Conflict over Hallowed Ground," *New Orleans Times-Picayune*, June 11, 1998. For a brief description of the events, see Lisa Reuter, "Gettysburg: The World Did Long Remember," *Columbus Dispatch,* Dec. 5, 1999: 1G ("At the wheat field alone, 6,000 men fell in $2^1/_2$ hours. One soldier would later write, 'Men were falling like leaves in autumn; my teeth chatter now when I think of it.' So many bodies covered the field, remembered another, that a person could walk across it without touching the ground").

3. See Rupert Cornwell, "Out of the West: Developers March on Killing Fields," *Independent (London)*, Dec. 18, 1991: 10.

4. The Kentucky Fried Chicken restaurant has long occupied the area near the monument and by now may have its own authenticity. Kentucky nominally never left the Union.

5. Will, "Hallowed Ground," B7.

6. Michael Shaara, *The Killer Angels: A Novel* (New York: McKay, 1974). For details about the effect on the visitor load, see Will, "Hallowed Ground," B7.

7. For a description of the Park Service plan and its history, see Edward T. Pound, "The Battle Over Gettysburg," *USA Today*, Sept. 26, 1997: 4A.

8. Stephen Barr, "Hill General Retreats on Gettysburg Plan," *Washington Post*, Oct. 2, 1998: A25. See also Ben White, "Lawmaker Criticizes Plan for Gettysburg," *Washington Post*, Feb. 12, 1999: A33.

9. Brett Lieberman, "Park Service Unveils Revised Gettysburg Plan," *Plain Dealer* (Cleveland), June 19, 1999: 14A.

10. APCWS Position on Proposed Gettysburg Development Plan (statement by Denis P. Galvin, Deputy Director, National Park Service, Feb. 24, 1998). Available online at: http://users.erols.com/va-udc/nps.html.

11. In fact, such a proposal is not as far-fetched as it sounds. See Heather Dewar, "Corporate Cash Eyed for Parks, Bill Puts Sponsorships at $10 Million Apiece," *Denver Post*, June 8, 1996: A1; and "Parks May Get 'Official' Sponsors, Senate Measure Would Lure Corporate Bucks," *St. Louis Post-Dispatch*, June 9, 1996: 1A. This plan was much derided. See, e.g., Joshua Reichert, "Commercializing Our National Parks: A Bad Joke," *Houston Chronicle*, Sept. 23, 1996: 19.

12. From the perspective of welfare economics, a regulation is rational – it promotes the welfare of society – only if it confers on members of society benefits in excess of costs. Since the benefits and costs may well accrue to different individuals, welfare economists may recognize two fundamental values in terms of which regulatory policy may be justified. The first is economic efficiency, which is to say, the extent to which total benefits of the policy exceed total costs. The second goal is equity, which is to say, the extent to which the distribution of costs and benefits is equitable or fair. For a presentation of this view, see generally Arthur M. Okun, *Equality and Efficiency: The Big Tradeoff* (Washington, DC: Brookings Institution, 1975). He writes, "This concept of efficiency implies that more is better, insofar as the 'more' consists in items people want to buy," p. 2. Kaplow and Shavell (cited in the previous chapter) along with many other welfare economists (such as Burton Weisbrod) include principles of fairness as preferences that thus might be entered into the general utility calculus. This latter view seems to me more consistent with the general thrust of environmental economics, which is to assert as a kind of revelation the empty tautology that preference satisfaction correlates with well-being and to count any other normative thesis as an expression of subjective or personal preference. See Weisbrod, "Income Redistribution Effects and Cost-Benefit Analysis," in *Problems in Public Expenditure Analysis*, Samuel B. Chase, ed. (Washington, DC: Brookings Institution, 1968), 177–222.

13. Dollywood attracts about 2 million patrons annually and is open only during the warmer months. See the Dollywood website at: http://company. monster.com/dolly/.

14. Proposed Gettysburg Development Plan (cited in note 10).

15. I would like to thank Rick Freeman for suggesting this example.
16. John V. Krutilla, "Conservation Reconsidered," *American Economics Review* 57(1967): 787–96.
17. See, e.g., William D. Nordhaus and James Tobin, "Is Economic Growth Obsolete?" *Economic Growth* 5(1972): 1.
18. William D. Nordhaus, *Invention, Growth, and Welfare: A Theoretical Treatment of Technological Change* (Cambridge, MA: MIT Press, 1969).
19. Robert M. Solow, "Is the End of the World at Hand?" in *The Economic Growth of Controversy*, Andrew Weintraub et al., eds. (London: Macmillan, 1974), pp. 39–53. Solow sought to establish that technological change, rather than the resource base, is essential to economic production. See, e.g., Robert M. Solow, "A Contribution to the Theory of Economic Growth," *Quarterly Journal of Economics* 70(1956): 60–84; Robert M. Solow, "Technical Change and the Aggregate Production Function," *Review of Economics and Statistics* 39(1957): 312–20.
20. Solow argued that if the future is like the past, raw materials will continually become more plentiful. See Solow, "Is the End of the World at Hand?" p. 49.
21. Nordhaus and Tobin, "Obsolete," p. 14. Many mainstream economists accept Solow's argument. As analyst Peter Drucker has written, "[W]here there is effective management, that is, application of knowledge to knowledge, we can always obtain the other resources." Peter Drucker, *Post Capitalist Society* (New York: HarperBusiness, 1993), p. 45. Others have argued that our technical ability to substitute resources for one another is so great that "the particular resources with which one starts increasingly become a matter of indifference. The reservation of particular resources for later use, therefore, may contribute little to the welfare of future generations." Harold J. Barnett and Chandler Morse, *Scarcity and Growth: The Economics of Natural Resource Availability* (Baltimore, MD: Resources for the Future, Johns Hopkins University Press, 1963), p. 11.
22. Krutilla, "Conservation Revisited," p. 777.
23. Ibid., p. 778.
24. Ibid., p. 784. See also, e.g., V. Kerry Smith, "The Effect of Technological Change on Different Uses of Environmental Resources in Natural Environments: Studies in Theoretical and Applied Analysis," *American Economics Review* 54 (1972): 54–87. Smith wrote, "[A]dvances in scientific knowledge and a mastery of techniques have been sufficiently pervasive and rapid to allow for an ever expanding supply of natural resource commodities at constant or falling supply prices," p. 54.
25. World Bank, *World Development Report: 1992* (Washington, DC: World Bank, 1992). This document contains a sustained argument against the views of ecological economics and defends the neoclassical assumption that, with technological advance and good government, resources do not limit growth.
26. See, e.g., Robert Costanza et al., "Goals, Agenda, and Policy Recommendations for Ecological Economics," in *Ecological Economics: The Science and*

Management of Sustainability (New York: Columbia University Press, 1991), p. 8 (arguing that we have "entered a new era" in which "the limiting factor in development is no longer manmade capital but remaining natural capital").

27. See, e.g., Edwin Mansfield, *Microeconomics: Theory and Applications*, 2d ed. (New York: W. W. Norton, 1975). Mansfield writes that economics is divided "into two parts: microeconomics and macroeconomics. Microeconomics deals with the economic behavior of individual units like consumers, firms, and resource owners; while macroeconomics deals with the behavior of economic aggregates like gross national product and the level of unemployment," p. 2.

28. See generally Tyler Cowen, *The Theory of Market Failure: A Critical Examination* (Fairfax, VA: George Mason University Press, 1988).

29. A. C. Pigou, *The Economics of Welfare*, 4th ed. (London: Macmillan & Co., 1932), 172–203.

30. Larry E. Ruff, "The Economic Common Sense of Pollution," *Public Interest* 19(1970): 69–85.

31. Since pollution is clearly a form of coercion rather than of exchange, to ask how much pollution society should permit is to ask how far one individual may use the person or property of another without his or her consent. Nothing in our law, shared ethical intuitions, or cultural history supports or even tolerates the utilitarian principle that one person can trespass upon another – indeed, should do so – whenever the benefits to society exceed the costs. See, e.g., *United States v. Kin-Buc, Inc.*, 532 F. Supp. 699, 702–03 (D.N.J. 1982) (holding that the Clean Air Act preempts federal common law claims of nuisance for air pollution). See also William C. Porter, "The Role of Private Nuisance Law in the Control of Air Pollution," *Arizona Law Review* 107 (1968): 108–17. The nonutilitarian basis of pollution-control law is so obvious that, as Maureen Cropper and Wallace Oates observe, "the cornerstones of federal environmental policy in the United States," such as the Clean Air and Clean Water Acts, "explicitly prohibited the weighing of benefits against costs in the setting of environmental standards." Maureen L. Cropper and Wallace E. Oates, "Environmental Economics: A Survey," *Journal of Economic Literature* 30(1992): 675.

32. For an illustrative example of this sort of reasoning, see E. B. Barbier et al., "Economic Value of Biodiversity," in *Global Biodiversity Assessment*, V. H. Heywood et al., eds. (New York: Cambridge University Press, 1995), pp. 823, 829. ("Moral or ethical concerns, like tastes and preferences, can be translated into a willingness to commit resources to conserve biodiversity.")

33. Krutilla, "Conservation Revisited," p. 781.

34. Ibid.

35. Ibid., p. 783 (arguing that "while the supply of fabricated goods and commercial services may be capable of continuous expansion from a given resource base by reason of scientific discovery and mastery of technique,

the supply of natural phenomena is virtually inelastic"). Krutilla had to show, however, that technology cannot provide substitutes for natural phenomena (such as the Grand Canyon) as it can for natural resources. Krutilla apparently infers from the inelasticity of the supply of natural phenomena that technology cannot offer substitutes for them. This is obviously a non sequitur. Technology can provide amusements – for example, IMAX® theater presentations of the Grand Canyon followed by a great party where one can meet celebrities – for which people may be willing to pay as much as to go to the Canyon itself. It is not clear, then, that inelasticities of supply bear on the question of whether technology can provide economic substitutes for intrinsically valuable objects of nature. Technology may provide goods and services for which people are willing to pay the same amount, which is the meaning of "substitute" relevant to economics.

36. Ibid., p. 778.
37. Ibid., p. 783.
38. Carlyle Murphy, "A Spiritual Lens on the Environment; Increasingly, Caring for Creation Is Viewed as a Religious Mandate," *Washington Post*, Feb. 3, 1998: A1.
39. Krutilla, "Conservation Revisited," p. 779.
40. Ibid.
41. "Market-determined prices," some economists claim, "are the only reliable, legally significant measures of value. . . . [T]he value of a natural resource is the sum of the value of all of its associated marketable commodities, such as timber, minerals, animals, and recreational use fees." Daniel S. Levy and David Friedman, "The Revenge of the Redwoods? Reconsidering Property Rights and the Economic Allocation of Natural Resources," *University of Chicago Law Review* 61 (1994): esp. pp. 500–501 (discussing the possibility of WTP estimates for existence values).
42. Economists have applied the WTP criterion to adjudicate the most important moral decisions that confront society. For example, economists have argued that the decision to wage war in Vietnam represented not a moral or political but a market failure because the decision to carry on the war failed to reflect the WTP demonstrators revealed, for example, in the travel costs they paid to protest against it. See generally Charles J. Cicchetti et al., "On the Economics of Mass Demonstrations: A Case Study of the November 1969 March on Washington," *American Economics Review* 61 (1971): 179–95.

Whatever the question, from segregation in housing to certain kinds of slavery, practices people oppose for moral reasons may also be characterized as objectionable for economic reasons, once the WTP of those opponents is factored into the cost-benefit analysis. See generally Duncan Kennedy, "Cost-Benefit Analysis of Entitlement Problems: A Critique," *Stanford Law Review* 33 (1981): 387–445.
43. If mainstream economics had determined that natural resources could be taken for granted, what sort of scarcity was left for environmental

economists to study? To find a "scarcity," Krutilla moved the focus of environmental economics from economic to ethical concerns. To do this, he had to analyze principled views antithetical to the assumptions of welfare economics as if they were preferences and thus indications of utility. The conflation of belief with benefit produced the industry of contingent valuation – an industry that rests, as I argue here, on a conceptual mistake.

44. The high-water mark of this approach to environmental evaluation may be found in Robert Costanza et al., "The Value of the World's Ecosystem Services and Natural Capital," *Nature* 253 (1997): 253–260. I criticize this article in a later chapter.

45. See, e.g., Pete Morton, "The Economic Benefits of Wilderness: Theory and Practice," *Denver University Law Review* 76(2) (1999): 465–518. Some environmentalists question the use of contingent valuation largely for technical reasons. See, e.g., Kristin M. Jakobsson and Andrew K. Dragun, *Contingent Valuation and Endangered Species* (Cheltenham, UK: Elgar, 1996), pp. 78–82.

46. For examples of this research agenda, see Raymond J. Kopp and V. Kerry Smith, *Valuing Natural Assets: The Economics of Natural Resource Damage Assessments* (Washington, DC: Resources for the Future, 1993).

47. For a good review of the literature, see generally A. Myrick Freeman III, *The Benefits of Environmental Improvement: Theory and Practice* (Baltimore, MD: Resources for the Future, Johns Hopkins University Press, 1979).

48. Krutilla, "Conservation Revisited," p. 779, n. 7 (describing environmentalists as having subjective reactions to, rather than objective opinions about, the loss of a species or the disfiguring of an environment).

49. For a general statement and defense of the position of welfare economics in environmental policy, see Daniel C. Esty, "Toward Optimal Environmental Governance," *New York University Law Review* 74 (1999). See also Louis Kaplow and Steven Shavell, "Property Rules Versus Liability Rules: An Economic Analysis," *Harvard Law Review* 109 (1996): 715–35 (taking the cost-benefit balance to define ideal regulation).

50. Edith Stokey and Richard Zeckhauser, *A Primer for Policy Analysis* (New York: W. W. Norton, 1978), p. 277.

51. A. Myrick Freeman III, *The Measurement of Environmental Resource Values* (Washington, DC: Resources for the Future, 1993), p. 6.

52. Eban S. Goodstein, *Economics and the Environment*, 2d ed. (Englewood Cliffs, NJ: Prentice Hall, 1999), p. 24.

53. Freeman, *Environmental Improvement*, p. 6.

54. For a discussion of Ford's beliefs, see Roland Marchand, *Advertising the American Dream: Making Way for Modernity, 1920–1940* (Berkeley: University of California Press, 1985), pp. 118, 156–58.

55. Following social choice theory, economists apply the principle of consumer sovereignty to all views but their own – in other words, they regard everyone else as having wants rather than ideas. For the classic statement of this position, see Joseph Schumpeter, "On the Concept of Social Value," *Quarterly Journal of Economics* 23 (1909): 213, 214–17.

56. Commentators generally refer to this idea as the principle of consumer sovereignty. For a general statement of how this principle fits within the foundations of economic theory, see Martha Nussbaum, "Flawed Foundations: The Philosophical Critique of (a Particular Type of) Economics," *University of Chicago Law Review* 64(1997): esp. pp. 1197–98.

57. See, e.g., Allen V. Kneese and Blair T. Bower, "Introduction," *Environmental Quality Analysis: Theory and Method in the Social Sciences* (Washington, DC: Resources for the Future, 1972), pp. 3–4.

58. Kennedy, "Entitlement Problems," pp. 401–21.

59. Critics of Krutilla's approach charged that it came primarily "from economists desperately eager to play a more significant role in environmental policy and environmental groups seeking to gain the support of conservatives." Fred L. Smith, Jr., "A Free-Market Environmental Program," *CATO Journal* 11(1992): esp. pp. 457, 468n.15.

60. Environmental economists typically ground economic valuation in the moral theory of utilitarianism according to which happiness has intrinsic value. As Goodstein points out, the "moral foundation underlying economic analysis, which has as its goal human happiness or utility, is known as utilitarianism." Goodstein, *Economics and the Environment*, p. 24.

61. Freeman, *Environmental Improvement*, p. 7.

62. Ibid.

63. Robert D. Rowe and Lauraine G. Chestnut, *The Value of Visibility: Theory and Application* (Cambridge, MA: Abbot Books, 1982), p. 9. Economists often use consumer surplus as the appropriate measure of economic value in calculating the benefits associated with environmental improvements. See, e.g., Richard E. Just et al., *Applied Welfare Economics and Public Policy* (New York: Prentice Hall, 1982), pp. 69–83; John R. Stoll et al., "A Framework for Identifying Economic Benefits and Beneficiaries of Outdoor Recreation," *Policy Study Review* 7(1987), esp. pp. 445–48. In a later chapter I contend that since WTP is anchored to market prices, consumer surplus cannot be observed.

64. Paul Milgrom, "Is Sympathy an Economic Value? Philosophy, Economics, and the Contingent Valuation Method," in *Contingent Valuation: A Critical Assessment*, J. A. Hausman, ed. (Amsterdam: Elsevier, 1993), p. 431.

65. For further discussion of the possibility that WTP estimates in contingent valuation studies refer to the value not of a policy but of a state of moral satisfaction, see Daniel Kahneman and Jack L. Knetsch, "Valuing Public Goods: The Purchase of Moral Satisfaction," *Environmental Economics and Management* 22(1992): 57–70.

66. Krutilla, "Conservation Revisited," p. 779.

67. Ibid., p. 781.

68. One can understand this argument in terms of an ambiguity between two senses – one logical, the other psychological – in the term "satisfaction." To satisfy a preference in the logical sense is to meet or fulfill it; this is the sense in which equations and conditions are satisfied. To satisfy a person

in the psychological sense is to cause contentment or a feeling of well-being. Krutilla seems to have assumed that to satisfy a preference in the logical sense is to cause a psychological sense of satisfaction. No evidence justifies this inference.

69. For commentaries, see generally John F. Daum, "Some Legal and Regulatory Aspects of Contingent Valuation," in *Contingent Valuation: A Critical Assessment*, J. Hansman, ed. (Amsterdam: Elsevier, 1993), p. 389; William H. Desvousges et al., "Measuring Natural Resource Damages with Contingent Valuation: Tests of Validity and Reliability," in *Contingent Valuation: A Critical Assessment*, J. Hansman, ed. (Amsterdam: Elsevier, 1993), p. 91.

70. James R. Kahn, *The Economic Approach to Environmental and Natural Resources*, 2d ed. (Mason, OH: South-Western College Publishing, 1998), p. 102.

71. Jonathan Lesser, Daniel Dodds, and Richard O. Zerbe Jr., *Environmental Economics and Policy* (Reading, MA: Addison-Wesley, 1997), p. 282.

72. Ibid.

73. Tom Tietenberg, *Environmental and Natural Resource Economics*, 5th ed. (New York: HarperCollins College, 2000), p. 37.

74. Tom Tietenberg, *Environmental Economics and Policy* (New York: Addison-Wesley, 1994), pp. 62–63.

75. D. A. Schkade and J. W. Payne, "How People Respond to Contingent Valuation Questions: A Verbal Protocol Analysis of Willingness to Pay for an Environmental Regulation," *Journal of Environmental Economics and Management* 26(1994): 88, 89.

76. Ibid.

77. Barbier et al., *Value of Biodiversity*, p. 836.

78. Ibid. [citing Amartya Sen, "Rational Fools: A Critique of the Behavior Foundations of Economic Theory," *Philosophy and Public Affairs* 16(1977): 317].

79. Ibid. The authors nicely summarize the question as follows: "Indeed, the debate over environmental values often turns on whether values are considered as ethical judgements or equivalence measures, i.e. whether environmental values are statements of principle or a reflection of social costs," p. 829.

80. R. Blamey et al., "Respondents to Contingent Valuation Surveys: Consumers or Citizens?" *Australian Journal of Agricultural Economics* 39(1995): 263, 285.

81. Daniel A. Farber and Paul A. Hemmersbaugh, "The Shadow of the Future: Discount Rates, Later Generations, and the Environment," *Vanderbilt Law Review* 46(1993): 267, 301.

82. Ronald Dworkin, *Life's Dominion: An Argument About Abortion, Euthanasia, and Individual Freedom* (New York: Knopf, 1993), pp. 69–77.

83. Ibid., pp. 71–72. See also Ibid., pp. 75–77 (discussing the preservation of animal species).

84. Ibid., pp. 69–70.

85. Experiments show again and again that responses to CV questionnaires express what the individual believes to be good in general or good for society and not – as the CV methods seek to determine – what individuals believe is good for them. See, e.g., Thomas H. Stevens et al., "Measuring the Existence Value of Wildlife: What Do CVM Estimates Really Show?" *Land Economics* 67 (1991): 390; Thomas H. Stevens et al., "Measuring the Existence Value of Wildlife: Reply," *Land Economics* 69 (1993): 309.

86. Some economists agree and write: "[I]t may be inappropriate to use the [contingent valuation methodology] as an input to [benefit cost analysis] studies, unless means can be found to extract information on consumer preferences from data predominantly generated by citizen judgments." Blamey et al., "Contingent Valuation Surveys," p. 285.

87. Kerry Turner et al., *Environmental Economics: An Elementary Introduction* (Baltimore, MD: John Hopkins University Press, 1993), p. 38.

88. Goodstein, *Economics and the Environment*, p. 24.

89. In fact, these states per se lack intrinsic value. Their value inheres in their appropriateness to the circumstances in which they arise. The joy sadists take in the pain of others, for example, has no positive value, intrinsic or otherwise; it is bad, not good. The sadness one feels in sympathy with others, in contrast, although a pain, possesses intrinsic value. Pleasure and pain have value insofar as they function cognitively, that is, as ways of knowing the moral qualities of the world. Pleasure and pain are both valuable, then, insofar as they constitute ways of knowing and are thus appropriate to their objects. I agree with Socrates, in other words, that knowledge not pleasure constitutes the ultimate intrinsic good.

90. Many empirical studies find that money does not buy happiness – or that preference-satisfaction does not correlate with perceived well-being after basic needs are met. See, for example, Robert Samuelson, *The Good Life and Its Discontents: The American Dream in the Age of Entitlement* (New York: Knopf, 1997), e.g., p. 56; R. E. Lane, *The Market Experience* (New York: Cambridge University Press, 1991); and Michael Argyle, "Causes and Correlates of Happiness," in *Well-Being: The Foundations of Hedonic Psychology*, Daniel Kahneman, Ed Diener, and Norbert Schwarz, eds. (New York: Russell Sage Foundation, 1999): pp. 353–73. The proposition that income – or the ability to satisfy preferences – does not vary with subjective happiness (after basic needs are met) is consistent with the finding that economic prosperity does correlate with happiness and thus that people in more prosperous countries are happier than those in less prosperous ones. The principal reason for this may be that employment in productive work does increase happiness, and prosperity increases employment. Thus, the Calvinists might be right in emphasizing production rather than consumption as a source of salvation. Joblessness reduces happiness more than any other single factor, including divorce. This finding refers to the "pure effect" of being unemployed, when income is kept constant. Andrew E. Clark and Andrew J. Oswald, "Unhappiness and Unemployment," *Economic Journal* 104 (1994): 648–59.

91. Ed Diener et al., "The Relationship Between Income and Subjective Well-Being: Relative or Absolute?" *Social Indicators Research* 28(1992): 253–81 (finding that people whose incomes went up, down, or stayed about the same over a 10-year period had approximately the same levels of subjective well-being). See also Ruut Veenhoven, "Is Happiness Relative?" *Social Indicators Research* 24(1991): 1–32.

92. Michael Argyle, *The Psychology of Happiness* (New York: Routledge, 1987), pp. 102–6. Richard A. Easterlin, "Does Economic Growth Improve the Human Lot? Some Empirical Evidence," in *Nations and Households in Economic Growth: Essays in Honor of Moses Abramovitz*, Paul A. David and Melvin W. Reder, eds. (New York: Academic Press, 1974), pp. 89, 106. See also generally F. E. Trainer, *Abandon Affluence* (London: Zed Books, 1985); Paul Wachtel, *The Poverty of Affluence* (Philadelphia: New Society Publishers, 1989); and Tibor Scitovsky, *The Joyless Economy: The Psychology of Human Satisfaction* (Foreword by Robert H. Frank) (New York: Oxford University Press, 1992).

93. David G. Myers, *Exploring Psychology*, 3rd ed. (New York: Worth Publishers, 1996), pp. 346–50. For all kinds of citations and charts, see The Study of Happiness. Available online at: http://www.hope.edu/academic/psychology/myerstxt/happy/happy2.html/.

94. See Michael Argyle and Maryanne Martin, "The Psychological Causes of Happiness," in *Subjective Well-Being: An Interdisciplinary Perspective*, Fritz Strack et al., eds. (Oxford: Pergamon Press, 1991, esp. p. 77); Paul Krugman, "A Good Reason Growth Doesn't Necessarily Make Us Happier," *Arizona Daily Star*, Apr. 2, 2000: F2.

95. For a general discussion, see Jonathan Freedman, *Happy People: What Happiness Is, Who Has It, and Why* (New York: Harcourt Brace Jovanovich, 1978).

96. See generally P. D. Rickman et al., "Lottery Winners and Accident Victims: Is Happiness Relative?" *Journal of Personality and Social Psychology* 36(1978): 917; Mary Jordan, "Millions Don't Turn Everything to Gold: Many Lottery Winners Keep Same Jobs, Cars," *Washington Post*, July 21, 1991: A1.

97. Argyle, *Psychology of Happiness*, p. 144.

98. Ed Diener et al., "Happiness of the Very Wealthy," *Social Indicators Research* 16(1985): 263.

99. Krugman, "Good Reason Growth," p. F2; Robert E. Lane, "Does Money Buy Happiness?" *Public Interest* 113 (Fall 1993): 56–65.

100. Richard Posner, *The Economics of Justice* (Cambridge, MA: Harvard University Press, 1981), p. 60.

101. Freeman, *Environmental Improvement*, p. 3.

102. Tietenberg, *Natural Resource Economics*, p. 20.

103. W. Michael Hanemann, "Contingent Valuation and Economics," in *Environmental Valuation: New Perspectives*, K. G. Willis and J. T. Corkindale, eds. (Cheltenham, UK: CAB International, 1995), pp. 79, 105.

104. Kenneth J. Arrow, *Social Choice and Individual Value*, 2d ed. (New Haven, CT: Yale University Press, 1963), p. 17.
105. Alan Randall, *Resource Economics: An Economic Approach to Natural Resource and Environmental Policy* (Columbus, OH: Grid Publishing, 1981), p. 156.
106. Ibid.
107. Notice that in denying that society should adopt preference-satisfaction as a goal of social policy, one implies nothing whatever about paternalism. A paternalistic policy would prevent individuals from making certain choices, e.g., with respect to the consumption of drugs. The argument offered here is consistent with the largest libertarian tolerance for this sort of choice. It extends only to social policy, to the goals the government pursues, not to anything the individual might do in his or her private life.
108. For discussion of this concept in the larger context of political theory, see generally Cass R. Sunstein, "Naked Preferences and the Constitution," *Columbia Law Review* 84(1984): 1689–1732.
109. Will, "Hallowed Ground," p. B7.
110. J. Balz, "Separation of Races Found OK by Many Young People," *Los Angeles Times*, Aug. 17, 1999: A10.
111. Elizabeth Stead Kaszubski, "Letter to the Editor, Park Plan Honors 'Hallowed Ground,'" *USA Today*, June 24, 1999: 14A (describing the events that transpired at the spot where the Park Service proposed to build its new Visitors' Center).
112. See generally Jürgen Habermas, *Justification and Application: Remarks on Discourse Ethics*, Ciaran Cronin, trans. (Cambridge, MA: MIT Press, 1993).
113. A regulatory agency can take important macroeconomic indicators of prosperity into account while paying no attention to the concepts of microeconomics, such as marginal benefits and costs. The microeconomic concepts central to environmental economics – such as allocatory efficiency, net benefits, utility, and externality – have no clear relation, empirical or conceptual, to macroeconomic goals such as prosperity, full employment, and low inflation. Microeconomic efficiency has little or no demonstrated relation to macroeconomic performance. See generally *Microeconomic Efficiency and Macroeconomic Performance*, David Shepherd, Jeremy Turk, and Aubrey Silberston, eds. (Oxford: P. Allan, 1983). Later in this book, I suggest that the microeconomic theory of competitive markets suggests that competition will drive prices down to costs, eliminating producer surplus or profit. Thus, microeconomic efficiency is the enemy of macroeconomic performance.
114. Clark and Oswald, "Unhappiness and Unemployment." According to research summarized at the Mining Company's economics website, people's reported happiness, as measured by the annual United States General Social Survey, correlates negatively with the misery index, the sum of inflation and unemployment rates. See Economics and Happiness. Available online at: http://economics.tqn.com/finance/economics/library/weekly/aa051498.htm.

115. Interpreted in this light, technology-forcing statutes, such as the Clean Air Act, attempt to achieve as much environmental improvement as possible without hobbling the performance of the economy. The EPA, since it has to defend its policies politically, must take costs into account, where "costs" are understood in macroeconomic terms, e.g., terms of inflation and unemployment. The agency would not consider "costs" in the microeconomic sense of changes in net welfare or utility. Plainly, people consider the performance of the economy, i.e., prosperity, important enough that agencies that threaten to undermine it are unlikely to succeed politically. This presents no reason, however, for an agency to bother with cost-benefit analysis. Microeconomic efficiency, which cost-benefit analysis measures, has never been shown to have any relation to macroeconomic performance. See Sidney A. Shapiro and Thomas O. McGarity, "Not So Paradoxical: The Rationale for Technology-Based Regulation," *Duke Law Journal* 729(1991): 741–42 (arguing that the "willingness to pay" criterion does not provide the context for understanding the economic rationality of health-based environmental standards).

116. For a macroeconomic approach to assessing costs of environmental regulation, see Paul R. Portney, *Economics and the Clean Air Act*, reprinted in 136 Cong. Rec. H12911.01, *H12916. Oct. 26 (1990).

117. Nicholas A. Ashford, "Understanding Technological Responses of Industrial Firms to Environmental Problems: Implications for Government Policy," in *Environmental Strategies for Industry*, Kurt Fischer and Johan Schot, eds. (Washington, DC: Island Press, 1993), p. 282.

118. *American Trucking Association v. EPA*, 175 F.3d 1027, 1035–39, 1051–53 (D.C. Cir. 1999), modified on rehearing, 195 F.3d 4 (D.C. Cir. 1999).

119. See generally A. Dan Tarlock, "The Creation of New Risk Sharing Water Entitlement Regimes: The Case of the Truckee-Carson Settlement," *Ecology Law Quarterly* 25(1999): 674 (discussing collateral habitat conservation plans); A. Dan Tarlock, "Biodiversity Federalism," *Maryland Law Review* 54(1995): 1315 (surveying place-based environmental decision-making).

    Courts have required that agencies open decision-making processes to public participation. See, e.g., *Scenic Hudson Preservation Conference v. Federal Power Comm'n*, 354 F.2d 608, 616 (2d Cir. 1965) (stating that the Federal Power Commission should solicit public comment on aesthetic, conservation, and recreational interests). For a critical view of participatory initiatives, see Jim Rossi, "Participation Run Amok: The Costs of Mass Participation for Deliberative Agency Decisionmaking," *Northwestern University Law Review* 92(1997): 173 (citing the vast literature on public participation in the regulatory process).

120. See, e.g., Les Line, "Microcosmic Captive Breeding Project Offers New Hope for Beleaguered Beetle," *Orange County Register*, Sept. 28, 1996: A14 (reporting that it cost less than $10,000 to protect and restore the beetle).

121. For an excellent introduction, see generally Jody Freeman, "Collaborative Governance in the Administrative State," *UCLA Law Review* 45 (1997): 1. See also generally Richard H. Pildes and Cass R. Sunstein, "Reinventing the Regulatory State," *University of Chicago Law Review* 62 (1995): 1; Lawrence E. Susskind and Joshua Secunda, "The Risks and the Advantages of Agency Discretion: Evidence from EPA's Project XL," *UCLA Journal of Environmental Law and Policy* 17 (1998–99): 67. For theoretical commentary on collaborative rulemaking, see Daniel Fiorino, "Toward a New System of Environmental Regulation: The Case for an Industry Sector Approach," *Environmental Law* 26 (1996): 457; Douglas Michael, "Cooperative Implementation of Federal Regulations," *Yale Journal on Regulation* 13 (1996): 535, 574–89. For criticism, see Rena I. Steinzor, "Regulatory Reinvention and Project XL: Does the Emperor Have Any Clothes?" *Environmental Law Reporter* 26 (1996).

122. See, e.g., William J. Clinton, Memorandum, Regulatory Reinvention Initiative, Mar. 4, 1995. Available online at: http://www.pub.whitehouse. gov/urires/I2R?urn:pdi://oma.eop.gov.us/1995/3/6/2.text.1. See also "EPA Emphasis on Stakeholder Process Exasperates Risk Experts," *Risk Policy Report*, Oct. 16, 1998: 6–7; John S. Applegate, "Beyond the Usual Suspects: The Use of Citizen Advisory Boards in Environmental Decisionmaking," *Indiana Law Journal* 73 (1998): 901–57.

123. Chief Justice William Rehnquist, reviewing the Occupational Safety and Health Act, described the phrase "to the extent feasible" as one of many examples of "Congress simply avoiding a choice which was both fundamental for purposes of the statute and yet politically so divisive that the necessary decision or compromise was difficult, if not impossible, to hammer out in the legislative forge." *Industrial Union Dep't, AFL-CIO v. American Petroleum Institute*, 448 U.S. 607, 687 (1980) (Rehnquist, C.J., concurring). He implored the Court to invalidate the vague and precatory laws that support today's regulatory state. These statutes, he said, "violate the doctrine against uncanalized delegations of legislative power." Ibid., p. 675. For discussion of the penchant of Congress to delegate hard choices to others, see, e.g., John P. Dwyer, "The Pathology of Symbolic Legislation," *Ecology Law Quarterly* 17 (1990): 233.

124. As Judge Williams remarked in *American Trucking*, "[I]t seems bizarre that a statute intended to improve human health would, as EPA claimed at argument, lock the agency into looking at only one half of a substance's health effects in determining the maximum level for that substance," *American Trucking Association v. EPA*. The point here is that the EPA, by citing the "knee-of-the-curve" or any other moral basis for its decision, could meet the requirements that Judge Williams and democratic theory impose on them. Utterly mired in the Progressive tradition, however, the EPA will not concede that it makes moral or political judgments but will hide these judgments behind a smokescreen of environmental science. Even the threat by the D.C. Circuit panel – that the EPA's interpretation of the statute might be voided for overdelegation unless the agency

acknowledges the ethical judgments it makes and must make – is unlikely to dislodge the agency from its scientism.

125. For commentary, see Sheila Jasanoff, *The Fifth Branch* (Cambridge, MA: Harvard University Press, 1990), p. 1 (arguing that appeals to science should not "take the politics out of policymaking"); Bruce Bimber and David H. Guston, "Politics by the Same Means: Government and Science in the United States," in *Handbook of Science and Technology Studies*, Sheila Jasanoff et al., eds. (1995), 559; Sheila Jasanoff, "Research Subpoenas and the Sociology of Knowledge," *Law and Contemporary Problems* 59(3)(1996): 95, 98–100 (describing the deleterious effect of the expectations of law on the community of scientists).

126. Pound, "Battle over Gettysburg," p. 4A.

127. Ibid. (quoting Robert Moore).

Chapter 3

1. B. F. Skinner, *Science and Human Behavior* (New York: Macmillan, 1953), p. 223.

2. Bernard Williams, "A Critique of Utilitarianism," in *Utilitarianism: For and Against*, J. J. C. Smart and Bernard Williams, eds. (Cambridge: Cambridge University Press, 1973), p. 147.

3. Alan Randall, *Resource Economics: An Economic Approach to Natural Resource and Environmental Policy* (Columbus, OH: Grid Publishing, 1981), p. 156.

4. See, e.g., Kurt Baier, "Rationality and Morality," *Erkenntnis* 11(1997): 197–223; and D. George, "Does the Market Create Preferred Preferences?" *Review of Social Economy* 5(1993): 323–46.

5. Aimee L. Ball, "Daddy Oldest," *Worth Magazine*, April 1, 1992: 60–64; quotation on p. 62.

6. Jeffery Holland, *Budget and Economic Outlook: An Update* (Washington, DC: Diane Publishing, 2002), p. 23.

7. David McNaughton, *Moral Vision: An Introduction to Ethics* (Oxford: Blackwell, 1988), p. 130.

8. Daniel Hausman, "Revealed Preference, Belief, and Game Theory," *Economics and Philosophy* 16(2000): 99–115.

9. Ian Little, "A Reformulation of the Theory of Consumers' Behavior," *Oxford Economics Papers* 1(1949): 90–99. Quotation at pp. 91–92.

10. For discussion, see A. K. Sen, "Rational Fools: A Critique of the Behavioral Foundations of Economic Theory," *Philosophy and Public Affairs* 6 (1976/1977): 327–44; Amartya Sen, "Liberty and Social Choice," *Journal of Philosophy* 80(1983): 5–28.

11. John Hicks, *Revision of Demand Theory* (Oxford: Clarendon Press, 1956), p. 6.

12. Ian Little, "Reformulation," p. 90.

13. Daniel Hausman, "Revealed Preference," p. 99.

14. Alexander Rosenberg, *Economics: Mathematical Politics or Science of Diminishing Returns?* (Chicago: University of Chicago Press, 1992), p. 119.

15. G. L. S. Shackle, *Epistemics and Economics* (Cambridge: Cambridge University Press, 1972); B. Hodgson, *Economics and Moral Science* (Berlin: Springer, 2001); Robert Frank, *Passions within Reason: The Strategic Role of the Emotions* (New York: W. W. Norton, 1988).

16. P. A. Samuelson, "Consumption Theory in Terms of Revealed Preference," *Economica* 15(1948): 25–243.

17. Amartya Sen, "Rational Fools," *Journal of Philosophy and Public Affairs* 6(4) (1977): 241.

18. Raymond J. Kopp, "Environmental Economics: Not Dead but Thriving," *Resources*, Spring (111)(1993): 7–12; quotation at p. 9.

19. See, e.g., Anthony M. Yezer, Robert Goldfarb, and Paul J. Poppen, "Does Studying Economics Discourage Cooperation? Watch What We Do, Not What We Say or How We Play," *Journal of Economic Perspectives* 10(1)(1996): 177–86; Robert H. Frank, Thomas Gilovich, and Dennis T. Regan, "Do Economists Make Bad Citizens?" *Journal of Economic Perspectives* 10(1)(1996): 187–92; and Robert H. Frank, Thomas Gilovich, and Dennis T. Regan, "Does Studying Economics Inhibit Cooperation?" *Journal of Economic Perspectives* 7(2)(1993): 159–71.

20. F. W. Bell, "The Pope and the Price of Fish," *American Economic Review* 57(5)(1968): 1346–50.

21. R. Varian, *Intermediate Microeconomics*, 4th ed. (New York: W. W. Norton, 1996), p. 117.

22. A. Tversky and D. Kahneman, "The Framing of Decisions and the Psychology of Choice," *Science* 211(1981): 453–58.

23. Tversky and Kahneman, "Framing," 453–58.

24. G. H. von Wright, *The Logic of Preference* (Edinburgh: Edinburgh University Press, 1963).

25. Nelson Goodman, *The Structure of Appearance* (Cambridge, MA: Harvard University Press, 1951); Rudolph Carnap, *The Logical Structure of the World: Pseudoproblems in Philosophy* (Berkeley: University of California Press, 1967).

26. Skinner, *Science and Human Behavior*, p. 30.

27. Michael Scriven, "A Study of Radical Behaviorism," in *The Foundations of Science and the Concepts of Psychology and Psychoanalysis*, H. Feigl and M. Scrived, eds., *Minnesota Studies in the Philosophy of Science I* (Minneapolis: University of Minnesota Press, 1956), pp. 88–130; Noam Chomsky, "A Review of B. F. Skinner's Verbal Behavior," *Language* 35(1)(1959): 26–58.

28. Raymond J. Kopp and Katherine A. Pease, "Contingent Valuation: Economics, Law, and Politics," in *Determining the Value of Non-marketed Goods*, R. J. Kopp, W. W. Pommerehne, and N. Schwarz, eds. (Boston: Kluwer Academic Publishers, 1997), pp. 7–58.

29. Roy Selby, "A Bit About Phrenology," *AANS Bulletin* (1993); available online at: http://www.neurosurgery.org/cybermuseum/pre20th/phren/phrenology.html. For discussion of phrenology as a science, see S. H. Greenblatt, "Phrenology in the Science and Culture of the 19th Century," *Neurosurgery* 37(1995): 790–805.

30. Robert Sugden, "Welfare, Resources, and Capabilities: A Review of Inequality Reexamined by Amartya Sen," *Journal of Economic Literature* 31(1993): 1947–62; quotation at p. 1948.
31. Edith Stokey and Richard Zeckhauser, *A Primer for Policy Analysis* (New York: W. W. Norton, 1978), p. 275.
32. A. Myrick Freeman III, *The Measurement of Environmental Resource Values* (Washington, DC: Resources for the Future, 1993), p. 6.
33. David W. Pearce and Tannis Seccombe-Hett, "Economic Valuation and Environmental Decision-making in Europe," *Environmental Science and Technology* 34(8)(2000): 1419–1425; quotation at p. 1419.
34. Charles Perrings, "Economic Values of Biodiversity," in *Social Norms and Social Roles: Global Biodiversity Assessment*, V. H. Heywood, ed. (Cambridge: Cambridge University Press, 1995), pp. 823–914; cf. Cass R. Sunstein, *Columbia Law Review* (May 1996): esp. 932–35.
35. Sen, "Rational Fools," p. 327.
36. R. E. Lane, *The Market Experience* (New York: Cambridge University Press, 1991), ch. 26; R. E. Lane, "Does Money Buy Happiness?" *The Public Interest* 113(Fall 1993): 56–65. E. Diener, Jeff Horwitz, and Robert A. Emmons, "Happiness of the Very Wealthy," *Social Indicators Research* 16(1985): 263–74; M. Argyle, *The Psychology of Happiness* (New York: Methuen & Co., 1986). P. D. Brickman, D. Coates, and R. Janoff-Bulman, "Lottery Winners and Accident Victims: Is Happiness Relative?" *Journal of Personality and Social Psychology* 36(8)(1978): 917–27. People in wealthier societies may be happier than those in impoverished ones, but this suggests nothing about the relation between income or preference-satisfaction and happiness. In wealthier societies basic needs are more likely to be met; people have employment and health care, which do contribute to well-being.
37. Kopp and Pease, "Contingent Valuation," pp. 7–58; quotation on p. 8.
38. See, e.g., "Decision Making and Valuation for Environmental Policy," NSF/EPA Partnership for Environmental Research. This program has supported research not just on economic valuation but on collaborative processes of environmental decision-making, including projects of my own. Available online at: http://www.nsf.gov/home/crssprgm/epa/start.htm.
39. Raymond J. Kopp, W. W. Pommerehne, and N. Schwarz, "Editors' Introduction," in *Determining the Value of Non-marketed Goods*, R. J. Kopp, W. W. Pommerehne, and N. Schwarz, eds. (Boston: Kluwer Academic Publishers, 1997), pp. 1–6; quotation on p. 3.

Chapter 4

1. A. Myrick Freeman III, *The Measure of Environmental and Resource Value: Theory and Methods* (Washington, DC: Resources for the Future, 2003).
2. James R. Kahn, *The Economic Approach to Environmental and Natural Resources* (Fort Worth, TX: Dryden Press, 1998).

3. For an argument for the same position I have taken in this chapter, see Frank Knight, "Value and Price," in *The Ethics of Competition* (New Brunswick, NJ: Transaction Press, 1997 [1935]), pp. 229–42. In this essay, published in 1935, Knight observes that Smith was right – and the "marginalists" wrong – with respect to the question whether prices are settled on the demand side by subjective utility or the supply side by producer cost. "Although at first all cost theory was discarded in favor of the marginal utility explanation of value, gradually it came to be recognized that, while price immediately depends on marginal utility, under competitive conditions of production it is ultimately determined by cost" (p. 232).

4. Aristotle, *Politics* (Indianapolis: Hackett Publishing, 1998), p. I, 9.

5. Adam Smith, *An Enquiry into the Nature and Causes of the Wealth of Nations* (New York: Penguin Books, 1776, 1997), p. I, iv.

6. Ibid.

7. A. Marshall, *Principles of Economics* (Philadelphia: Porcupine Press, 1890), p. V, iii, 7.

8. David Pearce, *Economics and the Environment* (Cheltenham, UK: Edward Elgar, 1998), p. 221.

9. Eban Goodstein, *Economics and the Environment* (Englewood Cliffs, NJ: Prentice Hall, 1995), pp. 88–89.

10. Anthony Boardman, David H. Greenberg, Aidan R. Vining, and David L. Weimer, *Cost-Benefit Analysis: Concepts and Practice* (Upper Saddle River, NJ: Prentice Hall, 1996).

11. Charles D. Kolstad, *Environmental Economics* (New York: Oxford University Press, 2000), p. 292.

12. For example, Sunil Gupta, "Impact of Sales Promotions on When, What, and How Much to Buy," *Journal of Marketing Research* 25(4) (1988): 342–56; Aradhna Krishna, "The Normative Impact of Consumer Price Expectations for Multiple Brands on Consumer Purchase Behavior," *Marketing Science* 11(3) (Summer 1992): 266–87.

13. Barry Aarons, "Don't Call – Just Send Me an E-Mail: The New Competition for Traditional Telecom" (Report 175) (Lewiston, TX: Institute for Policy Innovation, 2003).

14. D. L. Greene, "Transportation's Oil Dependence and Energy Security in the 21st Century," in *Environmental Change, Adaptation and Security*, Steven C. Lonergan, ed. (Dordrecht, Netherlands: Kluwer, 1999).

15. Daniel Kahneman, Jack L. Knetsch, and Richard Thaler, "Fairness as a Constraint on Profit Seeking: Entitlements in the Market," *The American Economic Review* 76(4) (September 1986): 728–41.

16. Icek Ajzen, L. H. Rosenthal, and T. C. Brown, "Effects of Perceived Fairness on Willingness to Pay," *Journal of Applied Social Psychology* 30(12) (2000): 2439–50.

17. Edward E. Zajac, *Fairness or Efficiency: An Introduction to Public Utility Pricing* (Cambridge, MA: Ballinger, 1978).

18. K. Eichenwald, "Ex-Trader at Enron Is Charged in California Power Case," *New York Times*, June 4, 2003, p. C6.

19. Amos Tversky, "Contrasting Rational and Psychological Principles of Choice," in *Wise Choices: Decisions, Games, and Negotiations,* Richard J. Zeckhauser et al., eds. (Boston: Harvard Business School Press, 1996), p. 17; Paul Slovic, "The Construction of Preference," *American Psychologist* (50)(May 1995): 364–71.

20. J. R. Bettman, M. F. Luce, and J. W. Payne, "Constructive Consumer Choice Processes," *Journal of Consumer Research* 25(3)(1998): 187–217.

21. Marshall, *Principles of Economics,* p. 325.

22. For example, L. L. Wilde and A. Schwartz, "Equilibrium Comparison Shopping," *Review of Economic Studies* 46(3)(1979): 543–53; S. Salop and J. Stiglitz, "Bargains and Rip-offs: A Model of Monopolistically Competitive Price Dispersion," *Elgar Reference Collection,* International Library of Critical Writing in Economics 53(1976); K. Burdett and K. L. Judd, "Equilibrium Price Dispersion," *Econometrica* 51(1983): 955–69; and J. A. Carlson and R. P. McAfee, "Discrete Equilibrium Price Dispersion," *Journal of Political Economy* 91(3)(1983): 480–93.

23. S. Lach, "Existence and Persistence of Price Dispersion: An Empirical Analysis," *Review of Economics and Statistics* 84(3)(2002): 433–44.

24. Jerzy D. Konieczny and Andrzej Skrzypacz, "The Behavior of Price Dispersion in a Natural Experiment," Stanford Business School Research Paper No. 1641 (2000).

25. C. Narasimhan, "A Price Discrimination Theory of Coupons," *Marketing Science* (3)(spring 1984): 128–47; J. Howell, "Potential Profitability and Decreased Consumer Welfare through Manufacturers' Cents-off Coupons," *Journal of Consumer Affairs* 25(1)(Summer 1991): 164–85.

26. H. Marvel, "The Economics of Information and Retail Gasoline Price Behavior: An Empirical Analysis," *Journal of Political Economy* 84(1976): 1033–60.

27. For example, Lach, "Existence," Wilde and Schwartz, "Equilibrium," Salop and Stiglitz, "Bargains," Burdett and Judd, "Price Dispersion," and Carlson and McAfee, "Discrete Equilibrium."

28. S. Freeman, "Chrysler Offers PT Cruiser Deals as Shrinking Market Cools Hot Car," *Wall Street Journal* February 8, 2002: B9.

29. Barry Field, *Environmental Economics: An Introduction* (New York: McGraw-Hill, 1994), pp. 4, 47.

30. Marshall, *Principles of Economics,* pp. III, vi, 5.

31. Gary Becker, "Irrational Behavior in Economic Theory," *Journal of Political Economy* 70(1)(February 1962): 1–13.

32. Jonathan Lesser, Daniel Dodds, and Richard O. Zerbe Jr., *Environmental Economics and Policy* (Reading, MA: Addison-Wesley, 1997), p. 282.

33. Field, *Environmental Economics,* p. 49.

34. David A. Barboza, "Misery Is Abundant for Potato Farmers; Bumper Crops Turned into Fertilizer," *Washington Post,* March 17, 2001: C1.

35. L. Line, "Microcosmic Captive Breeding Project Offers New Hope for Beleaguered Beetle," *New York Times*, September 17, 1996: p. 1.

36. R. Thaler, "Mental Accounting," *Marketing Science* 4(3)(1985): 199–214.

Chapter 5

1. H. H. Munro (Saki), "Clovis on Parental Responsibilities," *Beasts and Super Beasts* (Great Neck, NY: Core Collection Books, 1978).

2. Bertrand Russell, *Introduction to Mathematical Philosophy* (New York and London: Allen and Unwin, 1917), p. 71.

3. Herman B. Leonard and Richard Zeckhauser, "Cost-benefit Analysis Applied to Risks: Its Philosophy and Legitimacy," in *Values at Risk*, Douglas MacLean, ed. (Totowa, NJ: Rowman and Allanheld, 1986), pp. 31–48.

4. A. V. Kneese and Blair T. Bower, *Environmental Quality Analysis: Theory and Method in the Social Sciences* (Baltimore, MD: Johns Hopkins University Press and Resources for the Future, 1972), pp. 3–4.

5. Jonathan A. Lesser, Daniel E. Dodds, and Richard O. Zerbe, Jr., *Environmental Economics and Policy* (Reading, MA: Addison-Wesley, 1997), p. 115.

6. Clean Air Act. 29 U.S.C., Section 109(b)(1).

7. Occupational Safety and Health Act, Section 655(b)(5)(1976).

8. Larry Ruff, "The Economic Common Sense of Pollution," *The Public Interest* (19) (Spring 1970): 69–85. Reprinted in Robert Dorfman and Nancy Dorfman, *Economics of the Environment: Selected Readings*, 3rd ed. (New York: W. W. Norton, 1993), pp. 20–36, quotation at 20.

9. Ibid., p. 23.

10. Ibid.; italics omitted.

11. Ibid, p. 29; italics omitted.

12. Ibid., p. 29.

13. Ibid., p. 30.

14. Ibid., p. 24.

15. Tom Tietenburg, "Editor's Introduction," *The Evolution of Emissions Trading: Theoretical Foundations and Design Considerations* (London: Ashgate Publishing, 2001), p. 2.

16. Richard O. Zerbe, Jr. and Howard E. McCurdy, "The Failure of Market Failure," *Journal of Policy Analysis and Management* (Fall 1999) 18(4): 558–78; quotation on p. 565.

17. William J. Baumol and Wallace E. Oates, *The Theory of Environmental Policy* (New York: Cambridge University Press, 1988), p. 10.

18. David Freed, "U.S. to Sue 15 Firms Over Pollution," *L.A. Times*, Jan. 18, 1990: B1.

19. Dale B. Thompson, "Valuing the Environment: Courts' Struggles with Natural Resource Damages," *Environmental Law* 32(2002): 57–86.

20. Jerry A. Hausman, *Contingent Valuation: A Critical Assessment* (Amsterdam: North-Holland, 1993).

21. Thompson, "Valuing the Environment," 2002. Thompson argues that CV estimates have been presented as evidence in court proceedings only twice and were ruled inadmissible in both instances.

22. A. Myrick Freeman III, "The Measurement of Environmental and Resource Values," in *Free Market Environmentalism*, Terry Anderson and Donald Leal, eds. (Boulder, CO: Westview Press, PERC, 1991), 2–3, 147–48.

23. Joseph E. Stiglitz et al., *The Economic Role of the State* (London: Basil Blackwell, 1989), p. 37.

24. Charles Perrings, *Economy and Environment* (Cambridge: Cambridge University Press, 1987), p. 131.

25. Fred L. Smith, Jr., "The Market and Nature," *The Freeman*, 43(9) (September 1993): 350–57, quotation at p. 352.

26. Terry Anderson and Donald Leal, *Free Market Environmentalism* (San Francisco: Pacific Research Institute, 1991), p. 9.

27. E. K. Hunt, "A Radical Critique of Welfare Economics," in *Growth, Profits, and Property*, Ed Nell, ed. (Cambridge: Cambridge University Press, 1980), pp. 239–49, quotation at pp. 245–46.

28. Ibid.

29. Ibid. See also R. C. D'Arge and E. K. Hunt, "Environmental Pollution, Externalities, and Conventional Economic Wisdom: A Critique," *Environmental Affairs* 1(1971): 266–86.

30. Zerbe Jr. and McCurdy, "The Failure of Market Failure."

31. Alan Randall, "The Problem of Market Failure," in *Economics of the Environment: Selected Readings*, Robert Dorfman and Nancy S. Dorfman, eds. (New York: W. W. Norton, 1993), p. 145.

32. Randall, "Market Failure," 144–61, quotation at p. 144.

33. Ronald H. Coase, "The Problem of Social Cost," *Journal of Law and Economics* 3(1960): 1–44.

34. Katharine Q. Seelye, "Utility Buys Town It Choked, Lock, Stock and Blue Plume," *New York Times*, May 13, 2002: A1, 14.

35. Baumol and Oates, *Theory of Environmental Policy*, p. 10.

36. Ruff, "Economic Common Sense," p. 27.

37. C. J. Dahlman, "The Problem of Externality," *Journal of Law and Economics* 22(1979): 153.

38. Coase, "Problem of Social Cost," p. 15.

39. Dahlman, "Problem of Externality," p. 145.

40. Coase, "Problem of Social Cost," pp. 25–26.

41. Duncan Kennedy, "Cost Benefit Analysis," *Stanford Law Review* 33(1981): 387–421, quotation at p. 397.

42. Ibid.

43. Ronald H. Coase, *The Firm, the Market, and the Law* (Chicago: University of Chicago Press, 1988), p. 26.

44. Ruff, "Economic Common Sense," p. 20.

45. Guido Calabresi and Douglas Melamed, "Property Rules, Liability Rules, and Inalienability: One View of the Cathedral," *Harvard Law Review* 85 (6)(1972): 1089–1182.

46. Tibor Machan, "Pollution and Political Theory," in *Earthbound: New Introductory Essays in Environmental Ethics,* Tom Regan, ed. (New York: Random House, 1984), pp. 74–106; quotation at p. 97.

47. See John Hospers, "What Libertarianism Is," in *The Libertarian Alternative: Essays in Political and Social Philosophy,* Tibor Machan, ed. (Chicago: Nelson Hall, 1974), quoting Rothbard, p. 15.

48. Senate Comm. on Pub. Works, 93d Cong., 1st Sess., Legislative History of the Water Pollution Control Act Amendments of 1972, at 1133 (1973) (quoting Sen. Bayh); see also Carol M. Rose, "Rethinking Environmental Controls: Management Strategies for Common Resources," *Duke Law Journal* 1 (1991): 1–46; and Wendy E. Wagner, "The Triumph of Technology-Based Standard," *University of Illinois Law Review* (2000): 83–113.

49. Martin Anderson, quoted in Walter E. Block, ed., *Economics and the Environment: A Reconciliation* (Vancouver: Fraser Institute, 1990), p. x.

50. Jeffrey Friedman, "Politics or Scholarship?" *Critical Review* 6 (2–3) (1992): 429–45, quotation at p. 430.

51. For a defense of "creative compliance" with the law, see Thomas J. Schoenbaum and Richard B. Stewart, "The Role of Mitigation and Conservation Measures in Achieving Compliance with Regulatory Requirements: Lessons from Section 316 of the Clean Water Act," *N.Y. University Environmental Law Journal* 8 (2000).

52. R. Shep Melnick, *Regulation and the Courts: The Case of the Clean Air Act* (1983). In *Riverside v. Ruckelshaus,* 4 Environment Rep. Cas. (BNA) 1728, 1731 (C.D. Cal. 1972), a circuit court ordered EPA to take measures – which would have to ban most driving in California – to meet the smog standard. At a news conference, EPA Administrator Ruckelshaus joked, "'Faced with the choice between my freedom [from court contempt orders] and your mobility, my freedom wins'" (Melnick, *Regulation,* pp. 321–22).

53. For discussion see Daniel A. Farber, "Taking Slippage Seriously: Noncompliance and Creative Compliance in Environmental Law," *Harvard Environmental Law Review* 23 (1999).

54. John P. Dwyer, "The Pathology of Symbolic Legislation," *Ecology Law Quarterly* 17 (1990).

55. *Les v. Reilly,* 968 F.2d 985, 986 (9th Cir. 1992), cert. denied sub nom. *Nat'l Agric. Chems. Ass'n v. Les,* 507 U.S. 950 (1993).

56. In fact, environmental groups sometimes refrained from challenging halfway measures when full compliance with the law would cause social upheaval. "For example, environmental groups could have successfully challenged EPA's practice during the late 1980s of approving state implementation plans that contain unrealistic promises of achieving compliance with the ozone NAAQS but these groups declined to do so because more stringent and realistic SIP provisions would have required sharp limitations on automobile use." Richard B. Stewart, "A New Generation of Environmental Regulation?" *Capital University Law Review* 21 (2001): 29–141; quotation at p. 59.

57. *Industrial Union Dep't v. Am. Petroleum Inst.*, 448 U.S. 607 (1980) (the Benzene case), at n122 Industrial Union Dep't., 448 U.S. at 675.
58. Ibid.
59. Antonin Scalia, "A Note on the Benzene Case," *Regulation* (Jul.–Aug. 1980): 28.
60. National Ambient Air Quality Standards for Particulate Matter, 62 Fed. Reg. 38,652 (1997). The agency found that particulate matter in the air was responsible for 60,000 premature deaths in the United States each year. See "Particles in Air Help Kill 60,000 a Year, Study Says," *New York Times,* May 13, 1991: A13.
61. *Am. Trucking Ass'ns v. EPA*, 175 F.3d 1027, 1036 (D.C. Cir.), modified in part and reh'g en banc denied, 195 F.3d 4 (D.C. Cir. 1999), and rev'd in part sub nom. *Whitman v. Am. Trucking Ass'ns*, 531 U.S. 457 (2001), at 1037.
62. Ibid.
63. For an argument to this effect, see Lisa S. Bressman, "Disciplining Delegation after Whitman v. American Trucking Associations," *Cornell Law Review* 87 (2002): 452–85.
64. For a good introduction to the regime of regulatory contracting, see Jody Freeman, "Collaborative Governance in the Administrative State," *UCLA Law Review* 45 (1997).
65. Stewart, "Environmental Regulation," p. 60.
66. Ibid., p. 61.
67. William F. Pedersen, "Regulatory Reform Contracts and Regulatory Reform," *Environmental Law Reporter* (ELR) 2002, 32 (5): 10589–593; quotation at p. 10591.
68. Ibid.
69. Ibid., p. 10590.
70. Bruce A. Ackerman and William T. Hassler, *Clean Coal/Dirty Air: Or How the Clean Air Act Became a Multibillion-Dollar Bail-Out for High-Sulfur Coal Producers and What Should Be Done About It* (New Haven: Yale University Press, 1981).
71. The concept of "trading under a cap," exemplified by the market for sulfur-dioxide allowances under 1990 Amendments to the CAA, illustrates this approach. It has been so thoroughly discussed, celebrated, and criticized in the literature that there is little need to comment further about it here. An excellent "Tradable Permits Biography," compiled by Tom Tietenberg, is available online at: http://www.colby.edu/personal/t/thtieten/trade.html.

    Some good discussions of "cap-and-trade" strategies include: Daniel Dudek and John Palmisano, "Emissions Trading: Why Is This Thoroughbred Hobbled?" *Columbia Journal of Environmental Law* 13 (1988); Robert W. Hahnand and Robert N. Stavins, "Incentive-Based Environmental Regulation: A New Era from an Old Idea?" *Ecology Law Quarterly* 18 (1991); Lisa Heinzerling, "Selling Pollution, Forcing Democracy," *Stanford Environmental Law Journal* 14 (May 1995): 300–44; and Gary Bryner,

"Market Incentives in Air Pollution Control," in *Flashpoints in Environmental Policymaking: Controversies in Achieving Sustainability*, Sheldon Kamieniecki et al., eds. (Albany: State University of New York Press, 1997), pp. 85–102.

72. The polluter would not be required to use the "best available technology" in use elsewhere but to achieve at least as good results in whatever way it chooses. One goal of regulatory contracting is to give the polluter an incentive to develop better than state-of-the-art control technology, for example, by allowing excess reductions as offsets. For an excellent essay on the use of "benchmarking" in regulatory contracts – as well as a superb study of other instruments useful to a contracting state – see Michael C. Dorf and Charles F. Sabel, "A Constitution of Democratic Experimentalism," *Columbia Law Review* 98 (March 1998): 267–473.

73. For the history and careful description of negotiated rulemaking in the United States, see *Rulemaking: How Government Agencies Write Law and Make Policy*, 2d ed. (Washington, DC: CQ Press, 1998). For a comparison of environmental contracts in the United States and Europe, see *Environmental Contracts: Comparative Approaches to Regulatory Innovation in the United States and Europe*, Eric W. Orts and Kurt Deketelaere, eds. (Boston: Kluwer Law International, 2001).

74. Jody Freeman, "The Contracting State," *Florida State University Law Review* 28 (Fall 2000) 155–214; quotation at p. 155.

75. Ibid. p. 190.

76. For discussion, see Gert Winter, "Bartering Rationality in Regulation," *Law and Society Review*, 19 (1985): 219–35, and John T. Scholz, "Cooperation, Deterrence and the Ecology of Regulatory Enforcement," *Law and Society Review* 18 (1984): 179–224.

77. The literature on Project XL (for "Excellence and Leadership") is immense. For the government's own assessment, see USEPA, Office of the Administrator, "Project Results," pp. 6–38 in *Project XL: 1999 Comprehensive Report*, EPA-100-R-99-008 (Washington, DC: October 1999). For another positive account of examples, see Dennis Hirsch, "Project XL and the Special Case: The EPA's Untold Success Story," *Columbia Law Journal* 26 (2001): 219–57. See also Joshua Secunda and Laurence F. Susskind, "'Improving' Project XL: Helping Adaptive Management to Work Within EPA," *UCLA Journal of Environmental Law and Policy* 17 (1999): 50–63; Joshua Secunda and Lawrence E. Susskind, "The Risks and Advantages of Agency Discretion: Evidence from EPA's Project XL," *UCLA Journal of Environmental Law and Policy* 17 (1998/1999): 83–92; and Mark Seidenfeld, "Empowering Stakeholders: Limits on Collaboration as the Basis for Flexible Regulation," *William and Mary Law Review* 41 (2000): 411–40.

78. E. Donald Elliott, "Toward Ecological Law and Policy," in *Thinking Ecologically: The Next Generation of Environmental Policy*, Marian R. Chertow and Daniel C. Esty, eds. (New Haven, CT: Yale University Press, 1997); quotation at p. 183.

79. Royal C. Gardner, "Banking on Entrepreneurs: Wetlands, Mitigation Banking, and Takings," *Iowa Law Review* 81 (1996): 527–87.

80. Robert L. Fischman and Jaelith Hall-Rivera, "A Lesson for Conservation from Pollution Control Law: Cooperative Federalism for Recovery Under the Endangered Species Act," *Columbia Journal of Environmental Law* 27 (2002): 45–172.

81. See Charles C. Caldart and Nicholas A. Ashford, "Negotiation as a Means of Developing and Implementing Environmental and Occupational Health and Safety Policy," *Harvard Environmental Law Review* 23 (1999): 141–202.

82. See Project XL Site-Specific Rulemaking for Merck & Co., Inc. Stonewall Plant, 62 Fed. Reg. 52,622, 52,627 (1997).

83. For a good discussion of "knee-of-the-curve" regulation at the Federal Energy Regulatory Commssion, see Leonard Shabman and Kurt Stephenson, "Environmental Valuation and Its Economic Critics," *Journal of Water Resources Planning and Management* 126 (6) (November–December 2000): 382–88, esp. p. 386.

84. Richard Cookson makes this point well in a reply to an earlier version of this chapter. See R. Cookson, "Welfare Economic Dogmas: A Reply to Sagoff," *Environmental Values* 5 (1996): 59–74; available online at: http://www.erica.demon.co.uk/EV/EV504.html.

85. K. J. Arrow, "The Organisation of Economic Activity: Issues Pertinent to the Choice of Market Versus Nonmarket Allocation," *The Analysis and Evaluation of Public Expenditures: the PPB system, US Congress, Joint Economic Committee* 1 (1969): 47–64.

86. For discussion, Thomas H. Tietenberg, "Economic Instruments for Environmental Protection," *Oxford Review of Economic Policy* 17 (1990): 17–33.

87. In fact, sulfur dioxide emissions have been cut by about half. For a good technical account of how this happened, see Paul L. Joskow et al., "The Market for Sulfur Dioxide Emissions," *American Economic Review* 88 (1998): 669–85.

88. J. Clarence Davies and Jan Mazurek, *Pollution Control in the United States* (Washington, DC: Resources for the Future, 1998), p. 140. Even sophisticated "cap-and-trade" strategies, however, are not immune to old-fashioned market corruption. Enron was the nation's leading emission-allowance trader and, as of this writing, no one knows how its collapse will affect the program. Available online at: http://www.enron.com/wholesale/emissions/.

89. This is an overstatement. In fact, the political and technical issues involved in reducing sulfur dioxide may be more important than the economic ones. For a more jaundiced view of the incentives program, see Richard F. Kosobud, "Emissions Trading from the Shadows," *Emissions Trading: Environmental Policy's New Approach* (New York: John Wiley, 2000). For an excellent study of the immense complexities that surround this and

other "cap-and-trade" strategies, see Jonathan Remy Nash and Richard L. Revesz, "Markets and Geography: Designing Marketable Permit Schemes to Control Local and Regional Pollution," *Ecology Law Quarterly* 28(2001): 569–660.

Chapter 6

1. Doug Tomkins, "Remarks to the 2001 Land Trust Alliance Rally," Baltimore, MD, October 2, 2001; available online at: http://www.lta.org/training/rally2001_tompkins.htm.
2. James Langman, "Thinking Big: After Founding Esprit and North Face, Doug Tompkins Dresses Up an 800,000-Acre Park," *e-magazine.com*, September–October 1997 available online at: http://www.emagazine.com/september-october_1997/0997curr_esprit_html.
3. John Muir, *The Yosemite* (New York: Century Co., 1912), p. 256.
4. Char Miller, *Gifford Pinchot and the Making of Modern Environmentalism* (Washington, DC: Island Press, 2001), pp. 140–41.
5. John Muir, "Hetch-Hetchy Valley," *Sierra Club Bulletin* (January 1908): 220.
6. Gretchen C. Daily, Susan Alexander, Paul R. Ehrlich, et al., "Ecosystem Services: Benefits Supplied to Human Societies by Natural Ecosystems," published as a white paper by the Ecological Society of America. Available online at: http://esa.sdsc.edu/daily.htm and reprinted in *Issues in Ecology*, 2(Spring 1997).
7. Ibid.
8. Jocelyn Kaiser, "Role Model for Ecology's Generation X," *Science* 287(5456) (February 18, 2000): 1191.
9. Simon Levin, *Fragile Dominion* (Reading, MA: Perseus Books, 1999), p. 204.
10. Graciela Chichilnisky and Geoffrey Heal, "Economic Returns from the Biosphere," *Nature* 391 (February 1998): 629–30.
11. Levin, *Fragile Dominion*, p. 204.
12. Edward O. Wilson, "What Is Nature Worth?" *Wilson Quarterly* 26(1) (Winter 2002): 20–39, quotation at pp. 23–24.
13. National Science Board, *Task Force on the Environment, Environmental Science and Engineering for the 21ˢᵗ Century: The Role of the National Science Foundation*, available online at: http://www.nsf.gov/cgi-bin/getpub?nsb0022 and http://www.nsf.gov/nsb/tfe/nsb99133/box1.htm.
14. Robert B. Jackson, Stephen R. Carpenter, Clifford N. Dahm, Diane M. McKnight, et al., "Water in a Changing World," available online by the Ecological Society of America, Issues in Ecology, at http://www.esa.org/issues9.htm and reprinted in *Ecological Applications* August 11, 2001: 1027–45.
15. http://www.rand.org/scitech/stpi/ourfuture/NaturesServices/section1.html. This publication, IP-203, is part of the RAND Issue Papers series.

16. Chichilnisky and Heal, "Economic Returns from the Biosphere," pp. 629–30.

17. Committee to Review the New York City Watershed Management Strategy, National Research Council [NRC], *Watershed Management for a Potable Water Supply: Assessing the New York City Strategy* (Washington, DC: National Academy Press, 2000), p. 200; available online at: http://www.nap.edu/catalog/9677.html?se_side.

18. Ibid., p. 65.

19. Ibid., p. 194.

20. Ibid., p. 23.

21. Ibid., pp. 77, 181.

22. Ibid., p. 82.

23. Ibid., p. 161.

24. Ibid., p. 197.

25. Ibid., p. 160.

26. New York City Municipal Water Finance Authority at: http://www.nyc.gov/html/nyw/home.html.

27. Raymond Orlando, Head of Investor Relations, New York City Municipal Water Finance Authority, telephone conversation with the author February 5, 2002.

28. New York City Independent Budget Office, "The Clean Water/Clean Air Bond Act of 1996: Fiscal Impact on New York City," available online at: http://www.ibo.nyc.ny.us/iboreports/pubwater.html.

29. Surface Water Treatment Regulations, US EPA, 40 CFR, Part 141.

30. W. R. MacKenzie, N. J. Hoxie, M. E. Proctor, M. S. Gradus, et al., "A Massive Outbreak in Milwaukee of Cryptosporidium Infection Transmitted through the Public Water Supply," *New England Journal of Medicine* 331(3)(July 21, 1994):161–67.

31. American Water Works Association, E-Mainstream, available online at: http://www.awwa.org/mainstream/archives/2001/september/ms0901ww.htm.

32. New York City Department of Environmental Protection, "New York City's Water Supply System, Watershed Agreement Overview," available online at: http://www.ci.nyc.ny.us/html/dep/html/agreement.html.

33. NRC, *Watershed Management*, p. 107, citing NRC 1999, available online at: http://www.epa.gov/OWOW/watershed/framework.html.

34. Ibid., p. 503.

35. Ibid., p. 502.

36. World Resources Institute Report (2000–2001): p. 210 available online at: http://www.wri.org/wr2000/pdf/freshwater_nyc.pdf.

37. Richard Perez-Pena, "Court Blocks a Water Plant in Bronx Park," *New York Times* February 9, 2001: B1.

38. Eric A. Goldstein and Mark Izeman, "Plug the City's Leaky Water Supply," *Newsday*, April, 24, 2001: A36.

39. Winnie Hu, "Group Says City Fails to Keep Its Part of a Clean-Water Pact," *New York Times*, June 28, 2000: B4.

40. New York Department of Natural Resources News Release available online at: http://www.ci.nyc.ny.us/html/dep/html/press/01-50pr.html.

41. Office of the Mayor, New York City, PR-364-03, December 19, 2003. "Mayor Michael R. Bloomberg and EPA Administrator Michael Leavitt Announce $25 Million for Land Acquisition to Protect Croton Watershed." Available online at: http://www.nyc.gov/portal/index. jsp?.

42. According to the New York City Watershed Agreement, "The City will spend $250 million in the Catskill & Delaware Watershed and $10 million in the Croton Watershed to acquire property deemed important for drinking water quality protection." "Governor Pataki Signs Historic Agreement on NYC Watershed," *New York State Press Release*, January 21, 1997; available online at: http://www.dec.state.ny.us/website/press/govrel/jan21. html.

43. John Stuart Mill, "Nature," in *Three Essays on Religion*, the 1874 edition (New York: Greenwood Press, 1969). Available online at: http://www. lancs.ac.uk/users/philosophy/texts/mill_on.htm.

44. Ibid., p. 12

45. Robert Costanza, Ralph d'Arge, Rudolf de Groot, et al., "The Value of the World's Ecosystem Services and Natural Capital," *Nature* 387 (May 15, 1987), 253–60.

46. Andrew Balmford, Aaron Bruner, Philip Cooper, et al., "Economic Reasons for Conserving Wild Nature," *Science* 297 (August 9, 2002): 950–53.

47. William K. Stevens, "How Much Is Nature Worth? For You, $33 Trillion," *New York Times*, May 20, 1997, Section c, p. 1.

48. Charles Petit, "Natural Environment Gets a Price Tag – $33 Trillion," *San Francisco Chronicle*, May 15, 1997, p. A7.

49. Gretchen C. Daily, *Nature's Services: Societal Dependence on Natural Ecosystems* (Washington, DC: Island Press, 1997).

50. Quoted in Petit, "Natural Environment."

51. Stuart L. Pimm, "The Value of Everything," *Nature* 387 (6230) (May 15, 1997): 231–232.

52. Nancy E. Bockstael, A. Myrick Freeman III, Raymond J. Kopp, Paul R. Portney, and V. Kerry Smith. "On Measuring Economic Values for Nature," *Environmental Science and Technology* 34 (8) (2000): 1384–89.

53. Ibid., p. 1385.

54. Ibid.

55. Ibid.

56. Ibid.

57. Ibid.

58. E. P. Odum, "Prerequisites for Sustainability," *Biosphere 2 Newsletter*, (Fall 1993): 1–8.

59. Robert Costanza, Herman E. Daly, and Joy A. Bartholomew, "Goals, Agenda, and Policy Recommendations for Ecological Economics," in *Ecological Economics: The Science and Management of Sustainability*, Robert Costanza, ed. (New York: Columbia University Press, 1991), 1–20.

Chapter 7

1. Herman Daly, "Elements of Environmental Macroeconomics," in *Ecological Economics: The Science and Management of Sustainability*, R. Costanza, ed. (New York: Columbia University Press, 1996), pp. 32–46. I wish to thank Herman Daly for helping me at every step to make the argument of this chapter as strong as I could and for writing a fair and trenchant reply. See Herman Daly, "Reply to Mark Sagoff's 'Carrying Capacity and Ecological Economics,'" *BioScience* 45(9) (Oct. 1995), pp. 621–24.
2. John Muir, *The Yosemite* (New York: Century Co., 1912), p. 256.
3. H. J. Barnett and C. Morse, *Scarcity and Growth: The Economics of Natural Resource Availability* (Baltimore, MD: Johns Hopkins University Press, 1963).
4. John V. Krutilla, "Conservation Reconsidered," *American Economics Review* 57(1967): 777.
5. Ibid., p. 777.
6. Ibid., p. 778.
7. World Bank, *World Development Report*, 1991. This document contains a sustained argument against the views of ecological economics and defends the neoclassical assumption that, with technological advance and good government, resources do not limit growth.
8. Herman Daly, "Moving to a Steady-state Economy," in *The Cassandra Conference: Resources and the Human Predicament*, P. R. Ehrlich and J. P. Holdren, eds. (College Station: Texas A&M Press, 1985), pp. 271–87.
9. Herman Daly, "Sustainable Growth: An Impossibility Theorem," in *Valuing the Earth: Economics, Ecology, Ethics*, H. E. Daly and K. N. Townsend, eds. (Cambridge, MA: MIT Press, 1993), pp. 267–74, quotation at p. 268.
10. R. Costanza, H. E. Daly, and J. A. Bartholomew, "Goals, Agenda, and Policy Recommendations for Ecological Economics," in *Ecological Economics: The Science and Management of Sustainability*. R. Costanza, ed. (New York: Columbia University Press, 1991), pp. 1–20, quotation at p. 8.
11. Peter Drucker, *Post Capitalist Society* (New York: Harper Business, 1993), p. 45.
12. Ibid., p. 8.
13. According to J. E. Stiglitz, "Comments: Some Retrospective Views on Growth Theory," in *Growth, Productivity, Unemployment*, Peter Diamond, ed. (Cambridge, MA: MIT Press, 1990), pp. 50–67, quotation at p. 53.
14. W. B. Nordhaus and J. Tobin, "Is Growth Obsolete?" in *Economic Growth* (New York: Columbia University Press, 1972), p. 14.
15. T. H. Lee, "Advanced Fossil Fuel Systems and Beyond," in *Technology and Environment*, J. H. Ausubel and H. E. Sladovich, eds. (Washington, DC: National Academy Press, 1989), pp. 114–36.
16. World Resources Institute, *World Resources 1994–95* (New York: Oxford University Press, 1995).
17. Ibid., p. 189.
18. World Bank, *World Development Report 1992: Development and the Environment* (New York: Oxford University Press, 1992), p. 38.

19. R. M. Solow, "A Contribution to the Theory of Economic Growth," *Quarterly Journal of Economics* 70(1956): 65–94, quotation at p. 53.
20. Herman Daly, *Steady State Economics*, 2d ed. (Washington, DC: Island Press, 1991), p. 108.
21. Robert Solow, "The Economics of Resources or the Resources of Economics," *American Economic Review* 64(1974): 1–14; quotation at pp. 10–11.
22. Vacliv Smil, *Global Ecology: Environmental Change and Social Flexibility* (London: Routledge, 1993); quotation at p. 57.
23. World Resources Institute, *World Resources*, p. 6.
24. Ibid., p. 5.
25. D. C. Hall and J. V. Hall, "Concepts and Measures of Natural Resource Scarcity with a Summary of Recent Trends," *Journal of Environmental Economics and Management* 11(1984): 363–79. See also Margaret E. Slade, "Trends in Natural-resources Commodity Prices: An Analysis of the Time Domain," *Journal of Environmental Economics and Management* 9(1982): 122–37.
26. P. Dasgupta and G. Heal, *Economic Theory and Exhaustible Resources* (Cambridge: Cambridge Economic Handbooks, 1979); see also A. C. Fisher, "Measures of Natural Resource Scarcity," in *Scarcity and Growth Reconsidered*, V. K. Smith, ed. (Baltimore, MD: Johns Hopkins University Press, 1979), pp. 249–75; and V. Kerry Smith and John V. Krutilla, "Toward Reformulating the Role of Natural Resources in Economic Models," in *Explorations in Natural Resource Economics*, V. Kerry Smith and John V. Krutilla, eds. (Baltimore, MD: Johns Hopkins University Press, 1982), pp. 3–29.
27. R. U. Ayres and A. V. Kneese, "Production, Consumption, and Externalities," *American Economic Review* 59(1969): 282–97. See also M. I. Kamien and N. L. Schwartz, "The Role of Common Property Resources in Optimal Planning Models with Exhaustible Resources," in *Explorations in Natural Resource Economics*, V. K. Smith and J. V. Krutilla, eds. (Baltimore, MD: Johns Hopkins University Press, 1982), pp. 47–66.
28. Talbot Page, *Conservation and Economic Efficiency: An Approach to Materials Policy*. (Baltimore, MD: Johns Hopkins University Press, 1977).
29. C. S. Holling, *Adaptive Environmental Assessment and Management* (New York: John Wiley, 1978); see also M. Common, *Sustainability and Policy: Limits to Economics* (New York: Cambridge University Press, 1985).
30. Paul and Anne Ehrlich, *The End of Affluence* (New York: Ballantine Books, 1974).
31. Daly, "Steady State Economy."
32. N. Georgescu-Roegen, "The Entropy Law and the Economic Problem," in *Toward a Steady-State Economy*, H. E. Daly, ed. (Baltimore, MD: Johns Hopkins University Press, 1973), pp. 37–49.
33. Herman Daly, "Entropy, Growth, and the Political Economy of Scarcity," in *Scarcity and Growth Reconsidered*, V. K. Smith, ed. (Baltimore, MD: Johns Hopkins University Press, 1979), pp. 67–94; quotation at p. 69.

34. John Holdren, "The Energy Predicament in Perspective," *Confronting Climate Change* (New York: Cambridge University Press, 1991), pp. 163–69.

35. World Bank, *World Development 1992*, p. 115.

36. K. N. Townsend, "Is Entropy Relevant to the Economics of Natural Resource Scarcity?" *Journal of Environmental Economics and Management* 23(1992): 96–100.

37. Georgescu-Roegen, "Entropy Law," pp. 37–49; quotation at p. 47.

38. P. Dunn, *Renewable Energies: Sources, Conversion and Application* (London: Peregrinus, Institution of Electrical Engineers, 1986), p. 26.

39. L. R. Brown, D. Denniston, C. Flavin, et al., *State of the World 1995* (New York: W. W. Norton, 1995), p. 64.

40. L. R. Brown, C. Flavin, and S. Postel, *Saving the Planet* (New York: W. W. Norton, 1991), p. 48.

41. P. Gleick, "Water and Energy," *Annual Review of Energy and the Environment* 19(1994): 267–99; see p. 290.

42. T. B. Johansson, H. Kelly, A. K. N. Reddy, and R. H. Williams, *Renewable Energy* (Washington, DC: Island Press, 1993), p. 1.

43. National Academy of Sciences, *Geothermal Energy Technology: Issues, R&D Needs, and Cooperative Arrangements* (Washington, DC: National Academy Press, 1987).

44. A. B. Lovins and H. L. Lovins, "Least-Cost Climatic Stabilization," *Annual Review of Energy and the Environment* 16(1991): 433–531; quotation at p. 433.

45. A. B. Lovins, "Energy, People, and Industrialization," in *Resources, Environment, and Population: Present Knowledge, Future Options*, K. Davis and N. S. Bernstam, eds. (New York: Oxford University Press, 1991), pp. 95–124.

46. C. Folke, M. Hammer, R. Costanza, and A. Jansson, "Investing in Natural Capital – Why, What, and How?" in *Investing in Natural Capital: The Ecological Economics Approach to Sustainability*, A. Jansson, M. Hammer, C. Folke, and R. Costanza, eds. (Washington, DC: Island Press, 1994), pp. 1–20.

47. "Ecological Economics and the Carrying Capacity of the Earth," in *Investing in Natural Capital*, A. Jansson et al., eds. (Washington, DC: Island Press, 1994), pp. 38–56.

48. "Operationalizing Sustainable Development by Investing in Natural Capital," *Investing in Natural Capital*, A. Jansson et al., eds. (Washington, DC: Island Press, 1994), pp. 22–37.

49. Herman Daly, "Toward Some Operational Principles of Sustainable Development," *Ecological Economics* 2(1990): 1–6; quotation at p. 3.

50. C. W. Clark, "Economic Biases Against Sustainable Development," in *Ecological Economics: The Science and Management of Sustainability*, R. Costanza, ed. (New York: Columbia University Press, 1991), pp. 319–30.

51. R. Heifner and R. Kinoshita, "Differences among Commodities in Real Price Variability and Drift," *Journal of Agricultural Economics Research* 45(1995): 10–20.

52. Robert Solow, *An Almost Practical Step Toward Sustainability* (Washington, DC: Resources for the Future, 1992), pp. 8–9.

53. Herman Daly, "Operationalizing Sustainable Development by Investing in Natural Capital," in *Investing in Natural Capital*, A. Jansson et al., eds. (Washington, DC: Island Press, 1994), pp. 22–37.

54. World Resources Institute, *World Resources*, p. 131.

55. Ibid., pp. 79, 134.

56. *The State of World Fisheries and Aquaculture 2000*. Rome: FAO, 2000. Available online at: http://www.fao.org/DOCREP/003/X8002E/X8002Eoo.htm.

57. N. Lord, "Born to Be Wild," *Sierra* (November/December 1994): 60–65, 73.

58. E. Hempel, "Norway's Salmon Capacity Is Now Nearly 300,000 Tons," *Fish Farming International* July 1994: 22–23.

59. Herman Daly, "Sustainable Development: From Concept and Theory to Operational Principles," in *Resources, Environment, and Population: Present Knowledge and Future Options*, K. Davis and M. S. Bernstein, eds. (New York: Oxford University Press, 1991), pp. 25–43.

60. Ibid.

61. Herman Daly, "On Wilfred Beckerman's Critique of Sustainable Development," *Environmental Values* 4(1)(1995): 49–55.

62. Folke, Hammer, Costanza, and Jansson, "Investing in Natural Capital."

63. H. E. Daly and K. N. Townsend, "Introduction," in *Valuing the Earth: Economics, Ecology, Ethics*, H. E. Daly and K. N. Townsend, eds. (Cambridge, MA: MIT Press, 1993), pp. 1–10.

64. Daly, "Sustainable Growth: An Impossibility Theorem," p. 267.

65. M. Brower, *Cool Energy* (Cambridge, MA: MIT Press, 1992), p. 13.

66. Department of Energy, United Kingdom, *Digest of United Kingdom Energy Statistics* (London: H.M.S.O., 1990) Table A1.

67. W. R. Moomaw and D. M. Tullis, "Charting Development Paths: A Multicountry Comparison of Carbon Dioxide Emissions," *G-DAE Discussion Paper #2, Global Development and Environment Institute* (Medford, MA: Tufts University Press, 1994).

68. N. Myers, "Population and Biodiversity," in *Population – the Complex Reality*, F. Graham-Smith, ed. (Golden, CO: North American Press, 1994), pp. 117–36.

69. N. Myers, "The Question of Linkages in Environment and Development," *BioScience* 43(5)(1993): 306.

70. R. Costanza, H. E. Daly, and J. A. Bartholomew, "Goals, Agenda, and Policy Recommendations for Ecological Economics," in *Ecological Economics: The Science and Management of Sustainability*, R. Costanza, ed. (New York: Columbia University Press, 1991), pp. 1–20.

71. R. Goodland, "The Case That the World Has Reached Its Limits," in *Population, Technology, and Lifestyle: The Transition to Sustainability*, R. Goodland, H. E. Daly, and S. El Serafy, eds. (Washington, DC: Island Press, 1993), pp. 3–22.

72. P. M. Vitousek, P. R. Ehrlich, A. H. Ehrlich, and P. Matson, "Human Appropriation of the Products of Photosynthesis," *BioScience* 36(6)(June 1986): 368–73; quotation at p. 372.

73. W. E. Rees and M. Wackernagel, "Ecological Footprints and Appropriated Carrying Capacity: Measuring the Natural Capital Requirement of the Human Economy," in *Investing in Natural Capital*, A. Jansson et al., eds. (Washington, DC: Island Press, 1994), pp. 362–90.
74. P. R. Ehrlich and A. H. Ehrlich, *The Population Explosion* (New York: Simon and Schuster, 1990), p. 269, n29.
75. Ibid., p. 37.
76. Richard Leakey and Roger Lewin, *The Sixth Extinction: Biodiversity and Its Survival* (London: Phoenix, 1998), ch. 13.
77. Stuart Pimm, *The World According to Pimm* (New York: McGraw-Hill, 2001), p. 9.
78. Ibid., p. 13.
79. Vitousek et al., "Appropriation," p. 369.
80. See also Pimm, *The World*, p. 18.
81. I follow Pimm's estimates, ibid., pp. 19–20.
82. Vacliv Smil, *The Earth's Biosphere: Evolution, Dynamics, and Change* (Cambridge, MA: MIT Press, 2002), p. 209.
83. Colin Tudge, "The Rise and Fall of Homo Sapiens," *Philosophical Transactions of the Royal Society of London* 325(1989), pp. 24–42.
84. Amartya Sen wrote in 1994, "food output is being held back by a lack of effective demand in the marketplace" rather than by ecological constraints on production. Amartya Sen, "Population: Delusion and Reality," *New York Review of Books*, Sept. 22, 1994. See also: Norman E. Borlaug, "Feeding a World of 10 Billion People: The Miracle Ahead," available online at: http://agriculture.tusk.ude/biotech/monfort2.html. "Had the world's food supply been distributed evenly, it would have provided an adequate diet (2,350 calories, principally from grain) in 1994 for 6.4 billion people – about 800 million more than the actual population."
85. Vitousek et al., "Appropriation," p. 370.
86. William Cronon, *Changes in the Land* (New York: Hill and Wang, 1983).
87. Vitousek et al., "Appropriation," p. 372.
88. P. E. Waggoner, *How Much Land Can Ten Billion People Spare for Nature?* (Ames, IA: Council for Agricultural Science and Technology, Task Force Report 121, 1994), pp. 26–27.
89. J. Anderson, "Feeding a Hungrier World," *Washington Post*, February 13, 1995: A3.
90. Vitousek et al., "Appropriation," p. 372.
91. Arthur Lovejoy, *The Great Chain of Being: A Study of the History of an Idea* (New York: Harper & Row, 1960).
92. G. P. Marsh, *Man and Nature; or Physical Geography as Modified by Human Action*, D. Lowenthal, ed. (Cambridge, MA: Harvard University Press, 1864, 1965).
93. A. M. Riabchikov, *The Changing Face of the Earth: The Structure and Dynamics of the Geosphere, Its Natural Development and the Changes Caused by Man.* John Williams, trans. (Moscow: Progress Publishers, 1975).
94. Bil McKibben, *The End of Nature* (New York: Random House, 1989).
95. Charles Mann, "1491." *Atlantic Monthly* (March 2000): 41–53. Available online at: http://www.theatlantic.com/issues/2002/03/ mann.htm.

96. N. Georgescu-Roegen, "Comments on the Papers by Daly and Stiglitz," in *Scarcity and Growth Reconsidered*, V. K. Smith, ed. (Baltimore, MD: Johns Hopkins University Press, 1979) p. 98. Available online at http://pareto. uab.es/wp/2002/51702.pdf.

97. Herman Daly, "Operationalizing Sustainable Development by Investing in Natural Capital," in *Investing in Natural Capital*, A. Jansson et al., eds. (Washington, DC: Island Press, 1994), pp. 22–37.

98. Stephen H. Schneider, "Climate and Food: Signs of Hope, Despair, and Opportunity," in *The Cassandra Conference*, P. Ehrlich and J. P. Holdren, eds. (College Station: Texas A&M Press, 1985), pp. 17–51.

99. E. O. Wilson, "Resolutions for the 80's," *Harvard Magazine* (January–February 1980): 22–26.

Chapter 8

1. James G. March, *A Primer in Decision Making* (New York: Free Press, 1994), p. viii.

2. Herman B. Leonard and Richard J. Zeckhauser, "Cost-Benefit Analysis Applied to Risks: Its Philosophy and Legitimacy," in *Values at Risk*, Douglas MacLean, ed. (Lanham, MD: Rowman and Allanheld, 1986), pp. 31–48, quotation at p. 34.

3. Barry C. Field, *Environmental Economics: An Introduction*, 2d ed. (New York: McGraw-Hill, 1997), p. 19.

4. Edith Stokey and Richard Zeckhauser, *A Primer for Policy Analysis* (New York: W. W. Norton, 1978), p. 151.

5. Kenneth J. Arrow, Maureen L. Cropper, George C. Eads, et al., "Is There a Role for Benefit-Cost Analysis in Environmental, Health, and Safety Regulation?" *Science* 272 (April 12, 1996): 221–22.

6. Ibid., p. 221.

7. Ibid., p. 222.

8. Ibid. Economic efficiency is the principal goal of environmental regulation, for example, pollution control, and redistributive issues should be handled separately. "[E]nvironmental, health, and safety regulations are neither effective or efficient tools for achieving redistributional goals."

9. Joseph E. Stiglitz, *Whither Socialism?* (Cambridge, MA: MIT Press, 1994), p. 2.

10. Ibid., p. 11.

11. Ronald Coase showed that the cooperative structure of a firm – as contrasted with the competitive structure of a market – is often more conducive to economic performance. R. H. Coase, *The Nature of the Firm* (1937), reprinted in *The Nature of the Firm*, Oliver E. Williamson and Sidney G. Winter, eds. (New York: Oxford University Press, 1991). The vertical integration of an industry (as contrasted with arms-length contractual bargains) can also be explained as an advantage of organization and cooperation over competition. See Oliver E. Williamson, *Markets and Hierarchies: Analysis and Antitrust Implications* (New York: Free Press, 1975); and Oliver E. Williamson, "Transaction-Cost Economics: The Governance of Contractual Relations," *Journal of Law and Economics* 22 (1979): 233–53.

12. Michael C. Dorf and Charles F. Sabel, "A Constitution of Democratic Experimentalism," *Columbia Law Review* 98 (March 1998): 267–473.

13. See Bradley C. Karkkainen, "Information as Environmental Regulation: TRI and Performance Benchmarking, Precursor to a New Paradigm?" *Georgetown Law Journal* 89 (January 2001): 257–370.

14. A vast literature describes and evaluates these methods of changing incentive structures to protect environmental quality. For a good general introduction, see Richard B. Stewart, "A New Generation of Environmental Regulation," *Capital University Law Review* 29(1)(2001): 21–182, and citations therein. See also Robert N. Stavins, "Lessons from the American Experiment with Market-Based Environmental Policies," *Social Science Network Electronic Paper Collection* (220). Available online at: http://papers.ssrn.com/abstract_id=285998. Much of the best work by economists who write on environmental policy identifies and analyzes the political economy of regulation, i.e., the political groups and forces that shape results. This is a far cry from cost-benefit analysis.

15. For facts and figures, see Robert H. Nelson, "How to Reform Grazing Policy: Creating Forage Rights on Federal Rangelands," *Fordham Environmental Law Journal* 8 (1997): 645–90.

16. These numbers are subject to fluctuation. See Richard Manning, *Grassland: The History, Biology, Politics, and Promise of the American Prairie* (New York: Viking, 1995), p. 132.

17. Nelson, "How to Reform Grazing Policy," esp. n. 44.

18. Nelson, "How to Reform Grazing Policy."

19. T. H. Watkins, "High Noon in Cattle Country," *Sierra Magazine* (March/ April) 2000. For discussion of the long-standing opposition of environmental groups to grazing, see Lynn Jacobs, *Waste of the West: Public Lands Ranching* (Tucson, AZ: Jacobs, 1992); Edward Abby, "Even the Bad Guys Wear White Hats," *Harper's* (Jan. 1986): 51–55; and Debra L. Donnahue, *The Western Range Revisited: Removing Livestock from the Public Range to Conserve Native Biodiversity* (Norman: University of Oklahoma Press, 1999).

20. L. Allen Torrell et al., "The Market Value of Public Land Forage Implied from Grazing Permits," in *Current Issues in Rangeland Economics*, Neil R. Rimbey and Diane E. Isaak, eds. (Moscow: University of Idaho, 1994), 80. Robert Nelson ("How to Reform Grazing Policy") estimates that if the typical AUM runs to 15 acres, the typical "buyout" price for a BLM permit would range between about $2.50 to $6.00 per acre.

21. B. Delworth Gardner, "A Proposal to Reduce Misallocation of Livestock Grazing Permits," *Journal of Farm Economics* 45 (1963): 109–28.

22. See, e.g., Jerry L Holechek, "Policy Changes on Federal Rangelands: A Perspective," *Journal of Soil and Water Conservation* (May–June) 1993; and William E. Martin, "Mitigating the Economic Impacts of Agency Programs for Public Rangelands," National Research Council/National Academy of Sciences, *Developing Strategies for Rangeland Management* (Washington, DC: NRC-NAS, 1994).

23. Dave Foreman, "Around the Campfire," *Wild Earth* (Fall 1995): 2–3.

24. Karl Hess, Jr., and Johanna H. Wald, "Grazing Reform: Here's the Answer," *High Country News*, Oct. 2, 1995: 14.

25. Sharman Russell, "Home on the Range," *Southwestern New Mexico Online*. Available at: http://www.southernnewmexico.com/snm/range.html

26. Ibid.

27. Andy Kerr, "Don't Try to Improve Grazing. Abolish It!" *High Country News*, 26(11)(June 13, 1994). Available online at: http://www.hcn.org/servlets/hcn.URLRemapper/1994/jun13/dir/othervoices.html.

28. Todd Wilkenson, "Ranchers Band Together to Resist Sprawl," *Christian Science Monitor*, July 29, 2002: p. 3.

29. Nelson, "How to Reform Grazing Policy."

30. Andy Kerr, "The Voluntary Retirement Option for Federal Public Land Grazing Permittees," *Wild Earth* 8(3)(Fall 1998): 63–67, quotation at pp. 66–67. Similarly, Dave Foreman, founder of the radical group Earth First!, has endorsed a strategy to "buy out grazing permittees in Wilderness Areas, National Parks, Wildlife Refuges, and other reserves. The butting-head battles with ranchers over grazing in Wilderness is bad news for all involved. The most practical way and fairest way to end grazing in Wilderness is to buy 'em out, instead of forcing its removal." Dave Foreman, "Around the Campfire," *Wild Earth* 5(Fall 1995): 2–3.

31. 43 C.F.R. § 4120.3-2 (2000); upheld in *Public Lands Council v. Babbitt*, 120 S. Ct. 1815 (U.S. 2000).

32. Dave Livermore, "Director's Report: Cows vs. Condos," *Basin Range and Ridgerock*, 2 (Newsletter of the Nature Conservancy of Utah, Fall 1996). The "Cows Are Better Than Condos" motto, now often seen on bumper stickers, has become a mantra. See, e.g., Eric Pooley, "Cows or Condos? Putting aside their Differences, Conservative Cattlemen and Left-Leaning Environmentalists Team up to Save a Valley," *Time*, July 7, 1997; available online at: http://www.time.com/time/reports/backbone/magstories/gunnison.html.

33. The exemplary negotiation that led to a consensus solution for regulating the Navajo Generating Station deserves more study than it has received. The basic bibliography includes: Steven H. Bergman, "To See or Not to See: The Viability of Visibility at the Grand Canyon," *UCLA Journal of Environmental Law and Policy* 13 (1994): 127–80; D. Michael Rappoport and John Cooney, "Visibility at the Grand Canyon: Regulatory Negotiations under the Clean Air Act," *Arizona State Law Journal* 24(1992): 627–42; and articles cited therein.

34. Steve Hinchman, "The Blurring of the West," *High Country News* 25(12), June 28, 1993: 1ff.

35. Leland Deck, "Visibility at the Grand Canyon and the Navajo Generating Station," in *Economic Analysis at EPA: Assessing Regulatory Impact*, Richard D. Morgenstern, ed. (Washington, DC: Resources for the Future, 1997), pp. 267–301.

36. National Research Council, *Protecting Visibility in National Parks and Wilderness Areas* (Washington, DC: National Academies Press, 1993).

37. See Robert D. Rowe and Lauraine G. Chestnut, *The Value of Visibility: Theory and Application* (Cambridge, MA: Abt Books, 1982); Robert D. Rowe and Lauraine G. Chestnut, eds., *Managing Air Quality and Scenic Resources at National Parks and Wilderness Areas* (Boulder, CO: Westview Press, 1983); United States Environmental Protection Agency, *Protecting Visibility: An EPA Report to Congress* (Washington, DC: GPO, 1979).

38. Walter J. Mead, "Review and Analysis of State-of-the-Art Contingent Valuation Studies," in *Contingent Valuation: A Critical Assessment*, Jerry A. Hausman, ed. (New York: North-Holland, 1993).

39. See Deck, "Visibility at the Grand Canyon, p. 278.

40. Ibid., p. 281.

41. I interviewed former EPA officials involved in the regulatory negotiation; this is what one said in a telephone interview.

42. Salt River Project, Navajo Generating Station BART Analysis, prepared by Decision Focus Inc. (Los Altos, CA: DFI, 1991). See also Decision Focus Inc., *Development and Design of a Contingent Valuation Survey Measuring the Public's Value for Visibility Improvements at the Grand Canyon National Park* (Los Altos, CA: DFI, 1990).

43. Deck, "Visibility at the Grand Canyon," p. 290.

44. Ibid., p. 293.

45. Ibid.

46. Ibid.

47. See Matthew L. Wald, "U.S. Agencies Use Negotiations to Pre-Empt Lawsuits Over Rules," *New York Times*, Sept. 23, 1991: A1.

48. *Central Ariz. Water Conservation Dist. v. EPA*, 990 F.2d 1531, 1544 (9th Cir. 1993).

49. E. Gundling, *The 3M Way to Innovation: Balancing People and Profit* (Tokyo: Kodansha, 2000).

50. Bill Clinton and Al Gore, "Reinventing Environmental Regulation," National Performance Review, Washington, DC, March 16, 1995. Available online at: http://govinfo.library.unit.edu/npr/library/rsreport/251a.html.

51. Alfred A. Marcus, Donald A. Geffen, and Ken Sexton, *Reinventing Environmental Regulation: Lessons from Project XL* (Washington, DC: Resources for the Future, 2002), p. 105. See also Allen Blackman and Jan Mazurek, "The Cost of Developing Site-Specific Environmental Regulations: Evidence from EPA's Project XL," Resources for the Future Discussion Paper #99-35, at 16 (Apr. 1999).

52. Marcus et al., *Reinventing Environmental Regulation*, pp. 85–86.

53. Intel Corporation, "Comments by Intel Corporation," prepared by J. Hatcher, Counsel before the Environmental Protection Agency, September 28, 1994.

54. Microelectronics Computer Technology Corporation, "Environmental Consciousness: A Strategic Competitiveness Issue for the Electronics and Computer Industry" (Austin, TX: MCC, 1993).

55. Marcus et al., *Reinventing Environmental Regulation*, pp. 119–20.

56. Jody Freeman, "Collaborative Governance in the Administrative State," *UCLA Law Review* 45 (October 1997): 1–98; see esp. n. 190.

57. Marcus et al., *Reinventing Environmental Regulation*, p. 145, n. 5, write that the "Production unit factor" was defined using as measures of units "the area of silicon processed divided by the line width of the smallest transistor on the chip." The stakeholder panel had to meet over 2,000 hours to wrap its collective mind around concepts such as this. There would seem to be no way that an economic analyst, environmentalist, or any other kibbitzer can get a handle on what is going on other than by committing a good deal of his or her life to mastering the technicalities. That is one reason why society needs to rely on representative stakeholder groups and stick with their results – rather than to allow all comers, however ill-informed, another bite at the apple at the agency, congressional, or administrative level. The penchant of various groups to end-run and to second-guess the stakeholder process by lobbying higher authorities doomed the 3M negotiations. Site-based environmental regulation requires good-faith negotiation by representatives of all major factions. There is no clear alternative.

58. James Boyd, Alan J. Krupnick, and Janice Mazurek, *Intel's XL Permit: A Framework for Evaluation* (Washington, DC: Discussion Paper, Resources for the Future, January 1998), p. 5.

59. Eileen Claussen and Lisa McNeilly, "Equity and Global Climate Change: The Complex Elements of Global Fairness," Washington, DC: Pew Center for Global Climate Change, 1998. Available online at: http://www.pewclimate.org/report2.html. See also Mark Sagoff, "Pollution Trading and the Global Environment," in *Property Rights, Economics, and the Environment*, Michael D. Kaplowitz, ed., Legal Relationship Series, 5 (Stamford, CT: JAI Press, 2000), pp. 241–257.

Chapter 9

1. Ed Marston, "The Timber Wars Evolve into a Divisive Attempt at Peace," *High Country News*, September 29, 1997; available online at: http://www.hcn.org/1997/sep29/dir/Feature_The_ timber.html. Many of the sources that follow are accessible through the website of the Quincy Library Group, at: http://qlg.org/public_html/contents/perspectives.htm.

2. Jane Braxton Little, "National Groups Object to Grassroots Power in D.C.," *High Country News*, March 31, 1997. Available online at: http://www.hcn.org/1997/mar31/dir/Western_National_g.html.

3. Karl Hess, "Beyond the Federal Range: Towards a Self-Governing West," lecture presented at the University of Colorado, Center for the American West, November 6, 1997.

4. John Milton Cooper, Jr., *The Warrior and the Priest: Woodrow Wilson and Theodore Roosevelt* (Cambridge, MA: Harvard University Press, 1983), p. 83; from a speech delivered in 1905 in Chicago.

5. See, e.g., Marion Clawson, *The Bureau of Land Management* (New York: Praeger, 1971), esp. pp. 71–72; and Julia Marie Wondolleck, *Public Lands: Conflict and Resolution* (New York: Plenum Press, 1988), pp. 20–22.

6. Hess, "Federal Range," p. 5.

7. Ibid.

8. Robert H. Nelson, *Public Lands and Private Rights: The Failure of Scientific Management* (Lanham, MD: Rowman and Littlefield, 1995), p. 230.

9. Gifford Pinchot, *Breaking New Ground* (New York: Harcourt, Brace & Co., 1947), p. 260.

10. U.S. Department of Agriculture, *A National Plan for Forestry: The Report of the Forest Service of the Agriculture Department on the Forest Problem of the United States* (Washington, DC: Government Printing Office, 1933), p. 141. Before World War II, "cut-and-run" timbering practices, which may have made economic sense when forests seemed to stretch forever, did denude landscapes, causing erosion, flooding, and so on. Only after the War, as Weyerhaeuser and other companies built up plantations for sustained yields, were private lands generally managed at least as well as the public forests. As demand for timber increased, private owners began to have an incentive to change from "cut-and-run" to "sustained-yield" forestry. For discussion, see Robert Nelson, *Public Lands and Private Rights*, Part II.

11. Quoted in Henry Clepper, *Professional Forestry in the United States* (Baltimore, MD: Johns Hopkins University Press, 1971), p. 291. Although timber reserves have always been more than adequate, Pinchot and his successors harped on the possibility of a "timber famine" to justify the policies, including fire suppression, they believed were necessary for the efficient and scientific management of the national forests. Since private producers handily satisfied demand prior to 1945, the public forests, if harvested, would glut the market, driving timber prices beneath costs. While fulminating against private timber companies, the Forest Service secured their tacit support by keeping public timber off the market except in extraordinary circumstances. The national forests, therefore, never contributed more than a few percent of national timber production before the Second World War. Harold K. Steen writes that the Forest Service sought to "avoid competing with private enterprise by withholding federal timber until private supplies were exhausted; sell only to meet purely local shortages; protect national forests from fire and other disasters." Harold K. Steen, *The U.S. Forest Service: A History* (Seattle: University of Washington Press, 1976), p. 113.

12. Quoted in Samuel P. Hays, *Conservation and the Gospel of Efficiency: The Progressive Conservation Movement, 1890–1920* (Cambridge, MA: Harvard University Press, 1959), p. 267.

13. Hays, *Conservation and the Gospel of Efficiency*, p. 28.

14. Ibid.

15. Eliza Wing-yee Lee, "Political Science, Public Administration, and the Rise of the American Administrative State," *Public Administration Review* 55 (November/December 1995): 538–48, quotation at p. 540.

16. For discussion, see Terry Anderson and Donald Leal, *Free Market Environmentalism* (Boulder, CO: Westview Press, 1991), ch. 4. These authors contend that "cut-and-run" timbering practices were economically efficient – as they probably were. It made more sense economically to turn trees to cash and invest the money in other industries than to reforest the land. From a strictly economic point of view, the most "profligate" timbering practices could well have been the most profitable, given the plentiful supply of forested land.

17. Robert H. Wiebe, *Self-Rule: A Cultural History of American Democracy* (Princeton, NJ: Princeton University Press, 1995), p. 143. Conservationists, as Robert Nelson has written, elevated "applied science from a practical tool to a new form of religious faith" with all the intolerance for dissent that implies. It is one thing for experts to speak truth to power; it is quite another for experts to wield power themselves. When they do, the tendency is always "to circle the wagons and defend established policy. Science would be enlisted for the defense rather than left free to inquire in any direction." Nelson, *Public Lands and Private Rights*, pp. 51, 53.

18. A wall-to-wall political consensus at the time favored maintaining federal control of Western public lands. Big timber interests generally supported policies to sequester millions of acres of public land. Although opposed in principle to the utilitarian ethic underlying scientific conservationism, preservationists, too, could support Pinchot's policies, since the Forest Service kept wilderness areas out of private ownership. Followers of John Muir did not then – as they do now – feel the political strength to demand zero-cut in the public forests; nevertheless, they could count on little cutting anyway, since private forests, which were more economical, sufficed for the nation's needs at the time. Besides, starting with Yosemite in 1872, preservationists had succeeded beyond their expectations in convincing Congress to create several immense national parks. In retrospect, we know that the Forest Service, inadvertently and against its will, preserved a vast natural reserve from which Congress could later carve several more "wilderness" areas. In the early twentieth century, no one suggested a better way to manage the national forests and other resources than to trust them to cadres of professionals and experts. Absent an alternative, reformers could honestly endorse the ideals of efficiency, specialization, hierarchy, and expertise upon which Pinchot founded the Forest Service. Wiebe comments, "Scientific government, the reformers believed, would bring opportunity, progress, order, and community" (*The Search for Order, 1877–1920*, New York: Hill and Wang, 1967, p. 107). The belief that land use decisions were justified scientifically allowed agency experts and bureaucrats to make those decisions stick politically. A study of public administration at the time concluded, "These men are not simply useful to legislators overwhelmed by the increasing flood of bills. They are the government." Leonard White, *Introduction to the Study of Public Administration* (New York: Macmillan, 1926).

19. Marston, "Timber Wars."

20. Ibid.
21. For discussion of the Forest Reserve Act, see Nelson, *Public Lands and Private Rights*, p. 46.
22. Hays, *Conservation and the Gospel of Efficiency*, pp. 41–42.
23. Pinchot and his politically savvy successors appeased the timber companies, moreover, by keeping production from public lands low, though after the War, the Forest Service had to increase production to meet greater demand. This meant giving the companies far more access to national forests. As for preservationists in the tradition of Muir, Pinchot famously dismissed their attitude as unscientific: "The object of our forest policy is not to preserve the forests because they are beautiful . . . or because they are refuges for the wild creatures of the wilderness . . . but the making of prosperous homes" (quoted by Hays, *Gospel*, pp. 41–42). Before the Second World War, the Forest Service used both its clear congressional mandate and the shield of scientific expertise to fend off challenges both from industry and from preservationist groups, making compromises as needed. Local communities lacked power to question or the expertise to oppose the will of federal agencies.
24. 16 U.S.C. Sec. 531 (1976 ed.).
25. Louis L. Jaffe, "The Illusion of the Ideal Administration," *Harvard Law Review* 86(1973): 1183–99; quotation at 1184.
26. Occupational Safety and Health Act, 29 U.S.C. Sec. 655(b)(5) (1976).
27. *Industrial Union Department, AFL-CIO v. American Petroleum Institute*, 448 U.S. 607 (1980) (the Benzene decision) (Justice William Rehnquist, concurring). The Clean Air Act, to cite another example, instructs the Environmental Protection Agency (EPA) to control air pollution so tightly that even the most sensitive groups are protected from harm with an adequate margin of safety. Laws this aspirational allow Congress to announce the good news – that the air shall be pollution-free – while leaving it to the agency to announce the bad news, *viz*, that this cannot be done at a price society is willing to pay. 42 U.S.C. Sec. 7408(f)(1)(C).
28. *Industrial Union Department, AFL-CIO v. American Petroleum Institute*, 448 U.S. 607(1980).
29. For this view, see, e.g., Eva H. Hanks and John L. Hanks, "An Environmental Bill of Rights: The Citizen Suit and the National Environment Policy Act of 1969," *Rutgers Law Review* 21(230) (1970).
30. "The most important feature of the Act," according to Senator Henry Jackson, its principal author, "is that it establishes new decision-making procedures for all agencies of the federal government." Henry Jackson, "Environmental Quality, the Courts, and Congress," *Michigan Law Review* 68(1079) (1970).
31. National Environmental Policy Act #102(2)(B); 42 U.S.C. #4332.
32. *National Resources Defense Council v. Morton*, 388 F. Supp. at 840 (1974).
33. Nelson, *Public Lands and Private Rights*, pp. 159–65.
34. Nothing resembling democratic deliberation or even compromise emerges from this zero-sum game. Gridlock is what Karl Hess calls "the brute reality of the iron triangle – the self-reinforcing relations between

entrenched special interests, ranchers, loggers, miners, and irrigators, and regulatory agencies . . . and the western congressional delegations who control the agencies' budgets and who rely on the political support of the monied interests to win re-election again and again." Hess, "Federal Range," p. 6.

35. John V. Krutilla, "Adaptive Responses to Forces for Change," paper presented at the Annual Meeting of the Society of American Foresters, Boston, MA, October 16, 1979: 6; cited and quoted in Nelson, *Public Lands and Private Rights*, p. 70.

36. John V. Krutilla and John V. Haigh, "An Integrated Approach to National Forest Management, *Environmental Law* 68(Winter 1978): 383.

37. Nelson, *Public Lands and Private Rights*, p. 70.

38. Executive Order 12,291, issued February 1, 1981. The Regulatory Reform Bill of 1981, nearly enacted, would have legislated economic efficiency as the goal of all regulation and mandated cost-benefit analysis to determine when a regulation is efficient. Senator John Glenn and Representative John Dingell opposed the bill; except for their opposition, it would have passed.

39. John V. Krutilla, *The Economics of Natural Environments: Studies in the Valuation of Commodity and Amenity Resources* (Washington, DC: Resources for the Future, 1985).

40. Sheila Jasanoff, *The Fifth Branch: Science Advisers as Policymakers* (Cambridge, MA: Harvard University Press, 1990).

41. The classic citation is Alvin Weinberg, "Science and Trans-Science," *Minerva* 10(1970): 209–22.

42. Sheila Jasanoff, "The Dilemma of Environmental Democracy," *Issues in Science and Technology* 13(Fall 1996): 63–70; quotation at 67.

43. Jasanoff, *The Fifth Branch*, p. 12.

44. James Madison, "Federalist no. 10," *The Federalist Papers*, Garry Wills, ed. (New York: Bantam Books, 1982), pp. 42–49.

45. John Baden and Richard Stroup, for example, have proposed that national forest lands "be put into the hands of qualified environmental groups such as the Sierra Club, the Audubon Society, and the Wilderness Society." John Baden and Richard Stroup, "Saving the Wilderness," *Reason* 13(July 1981): 35.

46. F. A. Hayek, *The Political Order of a Free People* (Chicago: University of Chicago Press, 1979), pp. 13, 15.

47. Joshua Cohen and Charles Sabel, "Directly Deliberative Polyarchy," *European Law Journal* 3(December 1997): 313–42; quotation at p. 325.

48. U.S. Forest Service, *Framework for the Future* (Washington, DC: Forest Service, February 1970); U.S. Forest Service, *Inform and Involve* (Washington, DC: Forest Service, February 1972).

49. See John Hendee et al., *Public Involvement and the Forest Service* (Seattle, WA: Pacific Northwest Forest and Range Experiment Station, May 1973). See also Rupert Cutler, "Public Involvement in USDA Decision-Making," *Journal of Soil and Water Conservation* 33(1978): 264–66.

50. Carmen Sirianni and Lewis Friedland, "Social Capital and Civic Innovation: Learning and Capacity-Building from the 1960s to the 1990s," *Change Magazine* 29 (January/February), 1997; Available online at: http://www.cpn.org/sections/new_citizenship/change.html.

51. These councils established lines of communication between competing groups and laid the foundations "for the kind of town meeting civic culture that was more common in the national and state forests of the Northeast" (Sirianni and Friedland, "Social Capital and Civic Innovation"). See also Paul Culhane, *Public Lands Politics: Interest Group Influence on the Forest Service and the Bureau of Land Management* (Baltimore, MD: Johns Hopkins University Press, 1981).

52. Sirianni and Friedland, "Social Capital and Civic Innovation."

53. Cohen and Sabel, "Directly Deliberative Polyarchy," p. 338.

54. Sirianni and Friedland, "Social Capital and Civic Innovation."

55. Ibid.

56. Robert Gottlieb and Helen Ingram, "The New Environmentalists," *Progressive*, August 1988: 14.

57. Aldo Leopold, "Land-Use Democracy," in *The River of the Mother of God and Other Essays*, Susan L. Flader and J. Baird Callicott, eds. (Madison: University of Wisconsin Press, 1991), p. 299.

58. Wondolleck, *Public Lands Conflict and Resolution*, p. 119.

59. Marston, "Timber Wars."

60. Ibid.

61. Patrick Mazza, "Co-optation or Constructive Engagement?: Quincy Library Group's Effort to Bring Together Loggers and Environmentalists under Fire," *The Cascadia Planet*, August 9, 1997. Available online at: http://www.tnews.com/text/quincy_library.html, quoting Freeman House, a founder of Northern California's Mattole Restoration Council, one of the oldest and most respected community-based ecological restoration efforts. House commented on the opposition of national environmental groups to the Quincy Library plan: "I tend to see the national environmental reaction coming from having developed a power base and feeling threatened by these community groups."

62. Quoted by Tom Philp, "Fallout from a Logging Consensus in the Sierra," *Sacramento Bee*, November 9, 1997. Available online at: http://www.sacbee.com/news/beetoday/newsroom/edit/110997/edit03.html.

63. Philp, "Fallout from a Logging Consensus."

64. Stephen Pyne, *Fire in America: A Cultural History of Wildland and Rural Fire* (Princeton, NJ: Princeton University Press, 1982), p. 71; details the extent to which Amerindian populations used fire as a management tool.

65. Marston, "Timber Wars."

66. Gifford Pinchot, *The Training of a Forester*, rev. 3rd ed. (Philadelphia: Lippincott, 1917), p. 32.

67. Robert Nelson, *A Burning Issue: Why the Forest Service Is Institutionally Incapable of Dealing with the Problem of Forest Fire, and How This Case Illustrates the Need to Abolish the Agency*. Working paper for the Competitive Enterprise Institute, February 1998: 15.

68. Ibid.

69. Megen J. Peterson, "Sierra Management Plan under Fire" (Berkeley, CA: Ecology Center, Summer 2000); available online at http://www. ecologycenter.org/terrain/2002summer/Sierra.html.

70. Mazza, "Co-optation or Constructive Engagement?"

71. Philp, "Fallout from a Logging Consensus."

72. Marston, "Timber Wars."

73. Mazza, "Co-optation or Constructive Engagement?"

74. Philp, "Fallout from a Logging Consensus."

75. "Prepared Testimony of Michael Jackson before the Senate Committee on Energy and Natural Resources Subcommittee on Forests and Public Land Management," July 24, 1997 (Federal News Service).

76. The precursor to the QLG plan, called the Conservationist Alternative to the Plumas National Forest Plan, was originally proposed in February 1986 by Friends of Plumas Wilderness, Mother Lode Chapter, Sierra Club, Northstate Wilderness Committee, and Altacal Audubon. The Wilderness Society and the Natural Resources Defense Council later provided financial and legal support for the plan.

77. Daniel P. Beard, "Dear Senator," letter from senior vice president of the National Audubon Society, Washington, D.C., September 17, 1997; available online at: http://qlg.org/public_html/Perspectives/audubonposition.htm.

78. Jane Braxton Little, "Critics Fear Quincy Bill Cedes Too Much Federal Power to Locals," *Sacramento Bee,* July 5, 1997; available online at: http://www.sacbee.com/news/beetoday/newsroom/local/070597/local07.html.

79. Philp, "Fallout from a Logging Consensus."

80. Beard, "Dear Senator."

81. Quoted in Mazza, "Co-optation or Constructive Engagement?"

82. Ibid.

83. Philp, "Fallout from a Logging Consensus."

84. Ed Marston writes, "Louis Blumberg of The Wilderness Society in San Francisco is not impressed by the QLG's impatience: 'We have all spent many years waiting for the Forest Service to make changes. It's slow to change, but to say that because the QLG is unable to have their plan adopted within two years is testimony to a failure of forest planning – I can't buy that. They're only one special interest group.'" Marston, "Timber Wars."

85. Letter of Deb Callahan, President, League of Conservation Voters to the House of Representatives opposing the Quincy Library Group Bill, H.R. 858, July 8, 1997. Available online at: http://www.lcv.org/eyeoncongress/letters97/Quincy.html.

86. Mazza, "Co-optation or Constructive Engagement?"

87. Michael Yost, Letter to the Editor, *High Country News,* November 24, 1997. Available online at: http://qlg.org/public_html/Perspectives/yost112497.htm.

88. Beard, "Dear Senator."

89. Sally Yost, President, and Sherry Yarnell, Conservation Chair, Plumas Audubon Society, Quincy, California, letter to Mike Leahy, Forest Campaign Coordinator, National Audubon Society, September 24, 1997; available online at: http://www.qlg.org/public_html/bill/audubon/pluaudo92497.htm. While the National Audubon Society acknowledged that "environmentalists who are participating in the QLG are legit and have the best of intentions," the Sierra Club published a full-page ad in the *New York Times* (National Edition, September 24, 1997: B10) questioning the bona fides of its local members, whom it described as an "industry-picked group."

90. Mazza, "Co-optation or Constructive Engagement?"

91. Ibid.

92. Quoted in Glen Martin, "Agriculture Dept. Oks Tough Rules for Forest Management," *San Francisco Chronicle*, December 28, 2001: A1.

93. Quoted in the January 2002 issue of the Forestry Source, "Rey Delays Decision of Sierra Nevada: Under Secretary Postpones Action of Controversial Plan." Available online at: http://www.safnet.org/archive/102_sierra.htm.

94. Quoted in Mike Taugher, "Lawyer Revives Logging Plan to Chorus of Criticism, Praise," *Contra Costa Times*, September 15, 2002; available online at: http://www.bayarea.com.

95. William E. Riebsame and James J. Robb, *Atlas of the New West* (New York: W. W. Norton, 1997), pp. 10, 108. In the arid area from the Sierra Nevada forests to the Colorado Plateau, more than half of the income people earn comes not from wages of any kind but from investments, retirement accounts, and other "transfer" payments. The rural West is now home to "modem" cowboys, highly educated, environmentally aware refugees from urban centers who love the landscape, conduct business over the Internet, and fly in and out of airports in easy reach of nearly every community. Ted Turner epitomizes the kind of rural hick the Sierra Club fears timber companies will co-opt. Quincy, an old logging and mining town where the Forest Service is the major employer, supports an economically and socially diverse population of 10,000 and a growing tourist industry. Instead of logging, one now logs in at Morning Thunder, the upscale bed and breakfast, or at other cafés in Quincy that serve cappuccino, latté, and espresso as well as campfire coffee.

96. All quotes from McCloskey can be found in Michael McCloskey, "The Skeptic: Collaboration Has Its Limits," *High Country News*, May 13, 1996; available online at: http://www.hcn.org/1996/may13/dir/Opinion_The_skepti.html. McCloskey's memo was also excerpted in *Harper's*, November 1996: 34–36.

97. "Robert Putnam Responds," *American Prospect* 25 (March–April 1996): 27.

98. Robert D. Putnam, "Bowling Alone: America's Declining Social Capital," *Journal of Democracy*, January 6, 1995: 65–78; quotation at p. 71.

99. The reverse may also be true: having arrived at a land ethic, they adopt the science that confirms it.

100. Reprinted as a *San Francisco Chronicle* editorial, July 23, 1997.
101. Donald Worster, "The Ecology of Order and Chaos," *Environmental History and Review* 14(1,2) (Spring/Summer 1990): 1–18; quotation at p. 13.
102. Gottlieb and Ingram, "The New Environmentalists," p. 14.
103. C. Jordan and D. Snow, "Diversification, Minorities, and the Mainstream," in D. Snow, ed., *Voices from the Environmental Movement: Perspectives for a New Era* (Washington, DC: Island Press, 1992): 71–84.
104. Lois Marie Gibbs and Karen J. Stults, "On Grassroots Environmentalism," in *Crossroads: Environmental Priorities for the Future*, Peter Borelli, ed. (Washington, DC: Island Press, 1988), p. 244.
105. See William M. Sullivan, "Making Civil Society Work: Democracy as a Problem of Civic Cooperation," in *Civic Society, Democracy, and Civic Renewal*, Robert K. Fullinwider, ed. (Lanham, MD: Rowman and Littlefield, 1999), pp. 31–54.
106. See Jean L. Cohen, "American Civil Society Talk" in *Civic Society, Democracy, and Civic Renewal*, Robert K. Fullinwider, ed. (Lanham, MD: Rowman and Littlefield, 1999), pp. 55–85.
107. Marston, "Timber Wars."

Index